Electricity and Energy Policy in Britain, France and the United States since 1945

For Pat, Peter, Freddy and Tom
with great love

Electricity and Energy Policy in Britain, France and the United States since 1945

Martin Chick

Senior Lecturer in Economic and Social History
University of Edinburgh, UK

Edward Elgar
Cheltenham, UK • Northampton, MA, USA

Published by
Edward Elgar Publishing Limited
The Lypiatts
15 Lansdown Road
Cheltenham
Glos GL50 2JA
UK

Edward Elgar Publishing, Inc.
William Pratt House
9 Dewey Court
Northampton
Massachusetts 01060
USA

Paperback edition 2009

A catalogue record for this book
is available from the British Library

Library of Congress Control Number: 2007921144

ISBN 978 1 84542 111 3 (cased)
ISBN 978 1 84844 591 8 (paperback)

Printed and bound by MPG Books Group, UK

Contents

Abbreviations

AGR	advanced gas-cooled reactor
ATIC	Association Technique de l'Importation Charbonnière
BP	British Petroleum
BST	bulk supply tariff
CCGT	combined-cycle gas turbine
CEB	Central Electricity Board
CEGB	Central Electricity Generating Board
CES	Conseil Économique et Social
CFP	Compagnie Française des Pétroles
CFR	Compagnie Française de Raffinage
CGP	Commissariat Général du Plan
CGT	Confédération Générale du Travail
CNRS	Centre National de la Recherche Scientifique
CPDE	Compagnie Parisienne de Distribution d'Électricité
CPRS	Central Policy Review Staff
CPUC	California Public Utilities Commission
DCF	discounted cash flow
DWT	deadweight tons
EC	European Community
ECA	Economic Co-operation Administration
ECSC	European Coal and Steel Community
EDC	European Defence Community
EDF	Électricité de France
EEC	European Economic Community
EFL	external finance limit
ERAP	Entreprise de Recherches et d'Activités Petrolières
ERCOT	Electric Reliability Council of Texas
ESC	Economic and Social Council (French: CES Conseil Economique et Social)
FCC	Féderation des Collectivités Concédantes
FERC	Federal Energy Regulatory Commission
FME	Fonds de Modernisation d'Équipement
FNCCR	Fédération Nationale des Collectivités Concédantes et Régies

FNCP	Fédération Nationale des Collectivités Publiques Électrifiées
FONT	Ministry of Industry archives, Centre des Archives Contemporaines, Fontainebleau
GDF	Gaz de France
GRECS	Groupe de Recherche Économique et Social
IEA	International Energy Agency
IOU	investor-owned utility
IPAA	Independent Petroleum Association of America
IPC	Iraq Petroleum Company
IPP	independent power producer
ISO	independent system operator
LILCO	Long Island Lighting Company
LOLP	loss of load probability
LPA	Labour Party Archives, Manchester
LRMC	long-run marginal cost
mbd	million barrels per day
NATO	North Atlantic Treaty Organisation
NCB	National Coal Board
NEDO	National Economic Development Office
NETA	new electricity trading arrangements
NGC	National Grid Company
NSHEB	North of Scotland Hydro-Electric Board
NYSPSC	New York State Public Service Commission
OECD	Organisation for European Co-operation and Development
OEEC	Organisation for European Economic Co-operation
OPEC	Organisation of Petroleum Exporting Countries
PG&E	Pacific Gas and Electric
PJM	Pennsylvania, New Jersey, and Maryland
PPP	pool purchasing price
PSP	pool selling price
PURPA	Public Utility Regulatory Policies Act
PWR	pressurised water reactor
PX	Power Exchange (California)
QF	qualifying facility
REC	regional electricity company
RRR	required rates of return
SAV	Centre des Archives Économiques et Financières, Savigny-le-Temple
SCE	Southern California Edison
SCNI	Select Committee on Nationalised Industries

SDGE	San Diego Gas and Electric
SEA	Single European Act
SMP	system marginal price
SNCF	La Société Nationale des Chemins de Fer
SOFRO	Société Française de Recherche Opérationnelle
SPR	Strategic Petroleum Reserve
SRMC	short-run marginal cost
SRO	Scottish Record Office
SSEB	South of Scotland Electricity Board
STPR	social time preference rate
tEC	*la tonne d'équivalent charbon* (UK: tC tonne of coal equivalent)
TDR	test discount rate
TFP	total factor productivity
TNA	The National Archives, London
TPA	third-party access
TVA	Tennessee Valley Authority
UNIMAREL	Union pour l'Étude du Marché de l'Électricité
UNIPEDE	Union Internationale des Producteurs et Distributeurs d'Énergie Électrique

Acknowledgements

The research for this book began with an ESRC-funded year in Paris and the time needed for writing up was provided by the Leverhulme Trust in the form of a research fellowship. In-between, funding and time was provided by the Carnegie Trust and the University of Edinburgh. I am extremely grateful to all of these institutions, funding councils and charities, for without them the book would never have been started, let alone finished. Moral support in Paris was provided by *les familles* Kohn, Martin, Mollot, Monnatte, Roux and the staff of the École Elémentaire, rue Clignancourt. In Paris, I was based at the Institut d'Histoire du Temps Présent under Henri Rousso, and I lived *en famille* and eponymously in rue Poulet in the 18th *arrondissement*. It was through the human bouillabaisse that surrounds the métro Château Rouge that I ventured each day to such various archives and libraries as: the National Archives in rue des Quatre Fils; the Ministry of Industry archives at Centre des Archives Contemporaines, Fontainebleau; the Centre des Archives Économiques et Financières at Savigny-le-Temple; the archives of Sciences Po; the Électricité de France archives, then in rue Messine; the library of École des Mines; Bibliothèque Cujas; and the Bibliothèque Nationale. In Britain, my main archives were the National Archives at Kew, the Scottish Record Office in Edinburgh, and the Labour Party archives in Manchester.

My debts to fellow academics are huge. In Edinburgh, Roger Davidson, David Greasley, John Banasik and Trevor Griffiths have offered valuable advice and coffee. In France, Patrick Fridenson, Dominique Barjot, Rang-Ri Park-Barjot, Michèle Ruffat, Alain Beltran, Christophe Bouneau, Françoise Verdon and François Crouzet have all been generous with their encouragement, wine and food. In Paris, Maurice Lévy-Leboyer, Jean-Marcel Jeanneney, Marcel Boiteux, François Caron, Pierre Lanthier, Hervé Joly, Denis Varaschin, Catherine Vuillermot and Isabelle Amboise have all patiently answered my questions about energy policy, while in Edinburgh Trish, MF, Elaine and the Thorburn and Shamash clans have kept me in good fettle. Above all, I am extremely grateful to Alan Beltran, Richard Hirsh and Bob Millward for their persistent interest in my work, and for all of the help which they have given me over the years of research and writing.

As anyone who knows me well will already know, none of this would have been possible without Hatty. To her, to Louisa, Deke, Verrall, Mary, Margaret, Tim, the two Andrews, Beth and Peter, much love and thanks. This book is dedicated to my sons, Freddy and Tom for bringing such joy, and to my parents, Pat and Peter, for working so hard to give me my early opportunities.

1. Introduction

On 8 May 1946, the electricity supply industry in France was nationalised and Électricité de France (EDF) was established. In 1947, the Electricity Act nationalised the electricity supply industry in Britain, with 1 April 1948 being set as the 'vesting' date for the transfer of assets into central public ownership. In the United States, regulation rather than nationalisation was the chosen means of exercising increased social control over the electricity utilities, and this found its legislative expression in the Public Utility Holding Company Act of 1935. In all three economies either national (France, Britain) or regional/state-based (USA), vertically-integrated monopolies were established and sanctioned by these legislative acts. The ownership, regulation and structure of each nation's electricity industry remained fundamentally unchanged throughout the almost 30 years of economic growth and low unemployment that followed the Second World War, that period being commonly referred to by economic historians as the Golden Age (1950–73) or *Les Trentes Glorieuses* (1945–75) (Fourastié, 1979; Crafts and Toniolo, 1996). Yet, as the Golden Age began to tarnish, as impure gold will, so too were questions raised about the durability of the monopolistic structure of the electricity supply industry and its continuance as a regulated or nationalised industry. The sources of such questioning differed in each country, as did each government's response. In France, EDF was able to separate itself from the broad contingent of nationalised industries and was allowed to negotiate new contractual arrangements between itself and the French government. Until very recently (2005), EDF was able to remain wholly in public ownership and to retain its effective domestic national monopoly. In the United States, the 1978 Public Utility Regulatory Policies Act (PURPA) encouraged new independent electricity producers to enter individual state electricity markets, but it was not until the 1992 Energy Policy Act that official, federal encouragement was given to the liberalisation of electricity markets in the United States. In Britain, the 1989 Electricity Act was preceded by a substantial restructuring of the industry and followed by determined efforts to promote greater competition in the industry. The 1989 Act itself effected the privatisation of the electricity supply industry in England and Wales, with the privatisation of the industry in Scotland following in 1991. In each case the policy response was shaped significantly by the perception of the industry's performance during the Golden Age. To that extent, the 'path development' weight of history hung heavily over this industry.

The development of the electricity supply industry in France, Britain and the United States during and after the Golden Age is the dominant concern of this book. The book is organised around five main political–economic themes: security (Chapter 2); pricing (Chapter 4); investment (Chapter 5); forms of ownership, and industrial and market structure (Chapter 6); with the fifth theme being the early development of the European Coal and Steel Community and the later efforts of the European Commission to promote competition in national and transnational electricity markets in Europe (Chapters 3 and 6). Electricity is of particular interest, not only because of its centrality to energy policy as a transformer of the potential energy of fuels into a flow of energy of such wide application, but also because its physical characteristics present particularly interesting problems for economists. Travelling at the speed of light and substantially incapable of being stored, its peak demand determines the industry's maximum capacity requirement and hence the industry's large, lumpy, sunk investments. In turn, its investments in transmission and distribution enjoy longevity and the large sunk costs of the transmission network contribute to its commonly being characterised as a natural monopoly. It was from either side of this natural monopoly that nationalising and regulating governments extended outwards to embrace the entire industry as a national and state/regional monopoly.

This blurring of the distinctions between the national/state monopoly and the industry's natural monopoly component provided an important target for the industry's critics, to whom politicians more readily lent an ear as the Golden Age lost its lustre (Gray, 1940). In particular, it was micro-economists who attracted political attention towards the end of the Golden Age, to some extent displacing in political affection the macroeconomists who were more readily associated with much of the Golden Age. Quite why fashions in the use of economists change is one of the running concerns of this book. What is it that affects the willingness of politicians to listen to economists and their often long-standing ideas? Why did work on utility by Jules Dupuit, dating back to the 1840s, and what we now, post-Marshall, term the 'consumers' surplus' become of such renewed and particular interest to economists during the 1970s, and through them to politicians? Why does the same economic idea gain a foothold in one country but not, until much later, in another? Why, to emphasise the central continuous theme of this book, was the marginalist approach to pricing and investment in the electricity supply industry adopted in France at least two decades before its partial adoption in Britain and the United States? Much more will be said on what is dubbed the 'marginalist' approach' in Chapter 4, but it is worth noting the considerable interest in marginalist theory among electricity managers and engineers in the early post-war years. International conferences on marginalist approaches to pricing in particular were held in Brussels, Louvain, Cologne and elsewhere (FONT, 1952, 1956). Such ideas were later to be evangelised in the United States by Cornell's Professor of Political Economy, Alfred Kahn, in his 1970–71 two-volume book, *The Economics of Regulation*. While advancing the case for marginal-cost pricing so as to reflect the social opportunity cost of resource use at the margin, Kahn acknowledged his debt to previous generations of economists, and in particular to the earlier post-war work done by the likes of Marcel Boiteux at EDF.

So far, we have noted the essentially similar technical characteristics of electricity supply and the apparent common mid-century political willingness in each country to sanction the organisation of the electricity supply industry in a vertically integrated monopoly form (FONT, 1948, 1949). Yet, in comparing the electricity supply industries in France, Britain and the United States, we are comparing industries of contrasting size, ownership and organisational structure. To begin with size: in terms of the total production of electricity, the ratio in 1950 between the USA, the UK and France was 11.8:2:1 and in 1970, 11.7:1.8:1 (see Appendix Table A1.1). In 1950 the ratio of per capita consumption of electricity in the United States, the UK, and France was 3.2:1.6:1, and by 1974, 2.7:1.4:1. There were also significant differences in the forms of electricity generation. In the early post-Second World War period, a higher proportion than now of electricity was generated from hydroelectric, as opposed to thermal, sources. That the proportionate contribution of hydroelectricity should fall is not surprising, given that relative fuel prices fell and that the industry itself was likely to hit diminishing returns as the best sites were used first. None the less its contribution was important and nowhere more so than in France, where it contributed 48.7 per cent of national electricity production in 1950 and 31.5 per cent in 1974. In Britain, hydroelectricity output was never important, but in the United States its contribution to total electricity output was 25.9 per cent in 1950 and 15.6 per cent in 1974 (see Appendix Table A1.2). So just before its great leap forward into a nuclear programme, in 1974 France still derived roughly just under one-third of its electricity output from hydroelectric sources and just under two-thirds from thermal-based generation. In 1978, this compared with 85.9 per cent in the UK where thermal sources had always been important (97.8 per cent in 1950) and 78.7 per cent in 1974 in the United States. This was little changed from 74.1 per cent in 1950, although in the intervening years thermal generators' share had risen (to 83.4 per cent by 1970) before being displaced at the margin by nuclear power.

A further source of continuing variety lay in the primary energy base of each economy (see Appendix Table A1.3). However, these national statistics need to be read in conjunction with those of each economy's exports and imports of primary energy (see Appendix Table A1.4). Not only did the United States always have a more balanced primary fuel base with coal, oil and gas all making significant contributions in contrast to the coal-based early fuel endowments of France and Britain, but the United States was also consistently more self-sufficient than the UK or France. In 1950, US primary energy imports formed 5.6 per cent of total primary energy production and only 13.15 per cent in 1970. The corresponding share for the UK was 13 per cent in 1950 and 107.4 per cent in 1970, and for France 64 per cent in 1950 and 295.7 per cent in 1970. This rise in fuel imports in France and Britain reflected the shift from coal to oil during the Golden Age, the comparative fuel poverty of France, and the intensification of its fuel dependency, which provided much of the background to the decisive shift towards nuclear power from the mid-1970s (see Chapters 2 and 5).

As well as contrasting in size, forms of generation and fuel base, there was also an obvious contrast between the publicly owned, nationalised electricity industries in France and Britain and the largely private, investor-owned utilities in the United States. However, both this contrast which was stark by 1948, as well as the similarities between the nationalised electricity monopolies of France and Britain, requires nuancing. Previously, the contrasts and similarities had been less clear. In the United States, as in Britain, there was a significant history of municipal involvement in electricity supply such that at its peak in 1921 there were 2,581 municipal systems. However, many of these systems were usually small, accounting for 41 per cent of all electric systems, but generating only 4.7 per cent of the total power output. Many of these small town systems were to be sold to private companies during the consolidation movement of the 1920s. Even so, the idea of municipalisation was still alive, and even reviving in the 1930s, as cheap loans from the federal government allowed local communities to buy their own electric system. From 1933 to 1938, the federal government paid approximately 45 per cent of the total cost of approved municipal projects and provided low-cost loans for the remaining 55 per cent as part of its public works programme (Joskow and Schmalensee, 1983, p. 17; Phillips, 1984, pp. 559–60; Millward, 2005, p. 77). While, in general, the municipal influence remained larger and stronger in Britain than in the United States, again this was in sharp contrast to France, where municipalisation was virtually unknown, much greater use being made of the concession system (ibid.).

While constitutional constraints affecting the division of power between the federal government and the states were always likely to make the nationalisation of the electricity supply industry in the United States improbable, the 1930s did see considerable direct federal government involvement in the industry. Most famously, there was the establishment of the Tennessee Valley Authority (TVA) which represented a greater direct involvement by central government in the electricity supply industry than was the case in Britain. While the British government had promoted the construction of the national grid from 1927, it had made a virtue of the fact that it did so without requiring a change of ownership, but rather 'the partial subordination of vested interests in generation' (Hannah, 1979, p. 94). However, the overseeing Central Electricity Board was given power in the establishing Electricity (Supply) Act of 1926 to close down inefficient stations (Hannah, 1979, pp. 94, 113). State involvement in the promotion of interconnection and the construction of a national grid was also advanced in France by supporters of the nationalisation of the industry, although by 1930 there were already some 4,000 km of high-tension transmission lines in France, more in per capita terms than in Britain where almost one-third of the lines were also less than 70 kV. However, the integrated nature of the British grid gave it a distinct advantage in transmitting the benefits of lower-cost electricity over that in France, which seemed to wait until Paris was fully connected before embarking seriously upon the promotion of a national network (Beltran and Picard, 1987; Millward, 2005, pp. 128–9). Yet lest British-focused historians be tempted to wave the development of their integrated system eastwards across the Channel, they would do well to look westwards over the Atlantic. While the United States did not develop a national grid in this period, in 1923 the electrical output of Britain was roughly the same as that of the state of California, and Britain's level of interconnection was inferior to a Californian network which stretched from one end of the state to the other (Hughes, 1983, p. 9). In the United States, the preferred route to greater security of supply and increased efficiency by means of improving the system load was to be through the use of regional reliability councils, interconnections and power pools.

That the interconnection of the electricity supply system in the United States was left mainly to a process of organic state- and regional-based development, rather than encouraged from above by central government as in Britain and France, highlights a third point of contrast between the industries in each country. The essentially state-based development of the industry in the United States was in sharp contrast to its increasingly national development in France and Britain. In an industry characterised by its organic development out of towns, cities and regions, the constitutional integrity of state-contained electricity which was not traded across state lines allied to the regional development of interconnection, maintained a strong state-based character to electricity supply in the

United States. This essentially state-based system was only strengthened by the Public Utilities Holding Company Act of 1935. Reflecting concern with holding company abuses and coming in the wake of some spectacular crashes, such as that of Samuel Insull's holding company empire, Middle West Utilities, the eventual Public Utilities Holding Company Act of 1935 required that holding companies be reduced to physically integrated systems, dealing solely with gas and electricity (Gordon, 1982, p. 95). This form of regulation had a number of important effects. First, it consolidated regulation (at state level) as the main form of utility supervision. Second, it effectively froze the structure of the industry in a series of regional monopolies (Newbery, 1999, p. 23). Third, it shifted investment risks towards customers, for so long as the regulator deemed the investment to be prudent and reasonable. Local monopoly vertically-integrated investor-owned utilities were effectively offered guaranteed rates of return on capital investment. The costs of poor investment decisions would be borne by customers, while in conditions of excess capacity prices would continue to reflect the return on asset base rather than potential excess supply (Hunt, 2002, p. 29).

Thus it was that at the beginning of the post-Second World War period, the electricity supply industries in Britain, France and the United States were structured as monopolies at either a national or state/regional level. This was politically tolerable so long as the industry was able to exploit economies of scale and technological progress to meet the 7 per cent annual growth in demand for electricity during the Golden Age, and to do so while maintaining price stability. In fact, as higher demand brought forth technologically advanced investment which was also able to exploit economies of scale, so unit costs fell, profit margins widened and price stability was ensured. It was only when this virtuous circle turned vicious from the end of the 1960s that the Golden Age assumptions concerning the ownership, regulation and structure of the electricity industry came to be challenged. The policy response in each country was shaped by the perception of how the industry had performed during the Golden Age. It is with that performance that this book is partly concerned. As a work of history, much of the book concentrates on the period for which the archives were open under the 30-year rule. The use of archival material is confined to the study of France and Britain, for no other reason than the sheer exigencies of time and energy. Time and energy themselves feature large in this book, which, while most obviously seeking to analyse the post-Second World War development of energy policy in each economy, also has a particular concern to trace and underline the importance of the marginalist approach to the allocation of resources in and among the fuel and power industries of Britain, France and the United States.

2.   Shifting from coal to oil: what price security?

The most substantial change which occurred in the international fuel economy from the end of the Second World War until the early 1970s was the shift in the proportionate use of coal and oil. In 1950, 61 per cent of the world's commercial energy requirements was obtained from solid fuels and 27 per cent from liquid fuels. In 1960 these shares were 52 per cent from solid fuels and 32 per cent from liquid fuels, and 32 and 45 per cent, respectively, in 1973 (United Nations, 1976; Robinson and Marshall, 1981, p. 35). The shift from coal to oil was particularly marked in Europe across the 1960s. In 1955, coal provided 75 per cent of total energy use in Western Europe, and petroleum just 23 per cent. By 1972, coal's share had shrunk to 22 per cent, while oil's had risen to 60 per cent (Ray, 1982, p. 201; Weyman-Jones, 1986, pp. 15–16; Yergin, 1991, p. 545). Measured in millions of tons of oil equivalent, domestic coal production fell by one-third in the UK and by almost one-half in France between 1960 and 1971; in physical terms, it fell by two-fifths in France and by one-quarter in the UK (Chick, 2006a, p. 146). In France, coal fell from providing over one-half of France's energy requirements in 1960 to furnishing under one-fifth by 1974, while in the UK, coal's contribution fell from almost three-quarters in 1960 to under one-third by 1974. In both economies, the falling proportionate contribution of coal was almost entirely made up by oil, its contribution in the UK rising from just over one-quarter in 1960 to over one-half in 1974, and in France from over one-third in 1960 to almost three-quarters by 1974. In the United States, between 1947 and 1956, coal production fell by 39 per cent as 3,000 mines closed and the number of mine workers was almost halved (Vietor, 1984, p. 163). Between 1947 and 1958, coal's share of the domestic energy market shrank from 47 to 22 per cent and was to drift down a little further to 19 per cent by 1974. This relative stabilising of its share of the domestic energy market across the 1960s was matched by oil, whose proportionate contribution to North America's energy requirements barely rose from 44 to 45 per cent between 1960 and 1974 (United Nations, 1976; Ray and Uhlmann, 1979, p. 6).

This international shift in the proportionate use of coal and oil reflected the fundamental change in their relative price, and in particular the low production costs of Middle Eastern oil. By the late 1940s, with oil selling for around $2.50 a barrel such that stripper-well operators in Texas could earn a 10 per cent profit, Middle East oil with a total cost of around 85 cents a barrel, was already highly price competitive. By the mid-1960s, the *maximum* economic finding cost of Middle East oil lay between 10 and 20 cents per barrel, about 5–10 per cent of the realised f.o.b. (free on board) price that had been set on world markets by the oil companies in the 1950s (Adelman, 1972, p. 77; Weyman-Jones, 1986, p. 55; Yergin, 1991, p. 432). Offering such substantial economic rents, oil production boomed in the Middle East after the Second World War. Between 1952 and 1973, the Middle East contributed 42 per cent of the world increase in production (excluding communist countries) but accounted for less than 4 per cent ($6 billion) of world-wide capital and exploration expenditures on crude oil production (Parra, 2004, p. 40). Proven reserves in the Middle East increased from 28 to 367 billion barrels between 1948 and 1972, such that of every ten barrels added to 'free' world oil reserves during that period, more than seven were found in the Middle East. The Middle East also had the world's largest oil fields. Even by the start of the twenty-first century, when the Middle East accounted for about two-thirds of the world's proven oil reserves, ten of the world's dozen largest oilfields in production were in the Middle East. So too were 14 of the next two dozen largest. While in 1950 the United States was the only country with a well-developed oil industry, between 1950 and 1973 the industry in the rest of the world grew ninefold, at an annual rate of increase of 10 per cent. Two hundred new refineries were built outside the United States, some older ones expanded, and about 1,750 tankers of ever-increasing size were launched. While American reserves increased from 21 to 38 billion barrels over the same period, its share of total world reserves fell from 34 to 7 per cent (Weyman-Jones, 1986, p. 55; Yergin, 1991, pp. 393, 500; Parra, 2004, pp. 33, 39).

  With the growth rate of the demand for oil being exceeded by the rate of increased supply of oil from low-cost fields in the Middle East, the international price of oil fell sufficiently to pose a competitive threat to domestic fuel industries in Britain, France and the United States. By the start of 1949, oil imports into the United States were increasing at a rate of 25 per cent a year, contributing to a daily excess supply of 300,000 barrels and making it likely that domestic oil prices would fall from over $3.00 per barrel to $2.00 per barrel within a few years. There was a danger that the major US companies who not only produced oil in the Middle East but also bought from the small independents in the United States might switch over to a greater reliance on imports (Vietor, 1984, p. 95; Parra, 2004, p. 44). Cheaper oil imports also threatened the domestic coal-mining industry. Even Venezuelan residual oil whose high transport cost: value ratio precluded its export to Europe, was dumped on the US East Coast market where it competed with bituminous coal (Bohi and Russell, 1978, pp. 144–5; Vietor, 1984, 53, 100, 163–4).[1] In Western Europe, post-war price controls on coal often obscured the movement in oil and coal price relativities, but by 1958 the competitive advantage of oil imports, and the pessimistic prospects for domestic coal-mining industries, were becoming very apparent. In France, the wholesale price indices for coal compared with heavy and domestic fuel oil began to diverge significantly from 1958. Therm for therm, the price of heavy fuel oil relative to French coal fell from a factor of 2.3 in 1958 to 1.2 by 1973, a reduction of 50 per cent (Lucas, 1985, p. 14; Caron, 1993, p. 1249; Chick, 2006a, p. 145).

Matters came to a head in 1958 as post-war coal shortages ended quickly in Europe and were replaced by mounting piles of unwanted coal at pit-heads. Unsurprisingly, coal producers in France and the UK began to join domestic coal and oil producers in the United States in calling for protection against oil imports. The lobbying on behalf of domestic oil producers by the likes of Senator Lyndon Johnson of Texas was resisted by the Truman and Eisenhower administrations. However, following the onset of the 1958 domestic recession, on 10 March 1959 President Dwight Eisenhower reluctantly replaced an existing voluntary programme with mandatory quotas on oil imports, such that oil imports were to amount to no more than 9 per cent of total consumption, later modified to 12.2 per cent of domestic production. These quotas were to last for the next 14 years, being tightened and loosened by the Kennedy and Johnson administrations, respectively, during the 1960s, during which time they became increasingly distorted as they mutated away from their original *raison d'être*. Behind import controls, the prorationing or limiting of output could occur as the major oil-producing states of Texas, Louisiana and Oklahoma as well as those of Alabama, Kansas, Michigan, New Mexico and North Dakota, restricted supply to maintain higher prices. It was never clear how those prices were settled, but the general effect was apparent (Gordon, 1981, p. 158). While the average US domestic wellhead price of oil was $2.90 a barrel in 1959, it was still $2.94 a decade later in 1968, and as such 60 to 70 per cent above the price of Middle East crude in East Coast markets (Vietor, 1984, pp. 97, 119, 120, 133, 144; Yergin, 1991, pp. 538, 539). Higher prices enabled higher-cost and, though not necessarily, small domestic producers to survive (Gordon, 1981, p. 160). These in turn contributed to the 29 per cent increase in domestic crude oil output between 1959 and 1968.

In the UK, the government also moved to protect the domestic nationalised coal industry. On the demand side, potential imported substitutes were either taxed or banned. In April 1961, a 2d (two old pence) per gallon duty was imposed on fuel oil, this tax being equivalent to 25–30 per cent of the industrial fuel oil price and estimated as being worth 10 million tons of coal and £20 million a year to the National Coal Board (NCB) (FONT, 1962, para. 8; TNA, 1962o, para. 14; Robinson, 1974, p. 41). In addition, imports of Russian oil and American coal were banned. The prohibition of even 2 million tons of Russian fuel oil imports was thought to be worth 3 million tons of coal and £5 million p.a. to the NCB, while excluding anywhere between 10 and 20 million tons of American coal was thought to be worth £5–£10 million p.a. to the NCB (TNA, 1962k, 1965c, p. 13). On the supply side, the Central Electricity Generating Board (CEGB) was effectively required to burn more NCB coal than it otherwise would have done. In a sense this was consistent with previous fuel policy, since in 1954, with the 1952 Ridley Committee Report having predicted that coal shortages would last until 1965, the Conservative Minister of Fuel and Power, Geoffrey Lloyd had pressured the Central Electricity Authority into increasing its dual-firing, oil-burning capability at power stations (Hannah, 1982, pp. 169–71). Now, with coal surpluses replacing shortages, that policy was simply reversed and from 1962, the CEGB was prompted to increase its coal-burn. In a scheme devised by the Coal Reappraisal Group and forced upon the CEGB by the Ministry, from 1963/64 a coal-burn target was set for the CEGB. If it burnt too little coal it was subject to a surcharge of 27 shillings (£1.35) for every ton of coal by which it fell short. Equally, in theory at least, if it burnt too much coal, then it received a rebate of 27 shillings (£1.35). However, this scheme proved to run in one direction only. While the CEGB dutifully paid a surcharge in 1963/64, when it overshot the target in 1964/65 the NCB contested the rebate (TNA, 1967b, paras 1, 3). At the NCB's request the scheme was abolished and replaced with another which effectively meant that in deciding its 'merit order' for bringing stations into operation, the CEGB should act as if oil cost 48 shillings (£2.40) more per ton than it actually did.

Although supposedly subject to annual review, something of which the CEGB frequently reminded ministers, this surcharge was still operating in 1966/67 at a CEGB estimated cost of £1.4 million to the electricity industry and at a value of £2.3 million tons of coal to the NCB (Cmnd. 2798, 1965, para. 83). As Middle East security concerns heightened during 1967, the government, having agreed that the electricity industry's costs of burning additional coal should be borne by public funds, took the chance to increase the preference to 60 shillings (£3.00) per ton from 1 August, which included a Middle East surcharge of 38 shillings (£1.90) from July. The total loading against oil was increased to 76 shillings (£3.80) from October, comprising 38 shillings (£1.90) Middle East surcharge plus 38 shillings (£1.90) preference. As the CEGB chairman, Sir Stanley Brown dryly observed, when this loading was added to the fuel oil tax, 'it undoubt-edly maximised coal-burn to the fullest extent compatible with maintain-ing the security of the system' (TNA, 1967d, paras 23–6). The effect of such measures was to slow down the rate of oil for coal substitution in the UK economy, remarkably so in the case of electricity generation. During the 1950s, the UK's consumption of oil products between 1955 and 1961 had doubled, including a marked rise in the use of fuel oil by electricity gener-ators, and left to itself the CEGB would have made increasing use of fuel oil (FONT, 1962, para. 8; TNA, 1962p, paras 14, 121; Robinson, 1974, p. 41; Chick, 2006a). It was a perverse success of UK fuel policy during the 1960s that by 1964 coal accounted for 88 per cent of fuel burnt to generate electricity and oil for only 11 per cent (TNA, 1964d, para. 20).

The French government's response to the appearance of coal surpluses in 1958 largely caused by falling oil prices differed from that of its UK and US counterparts. Like the British in having only one domestic fuel (coal) industry at the time, the French adopted an explicitly marginalist-based plan for its managed contraction, this plan bearing the name of the Minister of Industry, Jean-Marcel Jeanneney (Jeanneney, 1997). Appointed by Prime Minister Michel Debré at the start of the Fifth Republic, this recent professor of economics (1951–58) in the Faculty of Law and Economics in Paris and author of the legal and economics texts *Économie et Droit de l'Électricité* (with Claude-Albert Colliard) in 1950 and *Forces et Faiblesses de l'Économie Française* in 1956 was sym-pathetic to the approach of the marginalist economists. Pre-eminent among these in France in this period was Maurice Allais, Professor of Economics at l'École des Mines, where Jeanneney attended the series of seminars on energy policy organised by Allais during 1960. At the end of each seminar, at which the leaders of major fuel and power industries attended and gave papers, Allais would summarise the seminar's main issues and provide clear direction as to how such issues could, and should, be viewed from a marginalist point of view. The seminars provided a useful backdrop to the re-evaluation of French energy policy which Jeanneney ini-tiated in June 1959 and in which process he accorded an important role to the Energy Section of the government-advising Economic and Social Council (ESC). The membership of the Energy Section of the ESC included Allais, and Marcel Boiteux of EDF. In giving evidence to the hear-ings held by the ESC Energy Section, Jeanneney made clear his sympathy for the marginalist approach to the reappraisal of French energy policy which he hoped that the ESC would adopt, explicitly encouraging its members to treat bygones as bygones and to concentrate on marginal rather than average-cost-based prices (Chick, 2006a). The ESC Energy Section's report of 15 October 1959 ran along just such lines and formed the basis

for what became known more generally as the Jeanneney Plan for the contraction of the coal-mining industry in France. On 21 June 1960, Jeanneney
announced that coal output for 1965 would be targeted at 53 million tonnes
comprising 28 million tonnes for the mines of the Nord-Pas-de-Calais, 13.5
million tonnes for the Lorraine mines and 11.4 million tonnes for those in
the Centre-Midi (JMJ, 1960, col. 443).

Further cuts in coal output in 1965 and then again in 1968 meant that by
1973, French national coal production was no more than 27 million tonnes,
having been 58 million tons in 1958 (Desrousseaux, 1965; Chevalier et al.,
1986, pp. 56–7). Two-thirds of the coal-mining labour force had been shed
in that period, and EDF had not, unlike the CEGB, been made to burn
more coal than it wished to do. Not that EDF stopped purchasing coal.
In fact, EDF's purchases of coal almost doubled from 6 million tonnes to
11 million tonnes between 1959 and 1967, before falling back to 9 million
tonnes in 1969 and to 6 million tonnes in 1971. Faced with rising demand,
peak-hour load, and periodic droughts reducing hydroelectric output,
EDF continued to burn domestic and imported coal in older generating
stations (Morsel, 1996, p. 335). But it was not forced to burn more coal
than it otherwise would have done. Measured in kcal and kWh, the contribution of coal to French thermal electricity plant halved in France between
1967 and 1972, while oil's contribution more than doubled. In the UK, the
proportionate contribution of coal was twice that in France, and while
there was a doubling of the contribution of oil as the electricity industry
eventually gained greater freedom to burn oil, in 1972 the UK thermal electricity plants were only deriving one-third in kWh of their fuel-burn from
oil. That the UK government also restricted cheaper coal imports placed
the interests of the 454,700 NCB coalminers in 1965 before those of the
485,000 employees of the steel industry (TNA, 1961a, 1962i, para. 17;
Feinstein, 1972, table 59). The contrast was with the French willingness to
import Russian oil and to be tempted by Polish coal, at precisely the same
time as they were making cuts in their domestic coal-mining industry. In
part, this reflected a longer French tradition of importing coal, and indeed
coal imports declined at a slower rate than did indigenous coal output. Yet
it also reflected the broader marginalist thinking epitomised by Maurice
Allais that importing Polish coal and closing some mines in the Lorraine
district could produce financial savings which could in turn be used in the
retraining of laid-off miners (Allais, 1961a, pp. 217–18).

Thus, from 1958 in all three economies, there were major shifts in government fuel policy. In the United States and Britain, measures designed to
protect domestic fuel producers were detrimental to fuel users and, as such,
to the economic growth of the entire economy. In France, there was less
willingness to protect the single domestic fuel industry and to manage its

run-down at the expense of coal-burning industries. In part, this reflected the unusual influence of an explicitly marginalist school of economists, industrialists and politicians who were at the centre of fuel policy making from the start of the Fifth Republic in 1958. Running alongside this explicit marginalist approach to fuel policy making in France, there was also a different approach within the French central government towards the issue of national security. It is with this issue of the relationship between the perceived or presented national security interest, on the one hand, and the development of national fuel policy, on the other, that the rest of this chapter is concerned. The pertinence of national security to fuel policy is that it provides a patriotic cloak in which protection-seeking domestic fuel industries can wrap themselves. While national governments will be alive to the employment and political implications of increased competition from fuel imports, responding favourably to lobbying for protection on such grounds always runs the risk of appearing as favouring special and vested interests. In contrast, protecting domestic fuel industries in the interests of national security, while also incidentally shielding them from international competition, is a more politically attractive and defensible approach. Understandably, domestic fuel industries seeking protection from imports always played up the national security of domestic production and the risks of importing fuel. The main fuel import of concern was oil, and in analysing the perception, nature and mitigation of the risks of its importation, three broad categories of risk can be identified: the production of oil; the transport of oil; and the price of oil.

The most dramatic of the risks of importing fuel is that of suppliers being either unable or unwilling to supply fuel. When the source of increasing oil imports was the Middle East and when there was growing concern with Soviet activities in that area, it was easy for domestic oil producers in the United States to emphasise the vulnerability of such a source of oil imports. Groups such as the Independent Petroleum Association of America (IPAA) were always happy to point out the security dangers of importing from the Middle East, whose oilfields 'were only six hours bombing time from Russia' (Vietor, 1984, p. 96). This fear that the Soviets would destroy the means of production, or that they would encourage Middle East producers to halt production, was dramatic but not likely. It was not in the commercial interests of Middle East producers to halt production, and, even if they had wished to, that they were sufficiently organised to do so simultaneously seemed barely credible (LaCasse and Plourde, 1995, p. 4). They also had little to gain from breaking relations with the American and British oil companies, since they used the vast marketing organisations of the oil companies in order to best sell their oil (TNA, 1958, para. 9). As for the influence of the Soviets, it is true that towards the end of the Second World War, the Soviet Union had demanded an oil concession in Iran, and that Soviet troops had only withdrawn from Azerbaijan in northern Iran in 1946 under intense pressure from the United States and Britain. Yet it was never entirely clear what the Soviet Union would have done had it acquired greater influence in Iran. To quote the oil economist Morris Adelman:

> [In the] powerful legend or stereotype of the energy-famished bear stretching his greedy paw towards the Persian Gulf because he cannot 'satisfy his needs' with domestic supply . . . 'needs' should be spelled 'nonsense' [since] all that the USSR can get out of occupying the Persian Gulf is cheaper energy [and] this is not worth the cost, still less the risk of war. (Adelman, 1982, p. 6)

Even so, as the Soviet Union itself became an increasingly important producer of oil (and gas), so too did coal-protecting governments like that of the UK in 1959 ban oil imports from the Soviet Union on grounds of 'national security' (Ebel, 1961; Adelman, 1962, 1972, pp. 201–2; TNA, 1962h, para. 4a; 1970, paras 79–80; Campbell, 1968).

Where the influence of the Soviets in the Middle East was most suspected during the early post-war period was in the events leading up to the seizure of the refineries at Abadan in Iran in 1951. The Soviet Union was assumed both to have encouraged the Tudeh Party's organisation of demonstrations at Anglo-Iranian's Abadan refinery complex and to have been happy at the eventual seizure of the refineries. With Iran accounting for 40 per cent of total Middle Eastern oil production and being a particularly important source of aviation fuel in the Eastern Hemisphere, President Harry S Truman had accepted the advice of the National Security Council in June 1951, and moved to break the impasse which had set in between Iran and British Petroleum in the wake of the refinery's seizure (Vietor, 1984, p. 36; Yergin, 1991, pp. 420–21, 454). Yet, while the seizure of the Abadan refineries did highlight the vulnerability of oil operations in the Middle East, their seizure did not significantly imperil the supply of oil. Clearly, oil-producing companies had no wish to see their refineries appropriated, but this risk of appropriation did not necessarily imply any wish of nationalist governments to stop selling oil. Although the seizure of assets occasioned much political agitation, it was not clear that the long-run security implications were so serious. The obvious response to the seizure of refineries in the Middle East was to exploit the growing capability of oil tankers to ship Middle East crude oil to refineries located outside of the Middle East. This is what happened. While before the war, the UK with little domestic refinery capacity had annually imported 2.5 million tons of crude oil, exported 600,000 tons of oil, and met most of its requirements by importing about 9.5 million tons of refined products, by 1958, while refined oil imports remained at their pre-war level, crude oil imports had soared to 29 million tons and exports were of the order of 7.5 million tons (TNA, 1958, para. 5).

The loss of refineries in the Middle East could therefore be regarded as specific one-off losses which by definition could not be repeated. Indeed, given that refineries were always likely to be an obvious target for nationalist groups in the Middle East, then, as the oil expert Peter Odell argued, there was a case for relinquishing ownership of such Middle-East-based assets. In 1967, following calls at a Pan-Arab economic conference in Baghdad for the 'gradual nationalisation of the companies', Odell suggested to the Labour Party that: 'the time is opportune for the implementation of a little more socialism in our international and national oil supplies. Pragmatism and principle both indicate the desirability of our terminating the empire of British Petroleum (BP)' (LPA, 1967, p. 2). That in short, BP might be better off selling its assets to the national companies of Iraq, Kuwait, Libya and elsewhere in the Middle East. BP's earnings from the operations were only likely to be increasingly squeezed by the producing countries, and by selling the assets the countries would gain a strong incentive to abandon boycotts while providing BP with greater freedom as to where it bought supplies. Since relinquishing their fixed assets in oil-producing countries and states would give the oil companies greater scope as to where they sourced oil, any increased diversification of supply would bring further security enhancements. The UK Treasury was always mindful that the size of BP's presence in the Middle East carried associated defence costs, although the Treasury was alive to the balance of payments implications of operating in dollar areas (TNA, 1958, para. 6; 1963g, para. 2; LPA, 1968, p. 5). None the less, it was not uncommon for BP to be encouraged to reduce its presence in the Middle East. Yet it was always easier to list alternative or additional areas for exploration and development, such as the American shale oil deposits, the Arctic, the Athabasca and Venezuelan tar sands, Libya and Nigeria, than to demonstrate commercially how these areas, none of which was free of technical or political problems or both, were more attractive than continuing to operate in the Middle East (TNA, 1963g, para. 2; 1967e, para. 1). For most of the post-war period, it was difficult to beat the low development costs of Middle East oil, and any 'security' concerns encouraging diversification away from the Middle East would need to demonstrate why such a high security premium was worth paying (LPA, 1968, p. 4).

Even if it was the case that there were serious security risks to sourcing oil from particular areas of the world, it did not then necessarily follow that protecting domestic producers against imports was the logical policy response. If in times of war and/or international disputes, supplies of oil from outside a country were in danger of being cut off, then there was all the more reason to husband that country's domestic resources for that moment of peril. As the US Special Committee Investigating Petroleum Resources concluded in a report in January 1947: 'the reserves within our own borders are more likely than not to constitute the citadel of our defence' (Vietor, 1984, p. 93). This argument was reiterated by many experts in the United States in 1948, including Yale's Eugene Rostow in his book, *A National Policy for the Oil Industry* (Rostow, 1948) as well as by the National Security Resources Board. In a draft position paper, the Board reckoned that restricting oil production in the United States as well as in a co-operative Venezuela, Mexico and Canada, and presumably then importing large amounts of Middle Eastern oil, would allow a million barrels per day (mbd) of Western Hemisphere production to be shut in, in effect creating a military stockpile in the ground: 'the ideal storage place for petroleum' (Yergin, 1991, p. 428). In 1958, Clarence Randall, chairman of the Council on Foreign Economic Policy, was still making similar arguments to Secretary of State John Foster Dulles, and in 1960 the US National Security Council viewed American shut-in production as 'Europe's principal safety factor in the event of denial of Middle East oil' (Yergin, 1991, pp. 428, 537–8, 557). Yet such a use of imports in the interests of national security was not what domestic oil and coal producers were seeking. Tellingly perhaps, the National Security Resources Board's 1948 paper was never published because domestic producers 'were appalled by its financial and political implications' (Vietor, 1984, p. 93).

While the traditional argument that fuel imports represented a source of national insecurity could be turned on its head in this way, the counterargument that it was better to use imports so as to safeguard national fuel reserves for times of crisis rested on the assumption that the mother country would not be invaded. While this may have been a reasonable assumption for governments in the United States and, albeit less so, in the United Kingdom to make, it was more problematic in France which had hosted invading armies during the 1870–71 Franco-Prussian war, and the First and Second World Wars. France and its coal mines had a worrying tendency to be occupied in time of war, while her overseas sources of supply remained comparatively secure (FONT, 1959b). Had overseas oil reserves existed during the Second World War, they might well have assisted the efforts of the Free French (ibid., p. 11). In considering fuel policy at a time when any invasion of Western Europe might provoke a nuclear response, lobbying by the nationalised French coal-mining industry, Charbonnages de France, for the security benefits of national coal production could only be taken so far. If anything, the dominant mood of the Resistance literature and of the early post-war plans was to ascribe

France's past military insecurity to its economic weakness. In this context, it was possible to argue that in the interests of future French national security, it was vital that French economic performance be improved (Lynch, 1984). To this end, securing fuels on the most efficient and competitive basis was an issue of national security which overrode the particularist claims of French coalminers. As part of the review of French energy policy which was initiated by Jeanneney in 1959, the issue of the value of the 'security' benefits of domestic fuel production was addressed by the advisory ESC. Its report on French energy policy was of the view that 'security of energy supplies ought not to lead to insecurity for the whole of our economy in international competition' and that the 'fear of certain undefined risks ought not to cause Malthusian reflexes' (FONT, 1959c, p. 12). Or as the dominant economist on the ESC, Maurice Allais argued: 'All history shows that the inconveniences of a certain insecurity are relatively temporary, while a protectionist policy carries a permanent cost'. While regarding it as essential that France have secure sources of energy, Jeanneney was pleased that the ESC accepted Allais's proposal that such considerations should not increase energy prices by more than 10 per cent (Allais, 1961b, para. 94). Since Jeanneney opposed giving any 'absolute priority' to French coal mining if it placed coal-burning French industries at an international competitive disadvantage, he also viewed any talk of a protectionist fuel policy as contrary to French national interests (JMJ, 1960, col. 443).

That a domestic coal industry could be an important secure source of fuel in time of war, blockade or embargo was not doubted, but in the trade-off between oil imports and domestic coal production, policy was based on calculations of the minimum fuel requirements of French citizens in time of war. Crude calculations made by Lucien Gouni, Rapporteur Général to the Energy Commission of the Commissariat Général du Plan (CGP), indicated that in 1944 the per capita consumption of energy had fallen to half of its 1938 level, from 2 *tonnes d'équivalent-charbon* (tEC) per habitant in 1938 to no more than one in 1944. While recognising the dramatic wartime circumstances of the reduced consumption of 1944, Gouni estimated that if by 1975 2 tonnes per capita were supplied from domestic resources, then the 'minimum vital' per head could be put at the 1938 level of consumption, given an expected doubling in the standard of living between 1961 and 1975. Supplying 49 million inhabitants with 2 tonnes per head required a total national production of almost 100 million tonnes, or almost 45 per cent of current requirements. Nuclear and hydroelectricity were expected to supply the equivalent of 50–60 million tonnes of coal by 1975, leaving domestic coal to make up the gap of 40–50 million tonnes (Gouni, 1961, p. 349). Conveniently perhaps, the subsequent Jeanneney Plan for the contraction of the French coal-mining industry aimed to reduce output to 53 million tonnes.

In placing a lower premium on the national security benefits of domestic fuel production, the French government was pursuing a fuel policy significantly different from that of Britain and the United States. It was also a further point of contrast that the French planners were explicit as to the criteria and weightings being used in their formulation of future French energy policy. While it might be thought that national energy policy making would be a matter of rational economic calculation, this was not often so. As Adelman complained, a dominant characteristic of the making of energy policy was the absence of clear, explicit criteria and calculations underpinning national fuel policies. To take but one example, what reference price was used in the process of energy policy formulation? As Adelman observed: 'the reference price of oil is everywhere in the air, never on paper. The oral tradition is strong and clear. But estimated prices committed to writing, on the basis of which decisions are to be made, are rare'. Or again: 'It is a durable comforting illusion that governments listen to someone in the back room who has calculated the balance of private and social costs, national security, miners' retraining, etc. There is no evidence of it' (Adelman, 1972, pp. 224, 227). While this charge was generally true, it could not fairly be levelled at the French governments before and during the early years of the Fifth Republic. French planning did attempt to set out the criteria underpinning fuel policy, and indeed in doing so was to provoke an early major row concerning the appropriate mix of thermal and hydroelectric forms of electricity generation. The exposition of the criteria and reference costs became particularly explicit in the Fourth and Fifth Economic Plans, Adelman himself noting the exceptional nature of the Fourth Plan (ibid., p. 227; see also CGP, 1961, pp. 71–3, 253–57; 1965, pp. 53–77). The dominant concern of the energy sections of these two plans was with the balance to be struck between the production of domestic coal, and the importation of oil from the Middle East and, especially, Algeria.

While state-sponsored exploration had led to discoveries of oil and then gas at Lacq in France in 1949 and 1951, respectively, it was the finding of large deposits of Saharan oil and gas from 1956 which offered the greatest potential benefits to France. Excited by discoveries of oil (and gas) in Algeria, a *prix de référence* for the long-term development costs of both Middle Eastern and Saharan oil was estimated, and used to make comparisons with the cost of domestic coal production. Politics intruded into these calculations, since if Algeria achieved full independence from France, then this oil would almost certainly be taxed by the Algerian government, such a tax being expected to be around 25 new francs (NF) per tonne.[2] This would make for a total cost of between 83 and 100 NF per tonne, which for comparative purposes was converted into a coal equivalent (tEC) by dividing by 1.5 to produce a figure of 55–67 NF/tEC. Should Algeria remain a part of France, then the tEC development cost to France could be as low as 38 NF/tEC. The comparative development costs of Middle Eastern oil were put at 90–95 NF per tonne, or 60–65 NF/tEC (FONT, 1961, p. 75). These oil costs were compared in turn on a tEC basis with imports of American steam coal (63–70 NF per tonne according to port), European coal (67 NF per tonne) and European steam coal (61 NF per tonne). For domestic coal, the French Nord Pas-de-Calais output was used as the coal of reference and estimated at 67.0 NF per tonne in 1959 and 66.9 NF per tonne in 1960. As seen, the cost of African oil was estimated at 55–67 NF/tEC per tonne and that of Middle Eastern oil at 60–65 NF/tEC per tonne. In broad terms, it was not expected that there would be a fall in the comparative development costs of potential coal and oil substitutes (FONT, 1961, pp. 71, 76; Chick, 2006a).

If the approach of these French governments and planners towards striking a balance between domestic coal and imported oil was peculiarly economically rational, such calculations were always vulnerable to being distorted by the traditional long-standing wish of French governments to secure their own sources of oil. France had long sought *le pétrole franc* and *'l'indépendance pétrolière'* (Giraud et al., 1967; Adelman, 1972, p. 237). In 1924 the Compagnie Française des Pétroles (CFP) had been established, with the French government holding a 35 per cent interest and the CFP in turn holding a 23.75 per cent interest in the Iraq Petroleum Company (IPC) group. In 1928, a law had been passed by which the state reserved to itself the monopoly of oil importing and refining, which it then allocated through special licence to (mainly French) firms (Delavesne, 1960). The CFP and the Compagnie Française de Raffinage (CFR) had thus enjoyed a reserved share of a domestic market characterised by attractive prices. One common justification given for such protected high prices was that without them French oil companies 'would no longer be able to combat the foreign companies and after a very short time this could be harmful to our national security' (Adelman, 1972, p. 234; see also Giraud, 1968). However, as France had on average significantly higher oil prices than its European neighbours, the high profit margins in turn attracted foreign competitors to the French market, thereby intensifying protective measures in the interests of national independence (TNA, 1970, para. 19; Adelman, 1972, p. 235). Yet for all of its state support, the CFP had never produced significant amounts of oil, and President Charles de Gaulle is said to have exploded with rage on discovering CFP's low output volume (Yergin, 1991, p. 414). As part of the Gaullist continuing search for *le pétrole franc*, it was decided to merge the Bureau de Recherches des Pétroles and the Régie Autonome du Pétrole on 17 December 1965, thereby forming the group Elf-Entreprise de Recherches et d'Activités Petrolières (ERAP) which together with CFP was to pursue and develop the French search for oil in such countries as Iran, Iraq, Saudi Arabia, Libya and Canada (Caron, 1993, pp. 1252–3; Parra, 2004, pp. 50–51).

It was into this protected system that the French government hoped to funnel and nurture Algerian oil. Initially of course the hope was that Algeria would remain a part of France and provide a long overdue solution to France's fuel poverty at low development cost. Yet even after Algeria had gained its independence, her oil exports to France were given preferential treatment by the government in Paris. After the 1962 Evian agreements providing for Algerian independence, and their subsequent revision in 1965, the increased cost to France of Algerian oil was supported by maintaining high oil prices in the nationally controlled oil distribution system which, since the '*loi*' of 1928, had required a 90 per cent use of French refineries (Hartshorn, 1967, p. 263; Weyman-Jones, 1986, p. 69). Such a policy had an opportunity cost in that France paid prices for Algerian oil higher than those prevailing on the international oil market, as well as a direct financial cost. Ultimately, not only did Algerian oil disappoint the hopes of its early supporters, but it also proved to be not that much more 'secure' than other international sources of oil.

While supplies of Algerian oil came at a rising cost to France during the 1960s, during the 1970s French companies were to lose most of their oil assets in Algeria and the French government was forced to stand by as Algeria became a member of OPEC (Organisation of Petroleum Exporting Countries) and encouraged the organisation's moves to increase prices. Just prior to Algeria gaining its independence in 1962, French companies, of which the French government in turn held a large equity stake, accounted for a large share of Algeria's total oil production. However on 24 February 1971, President Houari Boumédienne announced that Algeria would take over a majority holding of 51 per cent in all French oil interests in Algeria and would nationalise all hydrocarbon transportation and gas resources. By 1972, French interests accounted for only 23 per cent of the country's production. Within five years, the French government companies gathered together in ERAP withdrew, leaving CFP to hang on for a further five years. Newly admitted into OPEC in July 1969, in October 1969, Algeria requested the opening of talks with France for an upward revision of tax-reference prices applicable to the French companies operating in Algeria, to take account of the Suez premium granted on Libyan and East Mediterranean crudes. On 6 January 1970, Boumédienne called for a fundamental revision of the 1965 Franco-Algerian oil agreement (Parra, 2004, pp. 50–51, 120–21, 132). Throughout the early 1970s, the Algerian government steadily raised the per-barrel tax payable by French companies. Since to boycott Algerian oil would hurt mainly the French companies, France found itself committed to paying an expensive price for such security of oil supply (Hartshorn, 1967, p. 263). At the same time, Algeria also supported Libya in pushing OPEC prices upwards (Parra, 2004, pp. 125, 132). With three-quarters of France's energy requirements being met by oil in 1973, even such a supposedly 'friendly' source of oil as Algeria was not looking particularly 'secure' or reliable. Economically rational at home in its calculation of the national fuel mix and playing down the national security benefits of domestic coal production, French fuel policy was overwhelmed by the political rationale affecting French governments' relations with Algeria. Ironically, the political instinct to nurture a 'special relationship' with a particular oil producer only heightened the security risk to France of importing oil and provided little evidence that such political arrangements were any more 'secure' than striking contracts in the market.

While our first category of risk, the sourcing of oil, easily resonated in the geopolitical minds of politicians, in fact the second category, that of transportation, was inherently much riskier. Essentially, the risk was higher because the transportation of oil involved its passing through third countries which were neither its producer nor its consumer. This was as true of oil passing in tankers through the Suez Canal as it was of oil moving through the 1,040-mile-long Tapline running across Syria from Saudi Arabia to the Mediterranean. Indeed, it was not unusual, as in 1967, for the closure of the Suez Canal and sabotage to the Tapline in Syria to coincide (Yergin, 1991, pp. 425–27, 488). Even so, despite the psychological shock for the French and the British in 1956 of President Gamal Abd al-Nasser's closure of the 100-mile-long Suez Canal linking the Red Sea to the Mediterranean, what was noticeable was the speed (about six months) with which the effects of the crisis were overcome (Malterre, 1956; TNA, 1957d, paras 1, 2; Viala, 1960). Similarly in 1967, the effects of the Canal's closure proved to be less severe than expected, with the major losers being those countries forgoing revenue by imposing ineffective embargoes (Laqueur, 1972, p. 153; Maull, 1980b, p. 4; Yergin, 1991, pp. 557–8). As had become evident during the Second World War, the essential fungibility of oil gave this, the largest item moving in international trade (10 per cent by value, 55 per cent by volume), an important basis of security (Chick, 2006b). In 1956, as in 1967, the main constraint on oil mobility was the availability, capacity and capability of oil tankers as the closure of the Suez Canal forced shipping to make the longer journey around the Cape of Good Hope, lengthening the journey of Persian oil to Southampton from 6,500 miles to 11,000 miles (Yergin, 1991, pp. 480, 493). Longer journeys increased the demand for tankers as companies like BP embarked upon 'the biggest charter operation ever' (LPA, 1968, p. 6). Access to transport was still the principal problem when the Canal was closed again in 1967 when there was another spate of new tanker ordering. With orders placed, the oil crisis eased and excess tanker capacity emerged. Shipbuilders, coping with the feast and famine fluctuations in demand, found that tankers ordered between 1967 and 1975 were no longer required as oil demand fell after 1973, and in 1974–75 tankers rolled down the slip-way and straight into mothballs (Zannetos, 1966, 1987; TNA, 1967e, para. 1).

Yet what was evident from the closure of the Suez Canal was that given the mobility of the international oil tanker fleets, providing sufficient tanker capacity could be found, cutting off transport oil arteries, while undoubtedly inconvenient, was unlikely to create insuperable problems for the West. Indeed, as tankers developed in size and technological capability, so the importance of the Canal, and the disruptive effects of its future closure, were likely to diminish. Exploiting economies of scale and associated improvements in welding, propulsion, loading and navigation, as well as increases in the size of refineries, markets, storage facilities, canals, channels and harbours, the largest vessels in operation increased from 105,000 deadweight tons (DWT) in 1959 to 546,000 DWT in 1979, and the long-run cost of transporting oil in a 475,000 DWT vessel in 1986 was only 41 per cent of that of a 75,000 DWT (the 'optimal' vessel of 1958) and only 23 per cent of the cost of a 30,000 DWT vessel. Indeed, when the Suez Canal was closed in 1973, the largest tankers, which were often simply too big to go through the Canal except in ballast, were more able than in 1956 to make the longer journey around the Cape although again forcing ships around the Cape did contribute to a tanker shortage (Koopmans, 1939; Tinbergen, 1959; Zannetos, 1966, 1987; TNA, 1967e, para. 1).

That the economic impact of the closure of the Suez Canal in 1956 and 1967 was short-lived, did not prevent it from having a large psychological impact on the geopolitical mindset of politicians. Now, in addition to perceived, often Soviet, threats to the initial production of oil, there could be added the additional threat to its subsequent transportation. The 1956 Suez 'crisis', only seemed to confirm to politicians the insecurity of oil imports. In the United States, the crisis could be seen as initiating the run-up to the 1959 sanctioning of the mandatory oil import programme. Either side of the Suez crisis, Congress gave the President the power to restrict oil imports through a 'National Security Amendment' to the 1955 Trade Act, should he regard the nation's security or its economic well-being as threatened (Yergin, 1991, p. 536). In France, EDF was able to use the crisis to persuade ministers to accept its new marginalist tariff structures for the electricity industry. In the UK, not only did the Suez crisis cause Prime Minister Anthony Eden to resign on medical grounds, but the crisis was interpreted by his successor Harold Macmillan as highlighting the insecurity of an increasing use of oil imports. Infamously, one of Macmillan's responses to the crisis was to sanction in 1957 a trebling of the essentially militarily designed civil nuclear power programme of 1955 which had provided for the installation of between 1,500 and 2,000 MW of nuclear capacity by 1965 (Cmd. 9389, 1955; TNA, 1963d). Without wishing to rehearse the history and economic cost of Macmillan's decision, it is perhaps useful to quote at length sections of a letter written by Aubrey Jones, Minister of Fuel and Power to the Chancellor of the Exchequer on 7 December 1956. The purpose of such extravagant quotation is to provide a sense of the extent to which otherwise intelligent people can allow perceived considerations of national security to override their usual notions of economic common sense. The extract runs thus:

> Now that the long series of Suez debates is over . . . it is most important that the Government should be seen to be tackling boldly and imaginatively the national weaknesses which the Suez crisis has revealed . . . in the field of fuel and power. . . . Our respective officials have been discussing this matter for some time and they seem to be agreed that we could announce a near-doubling of the programme for 1965, i.e. its raising from 1,500–2,000 megawatts to 3,000 or a bit more. Frankly, to merely near-double the programme does not seem to me to be good enough. The possibility of doubling has been canvassed for a long time; it has been known for months that each individual station will be doubled in capacity. To announce only a near-doubling therefore is to suggest that we are accepting the technological advances which industry has made and taking no initiative ourselves to expand the programme. It is vital that we should go further. How much more? The Atomic Energy Authority are of the opinion that technological resources would permit of a quadrupling of the programme; they have also taken steps to ensure that the requisite raw materials could be made available. They feel, however, that a quadrupling would be something of a crash action. Prudence therefore would seem to indicate a trebling as a minimum, with an undertaking to keep the situation constantly under review . . . As a Government I think we are going to be in great difficulties if we do not at least do this. The discussions of our officials seem to have been concerned with three points: first, the relative costs of nuclear and conventional electricity. These nice calculations, even if they are economically valid, cannot, however, take account of the political and strategic cost of our dependence on imported fuels which is surely the over-riding consideration. Secondly, the officials' discussions have been concerned with the energy budget – how much coal is likely to be available to satisfy the probable energy demand, how much oil, and how much remains to be found by nuclear power. We ought, I think, to seek to liberate ourselves from oil to the fullest extent possible. As for coal, the anomaly of having in an age of full employment a basic industry terribly dependent on manpower cannot but make us profoundly pessimistic about the coal prospect. I think it imperative in these circumstances to press on with nuclear power at the maximum speed; and if by chance it both enables us to contain the import of oil and leaves us with a surplus of coal, then either we export the coal or we can, perhaps, convert it into

oil . . . Once again therefore I cannot regard these neat calculations as really at the heart of the decision to be taken; we must not allow ourselves to become victims to the statisticians. Finally, the discussions between officials have raised the question whether the resources available for investment will allow of a greatly expanded nuclear power programme. Once again, what is needed is an act of Government will. The trebling of the nuclear power programme would substantially raise the capital cost over and above what would be required if we put in thermal stations. But if we mean to solve our energy problems high investment is inescapable. How can we possibly declare to the country that a trebling of the programme is both technically feasible and nationally vital but that we are not prepared to pursue policies which will make the investment resources available? In these circumstances, I would seek your authority to declare . . . that in the Government's view the country's fuel situation requires the maximum possible expansion of nuclear power, that a trebling of the programme as a minimum is now technically feasible, and that the Government is prepared to make the necessary investment resources available. (TNA, 1956)

If politicians were concerned by the impact of short-term interruptions to oil supply caused by such events as the closure of the Suez canal, then one obvious safeguard was to provide for a stockpile of oil for use during an emergency. The holding of stocks and the size of those stocks was a response to a perceived risk of interruption of supply. In insurance terms, the risk of importing oil involved an assessment of the probability, length and cost of an interruption or embargo of supply (Toman and Macauley, 1986). Unsurprisingly, given that two-thirds of Europe's oil supply passed through the Canal, in 1957 the UK government, as chair of the OEEC (Organisation for European Economic Co-operation) Oil Committee in 1957, cajoled Western European countries into expanding their oil stocks and storage facilities, as well as supporting schemes for OEEC/OECD (Organisation for Economic Co-operation and Development) countries to share supplies equitably between member countries in an emergency (TNA, 1957b, 1965d, ch. 5, para. 13; 1967c). By 1958, France was stocking the equivalent of three months of oil imports and in January 1961, the UK Economic Policy Committee reaffirmed previous moves to increase civil oil stocks to four months (FONT, 1961, p. 20). The difficult issue was who was to cover the cost of providing the tankage and holding stocks at this level. Governments inclined towards pushing the charges onto the oil companies, an inclination not viewed favourably by oil companies, especially when, as in Britain, a duty on heavy oils had just been introduced in the 1961 Budget (TNA, 1957e, para. 4). Aggrieved by the heavy oil duty, with oil and tankers plentiful, and with claims that their profit margins were under pressure, companies were reluctant to tie up more capital unproductively in stocks (TNA, 1962g, para. 4; Krapels, 1980, p. 47). In 1965, the policy in the UK was still to aim at an average level of stocks equivalent to at least four months consumption. At this level, assuming increased supplies from the USA and other sources mainly in the Western Hemisphere, it was thought possible without serious dislocation and with some degree of rationing to survive a crisis involving the complete cessation of imports from the Middle East for several months (TNA, 1965d, para. V. 13).

Stocks also had a potentially useful role in mitigating the third category of risk, that of sudden increases in the price of oil such as occurred during the 1970s (Randall Curlee and Wright, 1988, pp. 5–6). While between the start of 1970 and 1974, the price per barrel of Arabian light crude rose from $1.39 to $10.46, the single largest jump of over 130 per cent occurred between December 1973 and January 1974 during the Arab–Israeli war. Between 1 January 1973 and 1 January 1975 the price rose by over 475 per cent. What made these 1973 price increases (and those of 1979–81) disruptive in the short and medium terms was not so much their size but the abruptness with which they were introduced. OPEC had learnt to exploit a fortuitous rise in prices and, united in part by the anger of its Arab members, hold the price up. It was not capable of spontaneously engineering cuts in production and price rises; only of exploiting for a while a price rise which had occurred for other reasons. Even so, OPEC often struggled to maintain oil prices at a high level for long. While between 1 January 1979 and 10 January 1981, the oil price rose by 134 per cent from $14.55 per barrel to $34.00 per barrel, this followed a period when oil prices had fallen in real terms (Weyman-Jones, 1986, p. 20).

What was striking about the price hikes of the 1970s was that they often appeared to be driven by proportionately small reductions in oil supply. Both in 1973 and again in 1978–79 with the fall of the Shah of Iran and a temporary loss of Iranian oil production, while it was political crises which drove traders to the spot market, the actual loss of oil output was not that large. Even in the heat of the 1973 crisis, the amount of oil production lost was only around 5 mbd, as available Arab oil fell from 20.8 mbd in the first part of October to 15.8 mbd in December. While importantly there was no longer spare productive capacity in the United States, other producers like Iran were able to increase their throughput by a total of 600,000 barrels per day. At its worst, in December 1973, there was a net loss of supplies of 4.4 mbd, or about 9 per cent of the total 50.8 mbd that had been available in the 'free world' two months earlier. This amounted to 14 per cent of internationally traded oil, in a world whose oil consumption had been growing 7.5 per cent per year. Yet the dimensions of the loss of oil were less well known at the time (Yergin, 1991, p. 615). Given uncertainty, panic buying and speculation almost certainly occurred, not least because of the impact which a lack of fuel could have for users (Adelman, 1990, p. 1). Given short-term price inelasticity, the purchase of oil on the spot market reflected in part the speculative hope of higher prices in the future and with the cancellation of contracts by oil exporters so as to sell into the higher-priced spot market, the price hikes could be sudden and steep (Adelman, 1982, pp. 7–8). Yet in the longer term there remained large reserves of oil and higher price elasticities as consumers reduced demand.

While governments did move to increase their oil stocks during the 1970s, they envisaged them more as an ultimate source of security than as a means of trading down the oil price. In 1971, prior to the OPEC crisis, the OECD and the European Community (EC) regarded oil stocks equivalent to around 65 days of consumption as constituting a commercially reasonable level. In fact, stocks in the UK (72–99 days) and France (120 days) were often higher than this, while in Japan (45 days) and West Germany they were lower. The formal level was also low in the USA, but there 'stocks' were held in the ground in the form of reserve production capacity. After the first OPEC crisis, most OECD and EC countries with the notable exception of France moved to subsume their stockholding policy (now around 90 days) into the International Energy Agency's (IEA) emergency oil allocation scheme which was established in 1974 with the strong encouragement of Henry Kissinger (TNA, 1971, paras 40–41). France did not join for fear of upsetting Arab oil producers, French foreign policy being markedly pro-Arab at this time (Madelin, 1975; Krapels, 1980, p. 59). In the United States, the long-advocated Strategic Petroleum Reserve (SPR) was established in 1975 (Adelman, 1982, pp. 10–11; Weyman-Jones, 1986, pp. 72–3, 76).

In the United States and in the IEA there was little inclination to use these oil stocks as a means of acting on prices. Indeed it has been suggested that high prices, but not wild fluctuations, may have suited Kissinger's wider foreign policy aims, not least as high oil prices provided a means of supplying finance to Iran without the need to ask Congress for funds. Instead such funding was provided by high oil prices financed by Japanese and European purchasers of Middle Eastern oil (Kissinger, 1982, p. 855; 1990, p. 665; Yergin, 1991, p. 566; Parra, 2004, pp. 138–9, 197–8, 203–5).[3] This also accorded with the general political response of Western governments and the IEA which was to try to foster 'special', or at least, better relations with oil producers based on the mutual benefits of co-operation. In Paris in 1976, under the leadership of the fuel-poor French, but without support from the relatively fuel-rich UK and USA, the principal oil-consuming nations, OPEC and the non-oil developing countries met for a Conference on International Economic Cooperation in which the greater benefits of such co-operation were contrasted with the general losses resulting from conflict and sharp oil price movements. In the United States, President Jimmy Carter was to pursue a similarly co-operative approach in his dealings with Saudi Arabia, even to the point of agreeing in late 1978 to stop buying oil for the SPR in return for Saudi assurances that it would maintain a high rate of oil output. Whether emanating from Paris or Washington, such vaunting of the benefits of mutual co-operation looked distinctly jejune as oil prices shot up in 1979 and Saudi Arabia reduced oil output on 20 January 1979, from over 10 mbd to 8 mbd. As prices settled at a higher level, and excess capacity began to emerge by March 1979, Saudi Arabia cut output again in April–June 1979 and continued to withhold capacity during much of 1979 and 1980 as prices experienced what Sheikh Yamani referred to as 'another corrective action' like that of 1973–74. None the less, Carter kept to his side of the 1978 agreement with the Saudis for over two more years, until Congress overrode him and required that the SPR fill be resumed (Adelman, 1982, pp. 6, 11; 1990, p. 3; Weyman-Jones, 1986, pp. 71–2).

Even after the turbulent 1970s, considerable differences persisted concerning the nature and use of oil stockholdings. In 1984 the IEA emergency oil allocation scheme averaged about 17 per cent of annual consumption for European Economic Community (EEC) members, but it was never entirely clear as to how, in the event of a further embargo, such a strategic stock would be shared out given that the IEA members had differing fuel endowments (Scott, 1994). Countries like the UK and Norway with indigenous oil supplies might well have differing views from non-oil producers as to the timing and extent of any stock draw-down, while within countries there could well be a clash between the interests of private oil stockholding companies and the national government (Okogu, 1992). In the United States, as with the EEC, IEA and post-Suez schemes before it, the main issues of dispute affecting the SPR continued to concern its size, financing and operation (Teisberg, 1981). The level of the stockpile remained at only around half of the 1 and 2 billion barrels favoured by economists (Randall Curlee and Wright, 1988, pp. 7–9). As with the IEA stockpile, there were also differences between economists and politicians as to when the stockpile should be drawn down. The political tendency of politicians was to wait for the wettest of wet days to arrive. The IEA's emergency allocation scheme was not used in 1978–79 and the OPEC cartel was able to push through the second oil shock (Weyman-Jones, 1986, p. 60). At the heart of the problem of when to release stocks lay the choice of trigger mechanism. The SPR and IEA stockpiles were released by a quantitative trigger mechanism, whereas economists argued for a price trigger to be used. Initially, the SPR would only fire when the 'shortfall' reached 7 per cent, although this was later changed to 3 per cent (Okogu, 1992, pp. 81–2). During the 1979–80 crisis, it never went that high, and nothing was done. Yet the price nearly trebled (Adelman, 1982, p. 12). In 1990 the Bush administration was again to sit on the SPR waiting for a 'real physical shortage' to emerge (Adelman, 1990, p. 5; Gordon, 1992, p. 9). Waiting for a large quantitative shortfall or 'shortage' was likely to be a long wait. Any 'shortfall' trigger mechanism was unlikely to fire, because the level of physical supply short-fall experienced during oil 'crises' tended to be small, as price rises damp-ened demand and encouraged the bringing on-stream of previously shut-in production wells in non-disrupted producing countries, as happened in 1979/80 and 1990. Equally with the IEA programme, the stock release trigger point was much higher than any net shortage that had been encoun-tered since the formation of the IEA, and the concern was that the IEA pro-gramme might never be activated. Conversely, these comparatively small shortfalls provoked rapid price increases in spot prices, which rose seven-fold in late 1973, threefold in 1979 and roughly 2.5 times in 1990. Since a small shortfall could provoke a large price rise, not least as uncertainty and speculative activities began to drive the market, there was a case for gov-ernments releasing oil from the SPR and IEA stocks so as to reduce the rate of price increase by increasing supply. The stockpile could then be used to offset the short-term price inelasticity of demand and to lower expectations of future price increases so as to discourage hoarding (Adelman, 1982, pp. 12–13; Gordon, 1992, p. 9; Okogu, 1992, p. 82).

The periodic oil crises of the 1970s had two particular effects on the political formulation of national fuel policies. First, the sharp price move-ments were interpreted by politicians as indicating the insecurity and unpredictability of oil imports, especially when oil price rises were also commonly and erroneously interpreted at the time as indicative of the steady depletion of oil resources. While obviously geologically finite, the economic availability of oil in the future was to be a function of its mar-ginal cost compared with other fuels. The second effect of the oil price rises was to improve the attraction of competing fuels, if comparisons were made with oil at its higher prices. When these two effects were combined with political notions of grandeur, decisions such as that of the French gov-ernment to veer heavily towards nuclear power could and did result. Not that this interest in nuclear power was new. The planners behind the Fourth Plan had warned that metropolitan France would be able to provide only a declining share of its energy requirements and had been keen that France should persevere with research into the competitiveness of nuclear energy (FONT, 1961). France had built nuclear stations as at Chinon in the Loire (TNA, 1959a). In the Sixth Plan experimentation with heavy water reactors was accorded a high place, and an attempt had also been made to develop a reactor which would run on natural uranium, obviating the need to buy enriched uranium (or enrichment services) from the United States (TNA, 1969, para. 11c). There was a persistent reluctance to use American technology, and little interest in the British Advanced Gas-Cooled Reactor (AGR) which was dismissed as costly and the 'new British coal mines' for the problems it was expected to cause. While the heavy water reactor was a technical success, its cost was considered to be too high.

Consequently, it had been recommended in early 1968 that the programme be ended, but that France do enough building and operating of nuclear power plants to gain operating experience and readiness for the next more economic generation of plants. Ultimately, and unlike the case of Britain some 18 years previously, this move to nuclear power had the support of the nationalised electricity industry, EDF, and it was EDF management which made the technological choice of reactor, eventually preferring to build light-water reactors under an American licence rather than continue with the gas-graphite programme (Hecht, 1998, p. 297). By the end of 1986, 49 nuclear installations were in operation in France, representing 45 GW of power and accounting for 70 per cent of French production of electricity in 1986, which represented nearly 30 per cent of the country's total energy consumption (Chapuis, 1998, p. 31). That the nuclear programme should emerge from the 1970s concerns with high oil prices and uncertainty about future relations with Algeria, involved a considerable extrapolation from those circumstances to judgements about the long-term structure of relative fuel prices. Quite what test discount rate was applied to proposed nuclear projects in France is difficult to discover.

High oil prices also gave a boost to the nuclear programme in the United States. Early post-war commercial take-up of the technology had been slow, as no utility could afford to meet the cost of a serious accident and no insurance company was prepared to underwrite the risk. It was only after the Price–Anderson Act of 1957 in which government underwrote the liability up to a value of $500 million under a liability ceiling of $560 million (that is, the industry was liable for the remaining $60 million should costs exceed $500 million) that the technology became commercially interesting (Zimmerman, 1987; Tietenberg, 1996, p. 158). Construction of the first commercial plant started in 1964, at Oyster Creek in New Jersey. This boiling water reactor which the Jersey Central Power and Light Company had ordered from the General Electric Light Company in December 1963, was intended to come into operation in 1967, at what British observers regarded a 'sensational' cost of £39 per kW, compared with which 'the lowest cost for any American nuclear station under construction was £63 per kW; in Britain it was about £100' (TNA, 1965e). By that time, Britain had initiated a large nuclear power programme, much of it deriving from a trebling of an essentially military, plutonium programme in the wake of the Suez crisis.

While high oil prices improved the comparative attraction of nuclear power, in the UK they probably had their biggest impact on national fuel policy by encouraging the development of oil exploration and production in the North Sea (Bohi and Russell, 1978, p. 11; Parra, 2004, p. 143). Previously marginal fields could be developed and, depending on the discount rate used alongside anticipated future oil price increases, existing fields could be exploited. From the mid-1960s, the UK Treasury had long been aware that 'substantial discoveries of oil or gas in the North Sea would of course shift radically the balance of our security' and by the early 1970s there were hopes that North Sea oil would enable Britain to be self-sufficient in oil in 1980, while Norway, an insignificant consumer of oil, could be exporting close to 1 mbd. (TNA, 1965d, ch. V, paras 12, 29). Obviously, this affected the 'security' fuel concerns of oil producers like Britain and Norway, just as previously had the discovery of major oil and gas fields onshore in the Netherlands, but as well as improving world oil security by further diversifying sources of supply, this same diversification created new complications for those attempting to construct a European energy policy (Gordon, 1981, pp. 156, 176).

What was striking was that there was no substantial return in any of our three economies to a substantial use of coal. In part this was because many pits were closed, as the industry was run down during the 1960s. Clean air legislation also limited the types of coal which could be burned, and the perceptions of the security benefits of a domestic fuel industry were severely damaged in Britain by the role of the National Union of Mineworkers in the fall of the Heath government in 1974. It appeared that a monopoly supplier of coal at home offered no more security than a cartelised oil supplier abroad, especially when politicians and their appointed nationalised industry chairmen began to demonise miners and other unionised workers as 'The Enemies Within' (MacGregor, 1986). Natural gas now succeeded coal and then oil as the growth fuel, although any interruption to the flow of gas through pipelines was likely to have greater security implications than the interruptions to the movement of oil in tankers.

What was also striking was that politicians continued to dominate the formulation of fuel policy and continued to make decisions reflecting their essentially geopolitical view of fuel supply. One happy effect of the rise in oil prices was that it rendered oil import controls in the United States irrelevant. However, in response to oil price increases, Richard Nixon imposed 'anti-inflationary' price controls which exacerbated excess demand by discouraging domestic oil exploration and production and stimulating consumption. Throughout the 1970s, politicians responded to essentially short-term hikes in oil prices by announcing long-term programs of autarchy, whether it was Nixon's Project Independence Program or Carter's National Energy Plan . As usual, fuel policy making took little cognisance of what consumers might want, but the latter voted with their wallets showing little wish to lock themselves into costly sources of domestic oil. None the less, talk of securing the security of energy supplies continued to fall easily from political lips, and inevitably political rhetoric and consumer behaviour diverged. As Bohi and Russell observed:

> While laws were passed, research budgets increased, slogans adopted, international conferences called, solemn declarations signed, and developments in the oil market closely watched, the level of oil imports rose, the ratio of imported oil to domestic oil grew, the proportion of imported oil used in total energy consumption increased, and dependence on those nations which had sought to restrict oil supplies in 1973 was escalated. (Bohi and Russell, 1978, p. 3)

The importation of fuel involves risks which can be weighed against the benefits of cheaper fuel. As a risk whose probability and cost can be estimated, contingency measures and insurance provision can be organised in advance to cover the worst effects should the feared event occur. In insurance terms, a premium in the form of an import tax could be applied to imports (Gordon, 1981, p. 175). This premium could then help finance whatever contingency measures were put in place. Such measures usually included building up stocks. These can be used in the event of an embargo to provide a period of cover during which alternative sources of fuel are sought. Essentially this is the use of stock as a store of time. Such stocks can also be used during the more likely interruption to the transport, usually shipment, of fuel. By definition, as this is a blocking of a particular route such as the Suez Canal, then other routes can be found to carry a mobile, fungible, cargo. Blocking the movement of fuel down a pipeline is potentially more serious, since alternative pipeline routes are not as easily found. If there is only one pipeline leaving the source of production, then this is effectively more an interruption to supply than to transportation. In this case, reversion may be had to building sufficient stocks to provide time to find alternative sources of fuel.

As well as providing time in which to find alternative sources of, and routes for, fuel imports, a stock of fuel also provides a means of countering the risk of sudden hikes in the price of fuel. This is effectively the conversion of a stock into a flow so as to increase supply and dampen expectations of future excess demand. Just as a stock acts as a store of time, so a flow represents the conversion of that stored time into current time. Stored time in the form of accumulated output is released at a moment in time, which is what the market is, and has the added advantage of acting on perceptions of future time. In a sense, such a conversion of a stock into a flow offends common sense. It has been difficult, for example, to persuade politicians that the correct response to a price hike is to release stocks, rather than store them up for the worse days to come.

That reflects the dominant political concern with security of supply, although in fact the risk of ever being completely deprived of all fuel is among the lowest of risks. None the less, fuel policy is peculiarly vulnerable to political envisaging of nightmares which can result in expensive programmes such as nuclear power which bear little relation to the economic efficiency of fuel supply.

Political considerations also distort fuel policy inasmuch as they reflect local concerns with such domestic issues as making profits and safeguarding jobs. That such considerations should be close to the heart of politicians is proper and unsurprising. That they should intrude into fuel policy to the extent of protecting inefficient domestic industries and denying consumers an essentially cheaper supply of fuel is much more questionable. That the protection of employment and income should be cloaked in the flag of national security is scurrilous, not least in its lack of logic. That ultimately all politicians have favoured policies which maintained high fuel prices so as to protect failing industries such as coal, or to favour pet projects such as nuclear, is of interest as a constant in fuel policy. Even if the French followed a more rational approach to the sourcing of fuel, and had a heightened sense of the security implications of low economic growth, their treatment of Algeria remained strongly political. Again, politicians were willing to use established practices in the domestic refining and distribution system to maintain high prices to domestic consumers, and the subsequent substantial shift towards nuclear power was at least as much driven by considerations of security as of economics. As ever, the consumer voice in fuel policy decisions is the weakest and least organised, and seems quiescent so long as price levels remain steady. Consumer interest groups only seemed to raise their voices when fuel prices rose towards the end of the 1960s, seemingly less concerned at having overpaid for most of the preceding decade. Their interests had not been well served by their political representatives, whose dominant concern was with their local producer groups. There was a certain irony in the fact that it took the cartelised operations of OPEC to render the US import control and prorationing schemes irrelevant, although politicians continued to distort the domestic market with price controls. Security issues necessarily figure prominently in political approaches towards energy issues, but often in a context in which inadequate efforts are made to specify the probabilities and costs of risks, and the cost and benefits of precautionary measures. To an important extent, some of these political tendencies could be corrected by adopting a marginalist approach towards the making of energy policy, as occurred in discussions of the future of coal mining in France. Yet even then, while the economic benefits of oil imports were admitted in theory, they were reduced in practice by political preferences as to the sourcing of those imports.

Political interference in energy policy, predominantly on grounds of security, was also to pass beyond national boundaries and to exert a significant influence on the post-war reconstruction of Europe. Concerns with the sourcing and distribution of coal, and then oil, were to trouble in turn the European Coal and Steel Community (ECSC) and its successor community organisations, with a prolonged struggle to promote a more efficient use of energy resources within the ECSC only making some progress towards being won in the final years of the twentieth century. In seeking to comprehend how European energy policy developed during much of the second half of the twentieth century, an informed analytical understanding of the life, times and death of the ECSC is crucial. It is to just such an analysis that we now turn.

NOTES

1. Residual fuel oil is the viscous residuum of the refining process which strips the lighter molecules from crude oil. Because of its consistency, it cannot be transported long distances economically except by water. Although it contains more heat value per unit volume than other, lighter, petroleum products, its extra handling cost, limited application, and the availability of substitutes lowers its price per barrel relative to lighter fuels or gasoline (Vietor, 1984, p. 100).
2. The franc was revalued in January 1960, at a rate of 100 old francs to one new franc.
3. In Parra's view 'Kissinger was the best friend that the OPEC hawks ever had and his decision not to press seriously for lower prices was a monumental error' (2004, p. 205).

3. The European Coal and Steel Community

On 18 April 1951, the European Coal and Steel Community (ECSC) was established when the representatives of six countries, Belgium, France, the German Federal Republic, Italy, Luxembourg and the Netherlands, signed the 50-year Treaty of Paris. On 25 March 1957 the Treaty of Rome was signed by the same six countries, and the European Economic Community (EEC) was created in 1958. The UK chose not to join the ECSC in 1951 and was not allowed to join the EEC until 1973. At a press conference on 14 January 1963, President de Gaulle announced that he would veto the UK's application to join the EEC and on 27 November 1967, as the UK government prepared a second application for entry, de Gaulle countered with a fresh proposal of association which London rejected (Spierenburg and Poidevin, 1994, pp. 561, 571). Created as an economic institution to resolve political difficulties, the ECSC had developed into the economically successful EEC which for economic reasons UK politicians sought to join. That the Community should have enlarged out of the initial concentration on coal and steel reflected as much the pace of European economic development during the 1950s as the remarkable change in the economic fortunes of the coal-mining industry during the first two post-war decades.

The coal shortages which had caused fuel crises in Western Europe in 1947 and which had led to the continuance of domestic coal rationing in the UK until 1958, quickly gave way to mounting surplus coal stocks at pit-heads and major problems for national governments as to how, and at what rate, the industry was run down. In retrospect this fundamental change in the fortunes of the post-war coal-mining industry can be seen as part of the steady shift of Western European fuel economies away from coal and on to oil, and thence on to gas. As such, this shift posed a major challenge to the ECSC and in particular to its High Authority, since in conditions of excess supply it was supposed to deploy its supranational powers in a process of administered rationalisation in which the interests of the greater community would trump those of national governments. It was to such supranational powers that the UK is often cited as objecting, and therefore not joining the ECSC, but it was also simply not perceived as being in the National Coal Board's (NCB) interest to adhere. That the exercise of such supranational powers was blocked by national governments represented a major blow to the prospects of the ECSC from 1958, not least as the establishment of the EEC in that same year also began to shift the focus of political attention away from Luxembourg (ECSC) and towards Brussels (EEC). That the shift between coal and oil also became so apparent in 1958 in turn raised problems for a community which, with Euratom also being established, now had three separate communities among whom responsibility for fuel and power was scattered. In this context, the UK sought to join the ECSC both as part of its application to join the EEC and as a means of preventing the communities from moving towards a European fuel policy which would protect coal at the expense of oil. Happy to run just such a policy at home, the UK government had no wish to see the Western European interests of oil companies like Shell and BP damaged. Alive to the UK strategy, French ministers and officials used the negotiations over the UK's application to join the ECSC as one further means of blocking its joining of the EEC. By the time the UK did gain membership of the EEC, the ECSC itself had been merged out of existence, and the fuel concerns of an oil-dominated community were with OPEC price hikes and the security of fuel supply. None the less, the period of the ECSC's existence had spanned a crucial period of European fuel policy in Europe. Not only was that period of interest for the light which it shed on the hoary question of why the UK did not join the ECSC, and then not the EEC, at its inception, but it also encompassed the early development of both communities and their negotiation of the distribution of effective powers between national governments and community institutions. As well as coal providing the focus for the establishment of the ECSC, subsequent shifts in the relative cost of oil and coal were also to provide the community with many of the issues around which the tessellation of political, economic, central and local interests was to be settled.

On 9 May 1950, at a press conference in the Salon d'Horloge at the Quai d'Orsay, Paris, the French foreign minister, Robert Schuman, first publicly announced his plan for the establishment of the ECSC. The Schuman Plan was the outcome of post-war years of shifting international diplomacy, and the pragmatic tacking of the French to those changes in wind direction. The constant concern of the French was with the post-war political settlement of Germany, and the future of its coal and steel resources (Perron, 1996). The dominant changing influence on what it was possible for the French to achieve was the attitude of the United States to the post-war reconstruction of Germany and Western Europe. This American interest in securing the stability of Western European economies altered and intensified as its relations with its once wartime ally, the Soviet Union, deteriorated. In a succession of developments which included the failure of the

Moscow Council of Foreign Ministers in April 1947 to reach a four-power agreement on the future of Germany; the consequent decision of the new US Secretary of State George Marshall to give up the search for an agreement with the USSR and pursue the economic reconstruction of Western Europe as a bulwark against communist advance; and in 1949 the creation of the North Atlantic Treaty Organisation (NATO) which was militarily effective by the close of 1950, the United States moved to confirm its clear interest in the defence of Western Europe (Milward, 2002, p. 17).

In turn this developing American view of Western Europe altered what France could hope to extract from a post-war settlement.[1] In particular, it impacted on France's approach to the question of what should happen to the Ruhr. As part of its immediate post-war efforts to enhance its national security, the French had at first tried to detach the Ruhr area from Germany, or at least to give it extraterritorial status. Subsequently, given shifts in the US position, the French government thought in terms of international ownership for the Ruhr industries, and then the establishment of an International Authority for the Ruhr as part of a bargain by which the French agreed to the establishment of a West German government. Winning US support, France strengthened its proposals for an International Ruhr Authority which would allocate the output of Ruhr coal, coke and steel between German consumption and exports for European reconstruction, into a formal demand made at the London Conference on Germany which opened on 26 February 1948. By early March 1948, the Conference had agreed on the admission of the Western-occupied zones of Germany into the OEEC, and by June the Conference had formulated proposals to create the German Federal Republic. However, France did not get the International Ruhr Authority that she wanted. The US wanted the proposed Ruhr Authority to be responsible for the coal and steel industries in France and Benelux as well, but France still clung to the idea of an Authority in which French officials inside Ruhr mines would allocate coal to France. This was unacceptable to both the UK and the USA and in the Ruhr Agreement of December 1948 there emerged an International Ruhr Authority with only general supervisory powers to allocate Ruhr coal while the Ruhr was occupied, but with no executive power to enforce its decisions once the new German state would have come into existence (ibid., p. 43). The Agreement envisaged that in the indefinite future, the International Authority for the Ruhr might inherit from the Allied High Commission in Germany such powers of general management and investment control as might be necessary to maintain security and to promote economic co-operation. By the spring of 1950, however, it was apparent that the International Authority for the Ruhr was not functioning properly and had little chance of taking on fresh powers in the future.

The division of Ruhr coal supplies between internal consumption and export became at that time purely nominal, since the Ruhr industries were anxious to export all they could. In the field of discriminatory practices, the powers of the International Authority for the Ruhr overlapped those of the Allied High Commission which covered Western Germany and which inevitably had the last word. It was also made clear to the French in international discussions that the International Authority for the Ruhr was unlikely to inherit, at least for a long time, any further controls from the Allied High Commission. In the course of time it became clear to the French that they could not indefinitely exercise their powers on the Allied High Commission to limit German steel production and capacity, to determine the form of ownership of German heavy industry, or to prevent all forms of vertical combination between the coal and steel industries. The ultimate reasons for these changes were of course political. The federal government had been established and the position of Germany in international affairs was becoming very important. The US and the UK governments were pressing for an increasingly liberal policy designed to bring Germany into the Western camp (TNA, 1951b, paras 25, 26).

Given the concern with West Germany's future role in international affairs, Dean Acheson, Marshall's successor as Secretary of State, sought to clarify and strengthen the role of the new Federal Republic in Western Europe before Marshall Aid and occupation came to an end. One favoured means was the encouragement of further integrating institutions, and indeed Acheson declared 'the creation of supra-national institutions, operating on a less than unanimity basis for dealing with specific, economic, social and perhaps other problems' (Milward, 2002, p. 44) to be essential. In pushing towards an integrated Europe, US policy moved towards accepting that this might have to involve a customs union representing the triumph of US political over economic interests. Since Anglo-American financial agreements forbade commercial discrimination against US goods, the only way to strengthen ties with Western Europe might be 'the necessity of taking a single plunge into a full customs union' (Milward, 2002, p. 44). That would be permitted by existing American proposals for establishing regional, multilateral, commercial regimes providing they resulted in a lowering of the average level of previous duties of all their member states. The US was keen that Britain should play a pivotal and lead role in promoting the integration of Europe, as in a customs union. But, on this as on the eventual proposals for the ECSC, the UK government prevaricated. Certainly, Ernest Bevin, the UK Foreign Secretary, had no taste for discussing a customs union if it meant doing so as a principal agent of the US government. At the same time, the growing US involvement in Western Europe reduced the necessity of the immediate post-war Anglo-French alliance, since both countries could now get their security on the back of the USA and later NATO. All this made the UK see the USA as the only reliable provider of security beyond its own efforts. In a personal message to Acheson, Bevin emphasised that the UK could not 'accept obligations to Western Europe which would prevent or restrict the implementation of our responsibilities elsewhere' (Milward, 2002, p. 44). Five days after receiving Bevin's message Acheson made a direct appeal to Schuman. Only France, he wrote, could now devise a policy which could securely grapple the Federal Republic to the West European structures which had emerged from the Marshall Plan. Success depends 'on the assumption by your country of leadership in Europe on these problems' (Milward, 2002, p. 44).

For the French, unlike the British, there were clear, specific gains to be made from helping Acheson. Tying Germany into a larger European framework provided France's best chance of influencing Germany's future behaviour. Moreover, if French ambitions could be pursued within a broader European community then they might stand a better chance of realisation. In place of the previous French proposals for the International Ruhr Authority and the attempts at the London Conference to establish an 'association' controlling the Ruhr, Jean Monnet now drew together ideas for a common market in coal and steel between France, Benelux, Italy and the Federal Republic – and the UK if it would participate – which was likely to be more acceptable to the Americans. Such a common market would be supervised by a supranational authority (High Authority) composed of independent experts and of government representatives, with the Federal Republic being on equal terms with other members. This was effectively what Schuman announced in the proposals for the pooling of Western European coal and steel industries on 9 May 1950. But without American intervention even this French approach to limiting German power might have failed. The process of reorganising the German coal and steel industries which was occurring under the Allied High Commission would come to an end with the inception of the Schuman Plan. Knowing this, the Germans pushed to ensure that the reorganised units were of sufficient size, and that the steel companies had guaranteed access, preferably through ownership of coal mines, to their own coal supplies. This caused them to lock horns with the Allied High Commission in Germany and it was only American activity in brokering a settlement with the German federal government and trade unions that prevented the talks from breaking down in February 1951. For the United States, the political consequences of any breakdown of talks had proven unacceptable, representing as it would a major setback to attempts both to settle the German question and to promote a more integrated European Community. Once agreement had been reached between the federal Chancellor and the Allied High

Commission on 29 March 1951, Monnet went to Bonn on 4 April 1951 to negotiate the issues of French and German representation in the High Authority and the Assembly. Chancellor Konrad Adenauer wrung further concessions from the French concerning the possible removal of Allied controls on German heavy industry. Thus, as soon as the Treaty was signed on 18 April 1951, the French government sought the agreement of the US and the UK governments to a revision of the relevant intergovernmental agreements. Following tripartite negotiations, it was agreed in October 1951 that once the Schuman Treaty came into operation, restrictions on German steel capacity and production would cease (ibid., paras 9–11, 28).

For the French and the Americans, the political advantages of tying West Germany into a Western European bloc, out of the Soviet orbit and in place of an independent German national state, were clear. The potential for further integration was also clear and the political aspirations of the Schuman Plan were incorporated into the Preamble to the Paris Treaty. For the French, the Treaty was a first practical step towards the creation of a closely knit European Community, in line with the Pflimlin Plan for the pooling of agricultural produce and with the Pleven Plan for a European army. The French saw a potential role for Western Europe as an important international player in the free world along with the United States and the British Commonwealth. In promoting European integration they knew that they enjoyed the support of the United States. While the French would welcome UK support for the idea of Western European integration and would no doubt welcome UK participation as providing another possible brake against any attempt by the Germans to dominate the Community, they were suspicious that the British would use their position in the Community to reduce the effectiveness of the High Authority. The French were also not averse to maintaining the undisputed moral leadership among the participant countries. In short, the French stood to gain from UK approval, support and friendly association for, rather than member-ship of, the Schuman Community. Indeed there remains a strong suspicion that the French insisted on prior agreement to the principle of pooling their coal and steel industries under an International High Authority knowing that this would be unacceptable to the UK government (ibid., paras 3, 12, 13, 21, 22, 24). Nor did the French give the British early sight of the Schuman Plan, the text of which had been hurriedly pulled together by Monnet and his planners in under a week before Acheson's arrival in Paris on 8 May 1950 prior to a meeting in London of the foreign ministers of the three Western occupying powers on 10 May. Acheson was shown the text personally by Schuman on 8 May, and he agreed to keep it confidential, notably from the British government. On the morning of 9 May, Adenauer was shown the text and it was only on the afternoon of the same day that

René Massigli, the ambassador in London, provided Bevin with a summary. At six that evening, Schuman announced his proposal and invited the Federal Republic, Italy, the Benelux countries, and the United Kingdom to a conference to negotiate the creation of a European Coal and Steel Community as set out in the proposal. They were also invited to commit themselves before the conference started to the creation of a supranational authority.

For the UK, the ECSC was never to be bestowed with the same political importance as it received in France. It was essential neither for UK national security nor, with NATO established, for British defence of Western Europe. Rather, in London any acceptance of supranationality was viewed as undermining some fundamental basis of foreign policy. That, in Milward's words:

> by entering into the commitment to supranationality the United Kingdom would be accepting obligations to its European neighbours which would reduce its independence from, and thus its status and influence with, the USA, while at the same time weakening its links with the Commonwealth and thus even further reducing its influence over the USA. (Milward, 2002, p. 75)

To British eyes, French policy throughout this early post-war period was one of pragmatically backing into the ECSC, as its more ambitious plans for limiting German power were steadily closed down. In that light the Schuman Plan was but the latest attempt by the French to retain some control over German heavy industry, for which they were willing to surrender some of their own sovereignty to a supranational body. Without such a surrender of sovereignty, the Authority's functions might be no more than those already performed by the OEEC in regard to steel development, and these were seen as insufficient by the French. In addition to the gains in terms of national security, there might also be some economic benefits for the French. They could benefit from the Treaty provisions abolishing transport discrimination and obtain an improved supply of coking coal for their steel industry without having to engage in the 'disagreeable hard bargaining' which attended the quarterly division of the Ruhr coal resources undertaken by the International Authority for the Ruhr. The British also suspected the French of seeking to use the deconcentration clauses of the Schuman Treaty to 'freeze' the German coal and steel industries in their current structure, and to use the control of investment provisions of the Treaty to limit the indefinite expansion of the German steel industry on American and other international capital (TNA, 1951b, para. 27).

For the British, it was less clear what, if any, would be the economic benefits of joining the ECSC. While then, as now, much political excitement was generated by the issue of the supranational powers of the High

Authority, the essential economic point was that neither the iron and steel nor the coal industries in Britain saw any great advantage, and in the NCB's case considerable disadvantages, to joining. To the British iron and steel industry, much of the rationale of, and for, the High Authority was very familiar. The argument that in militarily and economically vital high fixed-cost industries subject to trade cycles and periodic excess capacity, a form of industrial supervision was required to manage industrial capacity, was one long deployed by planners in the iron and steel industry. When the necessity was urged for a High Authority able to 'co-ordinate and mediate' investment, marketing schemes, and prices etc'; to 'investigate and report' in regard to discriminatory practices; to 'supervise' the operation of schemes agreed between members; and to 'act as court of reference', the insistent vocabulary might as easily have come from the leaders of the British iron and steel industry (TNA, 1950d, para. 54). In 1946, the British Iron and Steel Federation had prepared its own development plan, the First Steel Plan, urging the benefits of administered rationalisation, and the powers later sought for a Steel Board extended such a planning approach to include the suppression of private property rights (Chick, 1998, ch. 7). True, there was a fundamental political difference between the exercise of such powers within a nation, and their supranational application. Yet, while the French had no greater love than the British for conceding powers to a supranational authority, their incentive for agreeing to do so, at least initially, was to acquire greater influence over German coal and steel resources. The British had no such economic or political incentive. Given that, all of the political misgivings about the supranational powers of the High Authority came into play. The UK Working Party on the Schuman Plan, which had been established in May 1950, was by no means alone in expressing its doubts as to whether 'the Authority need be supra-national in order to ensure the effective discharge of its responsibilities'. Equally it questioned the need for 'the Authority [to] be given any outward form which marks it as a prototype of federal institution for Europe nor carry any implications for the future political unity of Europe' (TNA, 1950d, para. 115). As such, as made clear in the official communiqué issued on 3 June 1950, the British government felt unable to satisfy the French require-ment that all countries attending the conference to discuss the Schuman Plan should commit themselves in advance to the creation of a suprana-tional authority (TNA, 1951b, paras 3, 4, 6).

In fact, as might have been predicted, for all of the insistence on prior agreement, during the subsequent negotiations which opened on 20 June 1950, a restrained version of the High Authority was negotiated. The creation of a Council of Ministers and of a Common Assembly substan-tially modified the autocratic position originally proposed for the High

Authority; great emphasis was placed on voluntary agreement and full publicity for the High Authority's activities; and the temporary safeguards for national industries against the consequences of establishing the free market were greatly elaborated in the Treaty signed in Paris on 18 April 1951. But the British government was not at the negotiations, and it did not even send observers, claiming that it was concerned to do nothing which could be represented as obstructing negotiations. All that issued from Britain were restatements of British objections to a supranational authority (TNA, 1955d, para. 1). Shortly after the commencement of negotiations, the Schuman Plan was debated in the House of Commons, on 26 June 1950, and the Chancellor of the Exchequer, Sir Stafford Cripps simply reiterated that it did not seem 'either necessary or appropriate in order to achieve our purposes to invest a supra-national authority of independent persons with powers for overriding Governmental and Parliamentary decisions in the participating countries'. He also expressed his doubts as to whether any such scheme would be workable unless preceded by complete political federation, while the Prime Minister, although conceding that 'the old idea of sovereignty' must be modified, expressed his reluctance to surrender sovereignty to 'an irresponsible body appointed by no one' (TNA, 1951b, para. 14).

Political misgivings in Britain about the Schuman Plan were reinforced by the iron and steel industry's lack of interest in, and the hostility of the NCB to, membership of the ECSC (TNA, 1955d, para. 8). That in post-war conditions of coal shortage, the Western European countries would wish to improve their access to British coal was unsurprising. In 1952 the ECSC and UK coal industries were approximately the same size, their respective output being 240 and 230 million metric tons (TNA, 1953a, para. 1). Among Western European economies, Britain was by far the largest coal producer (219 million tonnes in 1950) compared with West Germany (110 million tonnes), France (50.5 million tonnes) and Belgium (27.3 million tonnes). By 1950 neither Britain nor West Germany had recovered their equivalent pre-war output levels, West German coal output being 20 per cent lower, and Britain's 10 per cent lower, than in 1937. While Germany was a large net exporter of coal to Western Europe, and the Saar exported largely to Germany and France, France and Italy were substantial net importers. Between 1951 and 1957, German coal exports were not to grow significantly as increasing quantities of coal were burned domestically, not least in electricity power stations. As had happened after the First World War, the immediate post-war shortage of coal in Western Europe was partially alleviated by US shipments of coal, this time to the European Coal Organisation. Negligible before the war, coal exports from the United States to Western Europe stood at 33,640 million tonnes in 1947, the main recipients being France/Saar (12,080 million tonnes), Italy (7,207 million tonnes) and Belgium (4,184 million tonnes). Such US coal exports continued to be important into the early 1950s, particularly so for France for whom they formed often half, but in 1947 three-quarters, of her total imports between 1945 and 1948. While American coal exports to the future ECSC countries fell steeply from their peak in 1947, they were to rise again significantly in 1951 during the ECSC negotiations, thereby underlining the value of potential NCB coal exports to Western Europe (United Nations, 1948, paras 22, 37; Picard, 1951, pp. 67–8; TNA, 1951b, paras 35, 147; 1952, para. 9; Milward, 1984, p. 136; 1992, pp. 50, 66–7).

For its part, the NCB seemed to have little interest in exporting coal. As a percentage of total coal production, net exports fell from 23 per cent in 1935 and 20.4 per cent in 1938, to 4.7 per cent in 1946, 7.9 per cent in 1950 and 1.2 per cent in 1955. Of these minimal exports, ECSC-equivalent countries received 22 per cent in 1948, and 32.5 per cent in 1950 compared with 38 per cent of the larger volume of exports in 1938 (Ministry of Power, 1958, tables 4 and 52). As the Ministry of Fuel and Power noted, ECSC countries received only 1.5 million tons of coal in 1951 and 3.5 million tons in 1952, making them a less important bloc of countries than Scandinavia, the Irish Republic and Commonwealth countries like Canada which bought 5 million tons of UK coal. Nor did Britain normally import coal from ECSC countries (TNA, 1953a, para. 1). That the NCB could have exploited the international export market was clear, and that it was more profitable to sell abroad than at home was indicated by the differential of at least £1 per ton between export and domestic coal prices. That the NCB chose not to export reflected a commitment to the domestic market born of intense government pressure to avoid any repetition of the 1947 fuel crisis, a reading of its obligations as a (newly) nationalised industry to maintain adequate domestic supply, and a willingness to cater to an administered price-controlled excess demand for coal by emphasising the need to expand domestic production. So long as coal shortages persisted, so too was the NCB guaranteed priority in the allocation of resources by central planners, and inasmuch as price controls contributed to coal shortages, the NCB had little incentive to lift them.

If Britain were to join the ECSC, then not only would the NCB come under strong pressure to increase its exports to other ECSC countries, but the ECSC principle of equality of access to raw materials would cause the differential between international and UK domestic coal prices to come under close scrutiny (TNA, 1950d, para. 21; Kipping, 2002, pp. 136–7). The Community was almost certain to seek the abolition of the UK domestic price controls which it criticised as constituting 'dual pricing', and at odds with the Schuman Plan's concern to secure 'fairness' of managed competition (TNA, 1950a; 1950d, para. 77; 1951b, paras 27, 138, 141; 1952, para. 11; 1953a, para. 96; 1953b, para. 94). The standard complaint against the UK was that with domestic coal prices being at least £1 per ton less than its export prices, UK exports of manufactured goods were being subsidised by a loss-making nationalised coal industry, and, at the same time, the NCB was provided with a protected domestic coal market. The OEEC had targeted dual pricing as an obstacle to the development of a common European market, and in 1949 the UK had had to dissent from criticisms made in an OEEC Trade Committee Report on dual pricing (TNA, 1950a, paras 51, 57; 1950b; 1950c). American criticism of the practice was strong and persistent (TNA, 1950d, para. 21). While the British denied that the NCB deficit of £14.0 million between 1946 and 1952 constituted either a large or deliberate subsidy to other industries, it did implicitly admit some subsidy in recognising that entry into the ECSC was likely to cause domestic coal prices to rise, with a consequent impact on the better-quality coking coals used in steel coke ovens (TNA, 1953a, para. 96). In all, though, leaving aside the supranational issues, there was little industrial or political support for joining a coal community, membership of which was likely to require an increase in exports, a scrapping of dual pricing, and presumably a sharp increase in domestic coal prices. The coal industry was happy to associate itself with the sentiments of the Steel Trades Unions, the Engineering Advisory Council and the Iron and Steel Board whose opposition to ECSC membership was couched in terms of their preference for their relations with the Community being allowed to develop out of normal commercial negotiations (TNA, 1955d, para. 8).

Although the UK government chose not to join the ECSC in 1951, both it and leading Europeans were keen that some institutional links should be established between the two. In September 1952 shortly after the High Authority had begun its work, the UK established a permanent delegation at the seat of the High Authority. The President of the High Authority, Jean Monnet, was keen to strengthen this point of contact and he and the High Authority pressed for an agreement leading directly to UK association in the common market for coal and steel. In fact the Agreement signed on 21 December 1954 (Cmd. 9346) only created an institutional framework for discussion and negotiation, the Council of Association between the British Government and the High Authority coming into operation on 23 September 1955 (TNA, 1955c, para. 5; 1955d, paras 2–3, 10–13). Monnet's motives for promoting such an Association, which he had first mooted in a letter of 24 December 1953 were various. In part, it was always useful at various times to have a counterweight to Germany, while preserving what Monnet saw as French moral leadership in the community (TNA, 1955c, paras 4–5). More specifically, on occasions, Monnet found it useful to use evidence of London's interest in European integration to exert pressure on the French National Assembly to commit itself, for example, to ratifying the Treaty establishing a European Defence Community (EDC). In fact, to stay with that example, the advent of the Mendès-France government in Paris in mid-June 1954 and the French parliament's rejection of the EDC at the end of August had the effect of unsettling the High Authority, which became less certain of the French government's attitude towards a Europe in which the ECSC was the 'only existing European institution'. Shaken, Monnet and the High Authority moved to conclude the agreement with the British in December (Spierenburg and Poidevin, 1994, pp. 201–2, 204, 210). In general, after the resignation of Monnet as President of the High Authority in mid-1955 and the collapse of ambitions for an EDC, the political momentum of the ECSC began to fall away. Monnet's successor, René Mayer, tended to concentrate on improving the efficiency of the ECSC without expanding its powers (TNA, 1955d, para. 14; 1959b; Matláry, 1997, p. 15). For its part, the British used the Association Agreement and their influence in the OECD, where Sir Harold Hartley and Professor Austin Robinson had been mainly responsible for its two major policy reports on energy, as their main conduits of influence on ECSC fuel policy (TNA, 1963c).

The main potential commercial disadvantage of not joining the ECSC was the risk of being excluded from the Community's market in the event of a return of pre-war conditions of surplus production and capacity. Were there to be any reversion to quantitative restrictions, such as those imposed by France, Belgium and Holland before the war, there was little doubt that these would favour large ECSC coal producers, notably West Germany, while the French would toughen up the import controls which it operated through its Association Technique de l'Importation Charbonnière (ATIC) (TNA, 1950d, paras 103–4; 1962b, para. 5). Yet, at home, with the Ridley Committee Report in 1952 predicting domestic coal shortages until the mid-1960s and with the West German economy importing coal, the consequences for the NCB of being excluded from ECSC markets must have seemed distant (Cmd. 647, 1952; TNA, 1953b, para. 98). All the greater then was the shock of the slump when it came, earlier (1958) and deeper than ever expected. Between 1958 and 1959, ECSC coal stocks quadrupled (Viala, 1960; Weyman-Jones, 1986, p. 17). In part, the supply of European coal was rising as demand was increasingly satisfied by oil substitutes, but there was also increasing competition from American coal imports. Falling Atlantic freight rates from 1956 reflecting excess shipping capacity and a steady decline from early 1957 in the American wholesale price of coal, which was exacerbated by the impact of the 1958 American recession, all contributed to increasing and persistent competition from American coal.

American coal imports had steadily squeezed UK coal out of the German market, UK exports to Germany falling from 1.6 million tons in 1954 to only 0.5 million tons by 1957 (TNA, 1959c, para. 7; Milward, 1992, p. 89).

When the slump came in 1958, and as it became clear, as the French noted in 1959, that 'ce n'est plus la pénurie mais l'abondance qui se dessine à notre horizon', so too did national governments in the ECSC revert to protectionist fuel policies (FONT, 1959a). The immediate response of Belgium, France and West Germany was to restrict imports both from third countries and from each other, with Belgium pressing the High Authority to declare a state of 'manifest crisis', so as to restrict imports into the community as a whole (TNA, 1959c, para. 10, iii; 1960b, para. 4). On 2 September 1958, the West German government invoked Article XIX of the General Agreement on Tariffs and Trade (GATT) and moved to restrict coal imports from other countries, primarily the United States (TNA, 1959c, para. 1). UK complaints about the German presentation of high coal stocks as a political rather than an economic problem, about the base years used by the Germans in calculating British import restrictions, and about the Germans' later adjustment of the base period so as to cut the UK quota in half were all to no avail. Suddenly, British faith in working through the Council of Association looked shaky and the professed British view that 'our relations with the Community are based on the assumption that it will act as a Community and that member countries will not pursue independent policies' looked naive (ibid., paras 9–10).[2] In 1959, the Belgian government threatened the High Authority and the Council of Ministers with 'unilateral action', and forced them to agree to the introduction of import controls in 1960, this annual agreement being extended year by year after that (TNA, 1962c, para. 1). The crisis laid bare the political construct that was the ECSC, a community whose establishment had been driven by the geopolitical interests of France and the United States. It also exposed the weakness of the High Authority which had been unable to use any supranational powers to trump national self-interest. To that extent, when in 1962 the UK came to apply for membership of the ECSC as part of its wider application to the EEC, many of the previous obstacles to its membership had diminished in size (FONT, 1962, para. 1). In conditions of coal surplus, the issue of dual pricing was simply a quaint memory, as the NCB incurred substantial losses on exports in competition with American coal (TNA, 1960a, para. 2). The High Authority's powers had proved to be more limited than feared, and if the crisis had posed a first major test for the High Authority, it was one which it had failed. It had failed to exert authority over France and West Germany, it had failed to introduce production quotas because members refused to transfer policy making away from the national governments, and it had reaped the harvest of previous years when governments had used their effective control of nomination to the High Authority and the Authority's need for governments to sanction the secondment of their officials to the staff of the High Authority as a means of reducing its supranational, independent character (TNA, 1960c; Weyman-Jones, 1986, p. 17).

The UK government had originally intended to apply to join the ECSC and Euratom when substantial progress had been made in the negotiations for joining the EEC, but it was decided in February that, despite 'not altogether satisfactory' progress in the EEC negotiations, an application to join the ECSC should be considered by the ECSC Special Council of Ministers meeting in Luxembourg on 13 March (TNA, 1963a, paras 1–3). By this time the likely benefits to the UK coal industry of membership were regarded as slim. While the Community coal market was now by far the biggest overseas market for coal accessible to British exporters, the Ministry of Power thought that given the need to negotiate about quotas, and the competition from oil, the prospect of a 'net gain in exports would probably be limited', and that generally, 'in the case of coal the balance of economic advantage or disadvantage in joining the Community is small by comparison with the political considerations' (TNA, 1960b, paras 3, 4, 6).

Where the UK might benefit from ECSC membership was in its negative ability to prevent a coal-protecting energy policy being formulated. While as protective of its coal industry as other large producers, notably West Germany, the UK also had a keen interest in the increasingly important EEC oil market. In 1960, the EEC produced 110 million tons of oil products in its own refineries and imported over 10 million tons of products from outside the area. Some 80 per cent of the crude oil fed into the refineries was imported, mainly from the Middle East, and the remaining 20 per cent produced in the Community, including the Sahara. Although Shell had a small interest in Saharan oil production, the great bulk of the oil supplied to the EEC by UK companies came from outside the area. Just under 100 million tons of refined products were used in the EEC itself and the rest exported. Shell and BP had about 30 per cent of the community's total trade in oil, and in 1960 the companies' total receipts from trade in the area were valued at £530 million. In addition to their usual large investment in production and transport facilities, the companies had around £450 million worth of refinery and distribution networks in the community. In all, about half of the trade of the British/Dutch oil companies was with the Continent. Unsurprisingly, the major UK objective in this area was to see as little change as possible, with the movement of oil continuing between the Community and those non-EEC parts of the world from which UK companies overwhelmingly drew their supplies. There was particular distrust of any moves towards a community energy policy which might establish discriminatory protection for indigenous production and irritate the producing states from whom the companies drew their supplies (TNA, 1961b, paras 1, 2, 4, 5, 15, 30).

Prior to the UK's application to join the ECSC, progress towards a community energy policy had been extremely limited. In October 1957, on the eve of the creation of the Economic and Atomic Energy Communities, the Six did subscribe to an Energy Protocol affirming the need for a co-ordinated energy policy, and the High Authority was made responsible for the development of such a policy by the three communities (EEC, ECSC and Euratom) (TNA, 1962d, para. 1). Political and bureaucratic talk of 'co-ordination' led nowhere as usual, and the administrative response in 1959 of establishing a committee, an Energy Inter-Executive Committee chaired by Pierre Olivier Lapie of the High Authority, did little to help overcome fundamental differences of interest among Community members. While the mainly coal-consuming Dutch, Italians and Luxembourgeois favoured cheap supplies, the coal producers, notably Belgium and Germany, sought some form of protection from oil and coal imports. Similar differences existed between France and Italy with their oil interests, and the Benelux countries without, although it was agreed that the Community's common external tariff on crude oil, which was fixed in the Treaty of Rome, should be set at zero (TNA, 1957a; 1961b, paras 6,7, 24, 25; 1963a, para. 26). Refined oil tariffs remained to be agreed. The chances of formulating any common energy policy were reduced further by the symbolic and practical fact that while coal and solid fuels produced from coal were subject to the Treaty of Paris, the newer fuels such as oil, natural gas and secondary fuels came under the Treaty of Rome (ibid., para. 29). Neither Treaty made provision for a common energy policy, and indeed the Treaty of Paris specifically preserved the responsibility of individual governments as regarding their commercial policy towards third countries (TNA, 1957a, para. 1). Here, at least by 1961, some progress had been made inasmuch as the European Commission had secured agreement that there would be prior consultation by individual governments in advance of trade agreements with third countries.

In this context it was at best curious and at worst destructively hypocritical for the French to raise the issue of a common community energy policy during negotiations for UK accession to the ECSC. Interest in the prospects for a common energy policy had been revived in the European Commission by the recent success in agreeing a common agricultural policy. As Robert Marjolin of the European Commission unintentionally punned: '[if] an agreement is possible in the most difficult field of all both on short- and long-term policy objectives. . . . it should be possible to draw up . . . a common energy policy which could be achieved in the course of a few years' (TNA, 1962a). Emboldened by its success in agriculture and happy to use energy policy as a stick with which to beat the High Authority, in 1962 the European Commission pushed for a common energy policy or, at the very least, agreement on a common external tariff for refined oil products (TNA, 1957a, para. 3; 1962m, para. 2). Yet Marjolin also pressed the ECSC members to consider the long-term rationality of national energy policies designed to maintain high prices and thereby protect coal. Addressing the European Parliamentary Assembly in January 1962, Marjolin was blunt in his characterisation of what passed for the Community's energy policy: 'there is not one European country which does not protect its energy resources and, in fact, the oil policies of the Six countries, however different, have the same end in view, namely to charge relatively high prices to the consumer' (TNA, 1962a). In some ways, the British approach was much closer to that of Marjolin at the Commission with its interest in oil than to that of the High Authority, with its preponderant producers' interest in coal. But Britain's own stance was always ambivalent. For all of its liberal rhetoric, it was the UK's own fuel policy which imposed oil duties and effectively forced the nationalised electricity industry to burn coal. As the Treasury's J.L. Carr noted of the document on 'European Energy Policy':

> We should avoid using adjectives like liberal and outward-looking to describe policies which include a tax on oil designed to protect the coal industry, continued operation of a good many uneconomic pits, which would have to be subsidised if they were not under public ownership and carried by more profitable pits, and complete exclusion of Russian oil and American coal. (TNA, 1964a, para. 1)

In identifying major obstacles to the development of a common energy policy, it was at France that Marjolin pointed his largest accusatory finger. For Marjolin, the French law of 20 March 1928, which gave the French government extensive powers over oil imports and allowed it to protect indigenous crude oil production, constituted one of the major difficulties in securing the introduction of the Common Market for oil (TNA, 1961b). The mere threat of using the 1928 law had been sufficient to 'persuade' the major oil companies operating in France to contract with the French Saharan-producing countries to take considerable quantities of Saharan oil in preference to their usual, mainly Middle Eastern, sources of supply. With oil investments in Sahara and with Algeria being regarded as part of France, and therefore exempt from any import barriers established, the French had attempted to prevent a zero tariff being set on the community's crude oil imports, the successful resistance to this coming in particular from the Netherlands and Italy (TNA, 1961b, para. 11; 1962a, paras 9, 13, 25). Similarly, through the state-sponsored ATIC, France also exercised control over coal imports (FONT, 1959b, p. 3). Although it was modified on the opening of the ECSC and the French government acceded to High Authority requests that French importers be allowed direct access to coal producers in other Community countries, there was not a significant increase in freedom of trade (FONT, 1960b, pp. 4–5; Viala, 1960). The ATIC retained the power to supervise the execution of contracts and the exclusive right to arrange transport. Importers handling less than 10,000 tons a year were barred from direct access to producers outside France and the ATIC retained its monopoly over imports from third countries (TNA, 1962c, para. 4; 1962e, para. 7).[3] While Jeanneney as Minister of Industry was prepared to use marginalist arguments to justify the reduction in size of the French domestic coal industry, French politicians in general maintained a firm preference for protecting French coal, and where substitution with oil was necessary, doing so from French Saharan sources.

Given Marjolin's strictures against the French, it was surprising that the French themselves began to call for a European common energy policy. In fact, there was a need for a stricter *appellation controllée*. Quite simply, what the French meant by a common energy policy was one which favoured French oil, disadvantaged oil imports from non-members such as the UK, and allowed France to retain controls over coal imports. In short, the French sought to perpetuate a highly regulated energy policy, and, as Jeanneney put it, not allow the British to 'free-wheel'. Aware of British concern at the prospect of any such energy policy, Jeanneney began to express his enthusiasm for laying down the '*grandes lignes*' of just such a common energy policy embracing coal, oil and gas. In the face of such talk, the strategy of UK officials was to confine themselves to a low-key formal response confirming their willingness 'to co-operate in arriving at a satisfactory energy policy' and 'happy to accept 1957 Protocol, although in many respects it is out of date' (TNA, 1962d, para. 4). At the same time, they expressed their preference for not participating in discussions on energy policy until a full member of the Communities, wary that although history made it doubtful that the Six could reach agreement on energy policy during 1962, the prospect of UK entry might just propel them into just such an achievement. The UK representatives were always mindful that 'our interest would be best served if the main place for consideration of general energy matters was EEC rather than in a coal-dominated ECSC' (TNA, 1962d, para. 4). However, stimulated by the UK application to join the ECSC, the French pressed for the negotiation of a common energy policy to be completed before entry occurred. The British were displeased, complaining to Jeanneney that:

it did not seem a happy arrangement that the ECSC should face us with a common policy which they had been stimulated to devise by our application. Any plans must surely be based on the assumption of a Community enlarged by the inclusion of Great Britain, and would it not be preferable that our plans for a common policy should be discussed with us after our adhesion to the Communities. (TNA, 1962f)

Both at the time when the UK's application to the ECSC was considered, and in subsequent reflections on de Gaulle's vetoing of the UK's application to the EEC, there was general agreement among participants that even though problems arose, 'given a minimum of French goodwill it should have been possible to resolve these questions without too much difficulty' (TNA, 1963a). That minimum was never forthcoming. From the start, on receiving the UK application, the German, Italian and the Benelux representatives were happy to send an encouraging response to the UK, expressing hopes for an early opening of negotiations. In contrast, Jeanneney considered the UK application as requiring only a formal acknowledgement and that any negotiations could wait until 'sufficient' progress had been made in Brussels. He also insisted that any negotiations should be conducted by the member governments, and not by the Council on a Community basis as the Benelux and Italian representatives wanted. This conflict remained unresolved, and an interim vague welcoming statement was agreed. On 22 May the ECSC Special Council of Ministers again discussed the UK application, this time for a whole day. Michel Maurice-Bokanowski, Jeanneney's successor as Minister of Industry, in a minority of one, repeated the French thesis that the negotiations should be between governments and that the discussions on the entry of the UK into the three European Communities should be considered at one intergovernmental conference. Ultimately, the French were to get their way, with formal bilateral relations effectively being closed off by the French-driven decision that negotiations should be intergovernmental. The French view was that since the negotiations were part of an intergovernmental conference for accession to all three communities, they should, like the EEC and Euratom negotiations, take place in Brussels. As it turned out, the fact that they took place in Luxembourg played straight into French hands. Had the ECSC negotiations been in Brussels, the representation of the Five might have been at an adequate level, or at least have been given adequate guidance. The French faced both ways at once. On the one hand, so long as the Luxembourg negotiations remained at a technical level (and it was in Brussels, not Luxembourg, that political decisions had to be taken), then, as the French director of the Conference Secretariat told the UK delegation, French ministers would always have an early train or, plane to catch. On the other hand, while it suited the French that the conference should in theory be one between seven member governments, in practice they succeeded in making it into a dialogue between the Community and the UK. Thus it became common practice for agreement to be reached at meetings among the Six before there was any discussion with the UK delegation. When the meetings *à Sept* took place, the discussion was in fact in the form of a dialogue between the chairman, tied to an agreed brief *à Six*, and the UK representative. The former sat at one end of the conference room, the latter at the other, with the other representatives of the Six mutely lining the two sides. As one of these representatives observed, it often seemed more like a courtroom, with the UK delegation in the dock, than an international conference. Despite pressure from the UK delegation for adequate time to be earmarked for discussion *à Sept*, the French managed to secure agreement that the representatives should not meet for more than two days a week (and not every week), and that the proportion of time spent *à Sept* should be very small. As the UK Report on the Luxembourg conference complained of the French:

> Their prime interest was not so much to devote time to finding solutions with the UK delegation, as to condition the thinking of the Five until they accepted the main French theses. In this, through the intellectual capacity and persistence of the leader of the French delegation (Morin), and his ability to trade on the strength of the 'esprit communautaire', they had some success'. (TNA, 1963a, Pt 2 paras 4, 5, 38, 39, 42, 46, 47)

The French also moved to shut out the NCB and Iron and Steel Board representatives from direct involvement in negotiations. The NCB representatives had assumed that because of the role which they had played in the Council of Association, they would also participate as full members of the UK delegation in negotiations for the accession of the UK to the ECSC. However, once it was decided that the negotiations would be intergovernmental, the Six made it clear that they did not consider it proper for the boards to be represented in the conference room, and they were reduced to being represented on the UK delegation by advisers who did not take a direct part in the negotiations. In practice, these advisers were judged to have been of little value.

Effectively minimising NCB involvement in discussions, the French then moved to stoke up fears within the ECSC of the impact which admittance of the large NCB monopoly would have on the ECSC. The political sensitivity of this issue was initially underestimated by British officials, this reflecting the narrowness of the coal industry's contacts with Europe during the 1950s. Their point of contact had been with the High Authority's Council of Association, but their discussions tended to be on technical matters. Certainly, the NCB failed to pick up sufficiently on its potential perception as 'a colossus, which would have no difficulty in a few years' time in capturing a large share of their markets' (TNA, 1963a, para. 16) and one whose size might enable it to shield marginal collieries at a time when the closure of the weakest mines was inevitable. Statements in Rome in the autumn of 1962 by the NCB chairman of a brighter future and of an export target of 10 million tons (whether in total or just to the Six was not clear) did little to quieten Community apprehension. Fears concerning the NCB's size were skilfully exploited by Morin, the leader of the French delegation, who questioned the practicality of reconciling the size of the NCB with the fundamental objectives of the Treaty of Paris. For Morin, since the Treaty had not been drafted with an enterprise of the size and influence of the NCB in mind, any safeguards contained in the Treaty were inadequate, not least as they were based on an assumption of a modicum of competition, which the NCB was likely to expunge. Given that the French view at one and the same time considered the NCB incompatible with the Treaty's objectives and ruled out the possibility of any revision of that Treaty, there was little room for manoeuvre.

The British came to have a grudging respect and dislike for Morin, whom they regarded as an able stonewaller, an exploiter of divisions, a master of his brief and the intellectual superior of his colleagues of the Six (TNA, 1963a, Pt 1, 3, 57, 60; Pt 2 paras 2, 4, 8, 10, 12–14, 16, 18, 27, 30, 58). To provide just some sense of the British delegation's feelings towards Morin, there was the evening of 13 November 1962, when Morin arrived late for dinner with Keith Stock and Warner of the UK delegation, having spent the day tearing a draft report to pieces. Perfectly affable over his 'truite estragon flambée, au ricard', he had then 'turned his tortuous mind to pricing rules' before leaving in the snow to continue his demolition of the draft report at the night session (TNA, 1962l). Or again, when the chairman of the representatives, Armand Simon, lunched with Warner and Stock on 28 November 1962:

> He [Simon] arrived late and described himself as furious. Over the aperitifs, he said that he had always been loyal to his colleagues in the Six, but his experience that morning had been too much for him. They had spent hours on procedural minutiae of no consequence ... It was clear that our French colleague, Monsieur Morin, was mainly responsible for the black rings around Monsieur Simon's eyes, and he was singled out for special mention. Monsieur Simon wanted us to know that his colleagues of the Six were ashamed of Monsieur Morin's obstructive behaviour at the Ministerial Meeting of November 19, when he had been left to lead the French Delegation after Monsieur Maurice-Bokanowski had left ... Monsieur Simon saw no substantive reason why our negotiations should not go ahead rapidly. The trouble was the obstruction of the French and the excessively technical zeal of other Representatives who were adept at 'splitting hairs into four parts'. . . . Over the coffee, a gleam came into

Monsieur Simon's eyes at the thought that he would have handed over the
Chairmanship before the next report was taken by Ministers. (TNA, 1962n)

In the end the negotiations to join the ECSC ended once the larger negotiations for accession to the EEC broke down in Brussels (TNA, 1963b).
Even so, the negotiations at Luxembourg had not shown the ECSC in a
favourable light and did not bode well for its future. The common energy
policy sought by Marjolin had been hijacked by the French for their own
purposes. While Jeanneney had attempted to force through a new, albeit
French, energy policy, his successor Maurice-Bokanowski 'was only interested in politics' and the vacuum which this left in the French administration was filled with the competitive squabbling of Leblond and Albi,
respectively directors of oil and coal in the Ministry of Industry. The
prospects of any common energy policy emerging dimmed further, when
the departures from the High Authority of Dirk Spierenburg and Simon
Nora left the ECSC even more under the protectionist influence of the coal
and steel 'cartels' (TNA, 1962m, paras 1, 5). While a Protocol was produced
in 1964 by the ECSC Special Council of Ministers after almost seven years
of argument, it did not make much progress towards a common energy
policy. The Dutch regarded it as a victory for those who, because of
national interests, were opposed to any serious Community energy policy
(TNA, 1964c). In preparing, again, in 1966 an application for membership
of the EEC, UK officials recognised that accession would imply subscrib-
ing to the 1964 Protocol, but did not regard this as risking any loss of
control over national energy policy since

> in practice each of the Six still basically follows its own policy, and their inter-
> ests in the field differ widely enough to make it unlikely that they will move
> rapidly towards a common energy policy. . . . If and as a genuine common
> energy policy came in the longer term to be developed, we ought, given the
> differing interests of the present members and our weight in each of the main
> sectors – coal, oil, nuclear power, and, as now seems likely, natural gas – to avoid
> being obliged to adopt a Community policy unacceptable to us'. (TNA, 1966f,
> para. 44)

Following the vetoing of the UK application in January 1963, the
Ministry of Power increasingly looked to Brussels as the main focus of its
contacts with the Six. Not only did the ministers of most of the Six seem
increasingly to bypass Luxembourg and concentrate on Brussels, but that
was where the European Economic Commission and the Euratom
Commission were located. Moreover, the growth industries of oil, electricity and gas were the responsibility of the European Commission, while the
ECSC was left to grapple with the intractable problems of a coal-mining

industry of diminishing economic importance (TNA, 1963c). In that task, the High Authority was permanently scarred by its handling of the 1958 coal crisis and its failure to secure the requisite qualified majority in the Council for the special measures available in the event of a 'manifest crisis'. That at much the same time the EEC and Euratom were established by separate treaties independently of the ECSC, and were responsible for other competing energies eroded further any of the ECSC's claims to pre-eminence (Spierenburg and Poidevin, 1994, pp. 569, 651–2).

Increasingly, the High Authority was reduced to arbitrating between competing national interests rather than exercising any supranational power of its own. It was striking that the supranational, interventionist and finance levying powers accorded to the High Authority in the Treaty of Paris in 1951 had no equivalent in the Treaty of Rome. Moreover, with the potential merger of the ECSC into the EEC, it was likely that the High Authority's powers would be reduced or abolished (TNA, 1966f, para. 32). Certainly, after 1958 the pretensions of the High Authority to supranational authority looked increasingly vain. When in 1963 at the start of the Del Bo presidency, Germany moved to set up the Rationalisierungsverband, which was to pay government subsidies to the German coal industry as part of its rationalisation programme, it mattered little that in October 1963 Lapie condemned the Rationalisierungsverband as obstructing any possibility of establishing a common energy policy. National interest was dominant, long-time beneficiaries of High Authority aid such as Belgium were now rationalising their coal industry without help from Luxembourg, and similar subsidies had been, or were about to be, paid by the French and Dutch governments. Steadily the High Authority's importance and powers ebbed until it was eventually put out of its misery with the merger of the communities on 1 July 1967 (TNA, 1966f, para. 32; Spierenburg and Poidevin, 1994, pp. 600–601).

Attempts at constructing a Community energy policy did continue but to little effect. The European Commission tried and failed in 1968. The Commission's formal competences concerned primarily coal and nuclear energy, both of which were diminishing in importance in comparison with oil. The growing importance of oil, the fuel over which the Community had least influence, suited the British and made the issue of European energy policy less of an obstacle to its future membership of the Community. As all countries came to import increasing quantities of oil, so too did the divisions between European fuel producers and consumers begin to blur. Indeed, it was the common concern with oil prices which led to some commonalty of response to the OPEC price hikes of the 1970s. However this response was articulated, not so much through the European Commission, but through the IEA which helped to organise the emergency oil-sharing mechanism. France, however, chose not to participate, arguably slowing again any moves towards a common energy initiative in the EEC. It was not to be until the mid-1980s that fresh and purposeful moves were made towards a European energy policy. From 1985, energy policy became one of the main concerns of the Commission's internal market programme. With the replacement of the unanimity voting rule for Council decision making with the introduction of qualified majority voting for internal market proposals in the Council of Ministers, it became easier, but not easy, to push through the waves of directives required for the realisation of the 1985 Single European Act (SEA). In seeking to implement the SEA, decision-making power shifted to the institutions of the EC, and primarily to the Council of Ministers, as member states had relinquished their right to veto decisions. In pursuing an internal community market alongside national moves towards deregulation, new regulatory powers were likely to be centralised within the EC or in the Commission itself (Matláry, 1997, pp. 1, 6, 18, 21, 120). While progress has not been smooth, faltering after 1992 and always running into resistance from countries like France, in historical perspective it is a striking development.

NOTES

1. The following two paragraphs lean on Milward (2002).
2. The British complaint stemmed in part from their restrictions being appraised using the base years of 1956/58, 1958 being regarded by the UK as having been an artificially bad year for UK exports of coal to Germany. The German argument that there was some precedent in GATT for choosing the previous three years as a base period when operating restrictions on imports, was not accepted by the British, who argued that there were in fact no generally accepted rules as to what in such circumstances constituted non-discrimination. Article XIII of GATT provided for countries imposing restrictions to choose a base period which took account of special factors which may have affected trade, with the countries affected then having the right to seek consultation if they were dissatisfied, something which the British were ready to do.
3. The NCB coveted such an arrangement but was told that ATIC was only tolerated as it had been in existence when the Common Market was established, with functions that were readily adaptable to the necessary supervision.

4. Moving the margin to the centre: pricing electricity

> The central policy prescription of microeconomics is the equation of price and marginal cost. If economic theory is to have any relevance to public utility pricing, that is the point at which the inquiry must begin. (Alfred Kahn, Professor of Political Economy, University of Cornell, *The Economics of Regulation*, 1970, vol. 1, p. 65)

In many ways, Alfred Kahn in the United States in the 1970s was only reiterating what his fellow economists James Meade in Britain and Maurice Allais in France had urged in the 1940s (Meade, 1948). While each economist's exposition of his ideas concerning marginal-cost pricing was of inherent interest, the main concern of this chapter is with the practical impact of their thinking. In Britain, although Director of the Cabinet-advising Economic Section within government, Meade was unable to persuade Herbert Morrison, the minister responsible for the legislative progress of the nationalisation programme, of the merits of marginal-, as against average-cost pricing. In France, Allais as Professor of Economics at the École des Mines in Paris taught a remarkable generation of post-war students who went on to implement and evangelise many of Allais's marginalist teachings. Notable among such students was Marcel Boiteux, who was to be a leading figure in the devising of marginal-cost-based 'tarification' in EDF from the 1950s and its Director-General from October 1967. It was to such tarification that Alfred Kahn looked with admiration in the 1970s as oil price hikes and fears of energy shortages gave an impetus to the development of marginal-cost-based energy policies in the United States. With its central concern with the efficiency of resource allocation, marginal-cost-based energy policies could improve the efficiency of use of both fuel inputs and capital investment. By the late 1960s in Britain, marginal-cost approaches to fuel pricing and investment were being pushed to the fore, notably in the 1967 White Paper on nationalised industries, although many of these efforts were to fall foul of wider government interference with prices during the 1970s (Cmnd. 3437, 1967). Nevertheless, in comparison with the opening years of the post-war Golden Age (*Les Trentes Glorieuses*), by the end of the 1960s in the United States and Britain there was a much greater interest in the use of microeconomic mechanisms within utilities, and as such, in making greater use of marginal-cost pricing. This chapter will trace and analyse the development of that growth of interest in marginal-cost pricing. In doing so, it will concentrate on the case of the electricity industry, not simply because of the size and intensity of its capital investment, but also because it presents particularly complex problems for the application of marginal-cost pricing. These arise partly from the budgetary break-even problems accompanying the application of marginal-cost pricing in increasing-returns industries, and also from the tight relationship between peak demand and total capacity requirements caused by the inability to store electricity (leaving aside pumped storage).

Marginal cost is the change in total costs caused by producing one more unit of output. In the short run, it might be thought of as the change in operating costs, with fixed costs remaining just that. In the long term, then, the cost of providing new capital investment will also be included. Marginal cost may also be thought of as the avoided cost of not producing one more unit of output. While this may be of interest to the individual producers, assuming optimistically that they know where their marginal-cost and marginal-revenue curves lie, the larger importance of marginal cost is its centrality to the assumptions made about resource allocation by economists. In theory, if a Paretian allocation of resources is to be achieved in which it is not possible to reallocate resources without making others worse off, then it is essential in perfectly competitive conditions that the price of every commodity should be equal to its marginal cost. Unless price equal marginal cost, then price will not accurately reflect the cost of producing that additional unit of output and would therefore fail to send the accurate resource signal to consumers. In implying an ability to do one thing rather than another, this assumption of choice at the margin and an ability to engage in substitution, made marginalism on the basis of opportunity cost, rather than utility theory, the main driver of the increasing use of mathematics in economics from 1870 (Blaug, 1962, p. 279). In a perfectly competitive market, therefore, all decisions are made at the margin, such that the market price provides consumers who would have paid higher prices and producers whose marginal calculations allowed them to supply at a lower price with consumer and producer surpluses, respectively.

In monopoly industries, if prices are set equal to marginal cost, then an issue of immediate concern is how total costs will be covered at those levels of demand where marginal cost lies below average cost (total costs divided by output). This is less likely to be a problem for (decreasing-returns) industries with classic, U-shaped average-cost curves, where marginal cost is likely to remain above average cost for a sufficient proportion of the range of output. However, in (increasing-returns) industries financial problems arise, often because fixed or sunk investment forms a large proportion of total costs, such that marginal cost lies below average cost for much of the range of output. Given that the fixed assets exist, so as to reflect accurately the resource costs of their additional use, recourse is had to pricing at marginal cost. This may not cover total costs, but to price at average cost would often lead to a higher price and a potentially lower demand. Setting output where marginal cost equalled marginal revenue could incur a deadweight loss represented by that section of demand which was willing to pay above and up to marginal cost, but was forced to forgo its consumer surplus. It was with this efficiency of resource use across the economy that welfare economics was particularly concerned, such that it promoted pricing at marginal cost while applying to fixed and sunk investment the maxim of letting 'bygones be bygones'. Such issues commonly arise in utilities like electricity, telecommunications and railways, although any consideration of railways needs to distinguish between losses arising from marginal-cost pricing and those arising from excess capacity.

Such problems of how to marry the maximisation of the total benefits to society of using existing assets with the financial need to cover total costs have occupied economists for at least a century and a half. The starting point for such formal analysis is usually identified as the 1844 paper 'On the measurement of the utility of public works' by Jules Dupuit (1804–66) of the École des Ponts et Chaussées (Dupuit, 1844; Munby, 1978; Etner, 2000, p. 179). In analysing the maximisation of the social benefits of using roads, canals and bridges, Dupuit sought to maximise the area under the marginal-utility curve, or what Alfred Marshall was later to term the 'consumers' surplus'. Since the cost of, say, using a bridge once it was built was close to zero, then the benefits of encouraging the use of the bridge, rather than, say, the building of new boats or bridges, were such as to justify the government reducing the toll of the bridge to encourage its use. The issue of how far price should fall depended on the measurement of maximised utility. While it was Marshall who was later to develop the marginalist implications of Dupuit's predominant concern with maximising utility, none the less Dupuit's importance lay in his initiating (passing over Cournot) of this fundamental area of welfare economic analysis. In France, Dupuit's work was developed by the likes of Clément Colson, Maurice Picard, François Divisia and René Roy not least in response to the tarification issues presented by railways (Colson, 1890; Etner, 2000, p. 182).

Railways, characterised by a natural monopoly network, indivisibilities, and very large-scale economies in relation to market demand, provided a striking example of the problem of squaring economically efficient pricing with covering total costs. In the United States, Harold Hotelling argued that while output should be priced at marginal cost, the resulting deficits should be met from lump-sum taxes, that is, taxes that did not affect behaviour at the margin (Hotelling, 1938; Lerner, 1944). In Britain, Frank Ramsey (1903–30), mathematician, philosopher and elder brother of Michael (1904–88), the future Archbishop of Canterbury, suggested in work on taxation designed to minimise deadweight loss, that the deficit be covered by pricing inversely to the price elasticity of demand (Ramsey, 1927; Dokic and Engle, 2001). While this represented a necessitous departure for financial reasons from pure marginal-cost pricing, it did coalesce with the common practice on the railways of pricing according to value of service rather than the cost of that service. While much of the work concerning railway tarification was of direct relevance to electricity, Allais was to break explicitly with the use of such discriminatory tariffs reflecting utility (what the traffic will bear) rather than cost, as had been developed out of the Dupuit tradition by Divisia, Colson and René Roy. Allais was supported in this break with the discriminatory tariffs interpretation of Dupuit by Charles Malégarie, head of the Compagnie Parisienne de Distribution d'Électricité (CPDE) (Malégarie, 1947; see also Bousquet, 1947; Boiteux, 1986; Glachant, 1989, p. 121). Increasingly the thermal-generating electricity firms supplying large cities were happy to break with the *tarifs monômes* offered by the early hydroelectricity producers, and to devise tariffs which increased consumption and hence the returns on their fixed costs. That still left open the question of how any financial shortfalls were to be covered, and Ramsey pricing was to remain an important approach to the problem.

The use of marginal-cost pricing became a widely discussed issue among economists in the middle of the twentieth century. In very broad terms, the development of economic planning in the Soviet Union had led to a renewed interest in marginal-cost pricing as a potential basis for pricing in a planned economy, as reflected in the Lange–Lerner rules for decentralised market socialism (Blaug, 1962, p. 586). It was in reviewing Abba Lerner's *Economics of Control* that James Meade in Britain became particularly interested in securing the pricing of public enterprises along marginalist lines. In general, Allais knew of Meade's work, a translation of Meade's 1936 book, *An Introduction to Economic Analysis and Policy*, having arrived in France in 1939 just prior to the outbreak of the Second World War (Meade, 1936; Glachant, 1989). In June 1941, Allais read in translation Meade's *Économie Politique et Politique Économique*, which Allais regarded as a 'major contribution' to the subject (Allais, 1994, p. 31).

After being demobilised in July 1940, Allais returned to his pre-war employment as an engineer with the Service des Mines in Nantes, which was in German-occupied France. Remarkably, he now added to the pre-war training in physics and mechanics which he had received at the École Polytechnique before entering the Service des Mines, a self-taught immersion in economics. Allais's motivation was 'determined by circumstances' (ibid., p. 19). Shocked by the unemployment which he had seen on a trip to the United States in the summer of 1933, and having seen at close hand the social disorder in France following the elections of 1936, aged 29, Allais now sat down after work and prepared for the post-war world by 'trying to resolve the fundamental issue in all economics: to promote the greatest economic efficiency possible while assuring a distribution of income which would be generally acceptable' (Allais, 1994, p. 19). From July 1940, Allais read any economics texts in French on which he could lay his hands, the dominant influences being Léon Walras, Vilfredo Pareto, Irving Fisher and, to a lesser extent, François Divisia, Professor of Economics at the École Polytechnique. In the 30 months between January 1941 and July 1943, Allais wrote the almost one thousand pages of *À la Recherche d'une Discipline Économique*, which was never published but appeared in type-written form in 1943 funded by subscription. In 1947, *Économie et Intérêt* was published and these two works formed the basis of the award of the Nobel prize in economics to Allais in 1988. It is not often that two works not translated into English, and one of which was not even published, should have ultimately won such acclaim.

While Allais's work was not always welcomed in the *Grandes écoles*, it provided both the basis and the evidence for making Allais the dominant force in macroeconomics and applied industrial economics in France in the post-war period (Etner, 2000, p. 330). The objections to Allais's work were that it was too mathematical and too liberal in a period of growing interest in economic planning. Some of these differences came to a head during the contest between René Roy and Allais, the latter backed by the industrialist and writer Auguste Detoeuf, for the chair in economics at the Écoles des Mines. Allais was eventually elected on 24 November 1944 by 23 votes to five to what was formally titled as the 'Chaire d'Économie Générale et Industrielle de l'École Nationale Supérieure des Mines de Paris' (Allais, 1994, pp. 20, 124). Allais was to provide a central focus and inspiration for the development of the marginalist approach in post-war France. The main centre for discussion was the 'Groupe de Recherche Économique et Social' (GRECS) founded by Allais and Detoeuf in 1945 and which was to run until 1969. For almost its first 10 years, the group met on the first floor of Café Céron, Place Saint-Sulpice, thereafter at l'École des Mines. Other important centres were the CNRS seminar in econometrics established by René Roy and then run later by Edmond Malinvaud, the Société Française de Recherche Opérationnelle (SOFRO) created by Georges Guilbaud, Gabriel Dessus and Marcel Boiteux, and later, under Pierre Massé's leadership, the Third Plan.

Like Meade, in the immediate post-war period, Allais wrote at length urging the adoption of marginal-cost pricing by the newly nationalised industries, these writings including a 116-page text on the application of marginal-cost pricing in the French nationalised coal mines, the Charbonnages de France (Allais, 1952a and 1952b). In addition to Boiteux, among the students to whom Allais exposed his marginalist approach in this immediate post-war period were Gérard Debreu, who had been admitted to the École Normale Supérieure along with Boiteux in 1941, and Dessus (Boiteux, 1989; Bungener and Joël, 1989; Morsel, 1996, p. 354). Contacts were also good with Massé, *directeur de l'équipement* at EDF and Detoeuf at Alsthom. Before the war, Dessus had worked at CPDE and his hand is discernible in that company's pre-war approach to tarification. Debreu was encouraged by Allais to take up a post in the United States where he was to make his career, receiving the Nobel prize in 1983 for his contribution to the theory of general equilibrium, six years after Meade (1977) but five years before Allais (1988) won theirs. For some years, Debreu maintained his interest in tarification issues, publishing on the tax-subsidy problem in 1952 and then working with Kenneth Arrow on a theory of value which incorporated the time of a commodity's production (Debreu, 1952; Arrow and Debreu, 1959). Dessus was to become the leading evangelist for the marginalist approach, being a dominant figure at early post-war international conferences on approaches to utility pricing and exhibiting a particular flair for writing accessible parables highlighting the marginalist issues. One such concerned the short- and long-run marginal costs of collecting wood and coal for householders in a village, in which the added complications of 'discontinuities' existed as a succession of cliffs had to be climbed in order to reach more trees. Another was the well-known parable of the traveller going by train from Paris-Nord to Calais, in which short- and long-run marginal costs, discontinuities and indivisibilities are all discussed in relation to pricing the last seat on the existing train and the pricing of the next seat on an additional new train (Dessus, 1949a; Nelson, 1964).

While Allais was writing and teaching out of the École des Mines, James Meade was arguing the case for the adoption of marginal-cost pricing by nationalised industries, both within the Cabinet-advising Economic Section and in the pages of the *Economic Journal*. In the run-up to the writing of the legislation nationalising the electricity industry in Britain, a lively debate erupted in the *Economic Journal* in 1944 and 1945 concerning the use of marginal-cost pricing in public enterprise. In addition to Meade, contributions to the debate in general, and to its relevance to electricity in particular, came from some distinguished economists including Ronald Coase and Tom Wilson (Meade and Fleming, 1944; Coase, 1945, 1946; Wilson, 1945). One feature of the debate was its tendency to bifurcate between those who viewed the socialised industries, as they were then known, as a group, and those who viewed pricing issues on an industry-by-industry basis. As an example of the first approach, Meade suggested that diminishing-returns nationalised industries like coal mining use profits arising from pricing at marginal cost to offset losses in increasing-returns nationalised industries like electricity. Against this, Coase preferred the use of multi-part tariffs within an industry. It was not just that he wished to treat each industry on an individual basis, but that he also questioned the appropriateness of the Hotelling–Lerner solution to covering deficits arising from the gap between pricing at marginal and average cost. It was not clear to Coase why taxpayers should cover deficits arsing from pricing at marginal cost in the electricity industry. Coase's objections concerned the maldistribution of factors of production among different users, the fact that it led to a redistribution of income, and that the additional tax would produce harmful effects. There would also be a redistribution of income in favour of consumers of goods produced under conditions of decreasing cost. Moreover, as Coase pointed out, the deficits arising from the use of marginal-cost pricing in decreasing-cost industries, would vary according to population density. Those consumers living in low-density areas would probably be unwilling to pay the total costs of supply, and would therefore forgo the utility service, while those consumers living in cities would find their gains limited because, with equipment there being relatively intensively used, the divergence between marginal and average cost would probably be much less than elsewhere (Coase, 1946).

Drawing on earlier academic work by Paine and Clemens, as well as on the practical experience of utilities, Coase advanced a more specific approach based on utility tariffs (Paine, 1937; Havlik, 1938; Clemens, 1941). In terms of the history of the electricity industry, such tariffs broadly hailed back at least to the previous century. In 1892, John Hopkinson had argued for two-part tariffs divided between standing and running costs (Hopkinson, 1892–93; Byatt, 1979, p. 132; 1963; Hausman and Neufeld, 1984). Similarly, Coase proposed the use of a two-part tariff in which the entry fee for receiving output was set at a level sufficient to cover the firm's total costs when paid by each consumer, with a marginal price (usage charge) then being set at the firm's marginal costs. This differed from the two-part, but declining-block, tariffs being used in the United States. While the price of each kilowatt-hour of electricity fell in a series of downward steps as consumption increased, some of its fixed costs were also recovered in the charge for the early units of consumption (Brown and Sibley, 1986, p. 1). This was a tariff structure designed to promote consumption and it involved some redistribution from small to large consumers. This redistributive element tended to be obscured by the effects of rising demand, which induced new, higher-productivity investment with beneficial effects on all prices to all consumers. In Britain, the most explicit redistribution was from urban to rural areas, and from large to small users. In both Britain and the United States, little cognisance was taken of time of use and its implications for long-run marginal cost. In both countries the overwhelming tendency was towards average- rather than marginal-cost pricing. That this should have been so was not surprising. That the French electricity industry explicitly chose a marginalist approach to pricing that factored in peak-hour pricing was unusual and requires explanation.

The electricity supply industry in France was nationalised by virtue of the legislation of 8 April 1946 and almost immediately acquired a marginalist bent to the development of its tariff structure (Picard et al., 1985, ch. 1). In 1947, Gabriel Dessus was asked to establish the National Commercial Service in EDF, thereby placing within EDF probably the most enthusiastic marginalist evangelist in France at that, or any other, time. In 1949 Dessus recruited Marcel Boiteux to join him in working on the development of EDF's pricing structure. Prior to joining Dessus, Boiteux had been at the Société Nationale des Chemins de Fer (SNCF), where Allais had sent him to work with Roger Hutter on an assessment of the applicability of Allais's work to the newly nationalised railways (Hutter, 1950a, 1950b; SAV, 1957). The early work on tariffs by Dessus and Boiteux gave rise to some experimental tariffs in the late 1940s, followed in turn by the *Tarif Jaune* of 1 January 1952. This practical experience and the theoretical writings of Boiteux provided much of the basis for the *Tarif Vert* which was introduced in 1958 for large and industrial users of electricity (Boiteux, 1949, 1951, 1956a, 1960; FONT, 1953; Monnier, 1983, pp. 34–5, 163).

In December 1956, some long-overdue changes were made to the standing charge which was increased to 1,500 F/kW having been frozen at 150 francs since 1935. The wartime addition of an equal sum (20 francs) to night, day and peak tariffs had effectively eradicated the pre-war tariff differentials (Bernard, 1986; Boiteux, 1996). In addition, the standing charges inherited by EDF from the 1,200 plus *sociétés concessionnaires* had not been indexed and as a result had been rendered meaningless by inflation. While the equivalent early post-war British *prime fixe* was around 5,000–7,000 F/kW, in France it had remained at the pre-war level of 165 F/kW. In the *Tarif Vert*, the *prime fixe* was to be increased to 1,500 francs. Following negotiations on the terms on which the *Tarif Vert* would be introduced, a new *cahiers des charges* was approved, and on 27 November 1958 a decree (*un arrêté*) made the *Tarif Vert* obligatory for all subscribers from 1 January 1962. The *Tarif Vert* divided the year into a winter (1 October–31 March) and summer (1 April–30 September) season. Each season was then subdivided according to the hourly use of electricity. Winter was divided into three periods: (i) the peak-hour periods of 7–9 a.m.

and 5–7 p.m., but excluding October and March; (ii) the periods of lowest
use between 10 p.m. and 6 a.m. and all day Sunday; and (iii) the remaining
hours. In the summer, there was no peak-hour tariff, and the tariff was
divided between: (i) the hours of lowest use, 10 p.m.–6 a.m., and Sundays;
and (ii) the remaining hours. For all periods, as consumption increased, so
too did the variable energy rate charged diminish, with the fixed charge also
being charged at a declining rate as capacity subscribed for increased
(Meek, 1963b, p. 51).

The *Tarif Vert* captured international attention, the British economist
Ronald Meek regarding it as 'probably the first serious attempt ever made
to engage in marginal planning . . . [and] . . . of exceptional interest and
importance' (Meek, 1963a, p. 217). It also brought Boiteux's earlier writings on peak-hour pricing in the late 1940s to a wider Anglo-American
audience, not least as the economist, Peter Steiner of the University of
Wisconsin, had independently published his paper on the same issue in
1957 (Steiner, 1957). The arguments of the two economists were subsequently melded by economists into what became known as the
Boiteux–Steiner model for peak-load pricing. Yet, while theoretically clear,
the actual implementation of the *Tarif Vert* was always distinctly pragmatic. When faced with deficits of between 4 and 7 per cent arising from
the gap between average- and marginal-cost receipts, these differences at
their lower end were dismissed as being small, while at their upper end they
were thought likely to be covered by increasing marginal prices where
necessary. Convenient distinctions were also drawn between financial and
economic values. In calculating the effects of revaluing costs so as to allow
for the effects of inflation, Boiteux argued that the difference between revalued average cost and average accounting cost was about the same as the
difference between revalued average cost and marginal cost. When promoting the use of marginal-cost principles, Boiteux was happy at times to
dismiss the terminology of 'budgetary equilibrium' and 'average cost' as
being the language of accountants rather than that of economists. Yet, in
practice, it was the accounting-style observation of the broad similarity of
differential between revalued average cost and both average accounting
cost and marginal cost which eased the practical introduction of the *Tarif
Vert*. What emerged was a hybrid form of pricing, which incorporated some
Ramsey-style exploitation of price-inelastic consumers, with a marginal-
cost approach to the targeting of peak-hour consumption (Mitchell et al.,
1978, p. 74; Monnier, 1983, pp. 106, 162). As such, in reverting to Ramsey
pricing, it marked a departure from the purity of Allais's teachings on the
application of marginal-cost pricing. Yet essentially, even setting to one
side the 'second-best' considerations which necessarily limited the pure
application of marginal-cost pricing, it was a significant advance in

marrying a wish to use marginalist principles with a practical need to break even. In including peak-hour pricing, it also moved towards throwing a bridge between short- and long-run marginal costs.

The international implications of these developments in France were to ripple slowly outwards, first across the Channel, and then on across the Atlantic. The introduction of the *Tarif Vert* in France excited interest in Britain because of increasing dissatisfaction there with electricity and nationalised industry pricing. The electricity industry had long been criticised for selling output at below its long-run marginal cost for much of the year, of failing to distinguish sufficiently between peak and off-peak non-industrial demand, and of running a domestic:industrial price ratio which was too low (TNA, 1962j, para. 1; 1965b, para. 2). In the United States in the 1970s, the *Tarif Vert* was to be cited by supporters of tariff reform and its formative influence adduced. Amidst the renewed interest in the 1970s in the development and implementation of pricing structures centred around the marginal cost, leading regulatory economists in the United States happily acknowledged their intellectual debt to the French economists centred around Allais and EDF. Both Alfred Kahn and his pupil, Paul Joskow, recognised the value of EDF's work (Drèze, 1964; Joskow, 1976, p. 199). A central question therefore is why, and how, such a tariff was introduced in France in the 1950s, and equally why it was not introduced, and then often partially, until much later in Britain and the United States. It is instructive to begin with the Franco-British comparison since in both countries serious efforts were made, with differing results, to establish marginal-cost-based tariffs (Boiteux, 1949; Steiner, 1957; Hirshleifer, 1958a; Brown and Bruce Johnson, 1969; Baumol and Bradford, 1970; Mohring, 1970; Bailey and White, 1974; Wenders, 1976; Crew and Kleindorfer, 1978; Mitchell et al., 1978; Sherman and Visscher, 1978; Crew et al., 1995).

It is almost the disparity between the intellectual weight of the discussions on nationalised industry pricing occurring in Britain in the run-up to nationalisation and the virtually nil effect of such discussions on the principles for pricing written into the nationalising legislation which provides an immediate contrast between the British and French experience. This is especially marked given that in 1946 Meade was director of the Cabinet's advisory Economic Section of which he had been a member since 1940. Ironically the effect of Meade's advocacy of the case for marginal-cost pricing within government, was simply to point up the political objections to such pricing from major political figures such as Herbert Morrison. Before its attachment to the Treasury in 1953, the Economic Section reported to the Lord President, Herbert Morrison, who was not only a long-standing advocate of nationalisation but who also had responsibility for the progress of the legislative programme through parliament. Since one of the main political promises made by supporters of nationalisation was to make electricity more widely (and cheaply) available, then cross-subsidies between urban and rural and lower-income consumers were going to be necessary. On this basis, and having little sympathy for the alleged 'efficiency' of the financial losses represented by marginal-cost pricing in increasing-returns industries, politicians opted for the 'common-sense' appeal of average-cost pricing. Nationalised industries were simply required to cover their costs 'taking one year with another', these costs being average ones. Despairing, Meade left the Economic Section and returned to Cambridge University in 1947. It was one thing to wrestle intellectually with Richard Kahn, and through him with John Maynard Keynes, as a member of the Cambridge circus developing the multiplier in the early 1930s. It was quite another dealing with the rubbery politician, Morrison.

While marginalist principles were no more written into the French nationalising legislation than into that of the UK, there was clearly a difference in the subsequent ability of economists and advocates of marginal-cost pricing to influence the nature of electricity tariffs (Morsel, 1996, pp. 344–5). This influence was exerted through what we might broadly call a network, and quite possibly a technocratic one at that. While both the UK and France had a respectable history of economic interest in marginalist approaches towards tarification, including the use of discriminatory tariffs, it was more likely in France than in Britain that those taught such economics would enter the electricity industry. The teaching of Allais and his marginalist forebears occurred mainly in the two *Grandes écoles* of Mines and Ponts et Chaussées (FONT, 1960a; Bergougnoux et al., 1986). The generations of *ingénieurs-économistes* taught in these *Grandes écoles* formed a peer network in each generation. Before nationalisation, almost half (42 of 96) of the leaders of the *sociétés privées concessionnaires de service public* were *polytecnicians*, over half of whom came from the *grands corps*, in particular Ponts et Chaussées (16), Mines (5) and Génie Maritime (4) (Lanthier, 1979; Barjot and Morsell, 1996; Joly, 1996). On nationalisation, EDF took on many of these ex-CPDE directors and tariff designers including Paul Stasi, Robert Comte and Gabriel Dessus. At the newly established EDF, Pierre Simon (its first Director-General), Roger Gaspard (Simon's Assistant Director-General, and later Director-General), Pierre Ailleret (Director of Research and Studies) and Pierre Massé (Director of Equipment) all came from the Ponts et Chaussées. While Marcel Boiteux as a mathematician came from l'École Normale Supérieure, outside of the Ponts et Chaussées/École des Mines network, he had attended with Dessus and Debreu, Allais's wartime and post-war econometric seminars (Bungener, 1986; Boiteux, 1989; Bungener and Joël, 1989; Morsel, 1996, p. 354).

In academic, university-teaching terms, there was no equivalent in the UK of this strong Écoles des Mines and Ponts et Chaussées nexus. Sporadic efforts by such economists as Christopher Dow in 1951 and Ronald Meek in 1965 to strengthen the links between academics and the nationalised industries came to nothing. Meek's efforts to establish a Nationalised Industries Economic Research Institute at Leicester University failed to win the support of the interdepartmental Committee on Economic Research (TNA, 1951a, 1966d, para. 35). While during the 1960s economists such as Ronald Edwards were to join the electricity industry and Ralph Turvey and Michael Posner were to advise the government on electricity economics, there was never any equivalent of the French economic training of a tightly-knit group of students who then went on to shape policy within the nationalised industries.

As important as educational networks in explaining the differing progress towards the introduction of marginalist-based electricity tariffs in each country was the difference which existed between the perceived role of the nationalised electricity industry in each country. In France, the prime role perceived for the industry was as a source and basis of industrial and economic modernisation which would in turn make a significant contribution to improving national security. In economic strength was seen the source of enhanced national security, and protection against being invaded for the fourth time in under one hundred years by Germany. It was as an instrument of foreign policy and national security that Jean Monnet's Ministry of National Production received crucial protection from the Quai d'Orsay (Ministry of Foreign Affairs) against attacks from the Ministry of Finance in the immediate post-war period (Lynch, 1984). This central role of electricity in industrial modernisation was in sharp contrast to its perceived post-war role in Britain. There, the dominant early post-war mood was that wartime promises of improved post-war welfare and living conditions should be met. While William Beveridge's Report on Social Insurance and Allied Services published on 1 December 1942 was seen almost as a social contract forced from a reluctant government by a population subject to the risks of total war, it built on a growing mood reflected in the Jowitt Committee's report on electricity in August 1942 that the supply of electricity should be extended to more domestic consumers, not least as 'the Public have increasingly come to regard electricity as a necessity and not a mere luxury: and it should be regarded from the same point of view as sewerage or water' (TNA, 1942; Chick, 1995, p. 270). It was on just such a basis that Morrison had rejected Meade's marginal-cost proposals, preferring the cross-subsidising urban–rural pooling opportunities offered by an average cost-pricing structure, preferably in a single national distribution authority, for the extension 'of cheap electricity to rural areas where . . . electricity was either not available or unreasonably expensive' (TNA, 1946).

This concern with the related issues of French national security and industrial competitiveness persisted long into the post-war period, and significantly affected the balance struck between industrial and domestic electricity users. Certainly, when in 1956 EDF's Paul Stasi made international price comparisons between the tariff structure of the electricity industries in France, the USA and the UK, there was considerable concern at finding that in comparison to their American counterparts, the largest and longest French consumers were disadvantaged, while small French consumers were favoured (Stasi, 1956a, 1956b). Subsequent tariff adjustments narrowed the French/US industrial electricity price gap, and the momentum and direction of which Stasi's researches were a part carried through into the *Tarif Vert*'s further adjustment of electricity prices to industry. In contrast to the France/USA comparison, that between France and the UK produced an industrial–domestic price ratio which Stasi characterised as '*très particulière*'. In the UK sample, the average high voltage price per kW/h at 300 kW (a factory of 100 workers, for example) was 7.23 francs for 1,500 hours (450,000 kWh per year) compared with 7.72 francs in France, while the domestic subscriber paid only 5.18 francs for 3,000 kWh per year for low voltage electricity in the UK, but 8.44 francs in France. Considering distribution costs alone, the UK industrial-domestic price ratio was unusual. With the subsequent French tariff reforms, this internationally comparative ratio between domestic and industrial price was to become even starker. By 1970, the ratio of low to high voltage rates was higher in France than elsewhere: in Britain, the ratio was 1.16:1; in West Germany it was 1.65:1; in the USA it was 1.83:1, while in France it was 2.3:1 (Nissel, 1976, p. 67, Frost, 1991, p. 151). Nor was EDF above exploiting the dominant national security concerns. It was in 1956, when the Suez crisis provided a timely reminder of the value of fuel resources, that Massé and Boiteux used a 45-minute meeting to overcome the objections of Minister of Industry André Morice to the proposed *Tarif Vert* and then moved to circumvent the opposition of Minister of Finance Paul Ramadier (Massé 1984, p. 113; Morsel, 1996, pp. 356–7). Alongside *sécurité*, the republican virtue of *égalité* was also emphasised. Customers would be charged on the same basis, but, crucially, this did not mean that they would pay the same charges (Dessus, 1949b; Boiteux, 1969; Margairaz, 1996).

That EDF could overcome political objections to tariff reform also reflected the smaller proportionate importance of domestic household consumers in France compared with their counterparts in Britain and the United States. The domestic load was much less developed in France than in the UK, both as a proportion of total sales, and in terms of average consumption per connected household. In 1961, domestic consumption was 15 per cent of total power delivered in France, compared with over 30 per cent in England. While on the eve of nationalisation there were 22.5 km of high-tension (over 100,000 V) lines per 1,000 km^2 in France, compared with 5, 15 and 18 km for the United States, Britain and Germany, respectively, the extension of low-voltage metered supply to rural areas of low consumption held few immediate economic attractions (Bouneau, 1996, p. 142). In the mid-1950s, with 40 per cent of the French compared with 70 per cent of the British living in urban centres of more than 100,000 inhabitants, connecting new consumers to the network was likely to be more costly in per capita terms in France (Stasi, 1956a). That French domestic consumers were lagging their international counterparts was well known within government, and not least within the Ministry of Economy and Finance where, in the run-up to the publication of the *Tarif Vert*, data from UNIMAREL (Union pour l'Étude du Marché de l'Électricité) was being studied and which confirmed that not only was the use of low-tension electricity in France among the lowest in Europe in 1954 on both a per capita and subscriber basis, but that the per capita rate of growth was the lowest in Europe during the 1950–54 period. While these were broad-brush international comparisons, evidence of the use of domestic household electrical equipment continued to reflect in particular the gap between France and Britain, only sales of refrigerators in the warmer France being ahead of those in Britain (Appendix Table A1.5). While the French household electricity market was to grow from 12 million '*d'abonnés*' in 1950 to 25 million '*clients*' between 1950 and 1985, a specific tariff for domestic consumers, *le Tarif Universel*, was not adopted until 1965 (FONT, 1965; Morsel, 1996).

It was not that EDF did not wish to expand its domestic consumer market; quite the contrary. Pragmatic adjustments were often made in the application of the *Tarif Vert* so as not to preclude the use of electricity in low-density areas. To some extent, EDF had always received preferential treatment from the Ministry of Finance, and the authorisation of low-cost finance and capital grants to EDF may have gone some way towards funding system extensions. Yet, ultimately it was a cost which EDF chose to take on to itself, and to palliate some of the worst implications of a strict application of the *Tarif Vert* for regional development. Where the rigorous application of the *Tarif Vert* was thought likely to compromise the expansion of the low-density, non-industrialised departments of France, a fictitious value for density of consumption was invented, anticipating the later development of consumption. Since in 1957 two-thirds of the country was held to be non-industrialised, this was a significant but necessary departure from marginal-cost principles (Boiteux, 1957, p. 148; Meek, 1963b, p. 55). Rather than having any perverse distaste for not developing the domestic household market, it was just that given the greater proportionate importance of industrial demand in France as compared with Britain and the United States, it was easier to persuade industry of the benefits likely to accrue to them by using the *Tarif Vert*, and then to make concessions to other groups who believed themselves to be disadvantaged. Indeed, in the run-up to the introduction of the *Tarif Vert*, concessions were made to such an extent that Dessus felt unable to remain any longer at EDF, given its departure from the purer principles of marginal-cost pricing. Following a spectacular clash in 1956 over the new *cahiers* between Dessus and the local communes' representative, Georges Gilberton, Dessus resigned from EDF leaving Boiteux to continue the negotiations with Gilberton. Yet, while Gilberton was able to win some concessions from Boiteux, inflation was effectively to erase their value. Although the subsequent negotiations over the low-voltage *cahier des charges type* for the concession to EDF of *la distribution publique* also saw some further concessions made, by November 1960 the issue had been settled.

The position of Gilberton within EDF epitomised a further important difference between the electricity industry in France and Britain. In France, a highly centralised organisational structure with decision making focused in Paris was chosen. In contrast, the British chose a decentralised organisational structure in which, crucially, centralised generation was separated from distributive area boards. To borrow an 'electricity' term, the transmission of the marginalist message from Paris and the implementation of marginal-cost-based tariffs was much easier in the centralised French industry than in Britain. In France, a central marginalist principle was established and diffused across the entire system, according to which all customers were treated on the same basis. They did not pay the same price, because their marginal costs varied. In Britain, responsibility for generating electricity and responsibility for pricing electricity was split between the CEGB and the area boards. Why was it, then, that such different organisational structures were chosen for the nationalised electricity industry in each country?

In both France and Britain, in the run-in to the nationalisation of the electricity industry, the issue of organisational structure provoked fierce political clashes and in-fighting. In Britain, Herbert Morrison favoured a centralised organisation, in part so as to facilitate cross-subsidisation. Indeed, Morrison, the man so closely associated with the public corporation model, considered subsuming the industry into government as a department and thereby removing any notion of it operating at 'arm's length' from the government (Chick, 1998, p. 89). His centralising plans were opposed by Emanuel Shinwell, the first post-war Minister of Fuel and Power, who successfully lobbied for the maintenance of regional independence. The outcome was that responsibility for tariffs became split between the industry's Central Authority and the area boards. The Central Authority fixed the Bulk Supply Tariff (BST) for the bulk supply of electricity to the boards, but the area boards in England and Wales were then free to set their own area tariffs. Similarly, while the Central Authority was responsible for generation, responsibility for sales and distribution was separately entrusted to the area boards. This broke with the common pre-war vertical integration of generating, distribution and sales, and ruled out the option of forming fully integrated nationalised 'power boards'. In continuance of the centralised/decentralised struggle, while most of the ex-CEB (Central Electricity Board) men on the Central Authority wanted to organise around six grid control regions, the more decentralised structure favoured by the area boards was chosen, in which 14 generating areas were established, effectively mirroring the 14 area boards. Thus with the BST split from area tariffs, and with generation split from distribution and sales, there was no mechanism for the centralised imposition of local tariffs which properly reflected generating costs. The Central Authority could and did make cost-reflecting adjustments to the BST, but there was no guarantee that area boards would pass this cost information on to consumers in its own tariffs (Hannah, 1982, pp. 19–20, 63, 88).

The early struggle over organisational structure between Shinwell and Morrison had its counterpart in France, although with a different outcome but for perversely similar reasons. In France their two equivalents were, respectively, the communist Marcel Paul and the reform socialist Paul Ramadier. As Minister of Industrial Production, Paul pushed in article 2 of the nationalising legislation for the creation of *établissements publics régionaux*. Against him stood Ramadier, the *rapporteur du projet de loi* in the constituent assembly (Maleville, 1996). Ramadier had long-standing connections from 1933 with the Fédération Nationale des Collectivités Publiques Électrifiées (FNCP) and, from 1937, with its successor organisation the Fédération Nationale des Collectivités Concédantes et Régies (FNCCR), whose struggle for improved tariffs and greater rural electrification Ramadier had crucially supported both as a lawyer and as Secretary of State for Energy during the Popular Front. Paradoxically, these local groups favoured a more centralised structure than that proposed by Marcel Paul, in part because Paul's proposal was both insufficiently centralised and decentralised at one and the same time. While Paul proposed to locate the units of organisation at a regional level, the local loyalties of the federation were at the level of the commune or the '*syndicat de communes*'. Federation leaders like Georges Gilberton recognised that power and credibility would accrue to them by negotiating on such matters as tariffs at a national level. The EDF senior management favoured a centralised structure, as too did the Confédération Générale du Travail (CGT) who feared that a more decentralised structure would encourage challenges to their position by the more decentralist *Force Ouvrière*.

Ultimately, Paul's proposals were buried, not so much by the 1948 Commission Commune de la Distribution which looked capable of supporting his thinking, but by some sharp twisting of the arms of Henri Queuille, President of the Conseil Supérieur de l'Électricité. In the face of worrying noises from the Commission Commune de la Distribution, the EDF Director-General, Roger Gaspard, approached the sympathetic Senator Alexis Jaubert for help. In turn, Jaubert informed Queuille that if article 2 of the nationalising legislation was passed, then Jaubert would stand against Queuille in the latter's electoral fief of La Corrèze (Picard et al., 1985, p. 138). Thus local representation was incorporated at the top of the EDF centralised structure. The Féderation des Collectivités Concédantes (FCC) and its leading representative, Georges Gilberton, were given seats on the EDF Conseil d'Administration, where Gilberton was to serve for over 30 years until his departure in 1979. This accommodation of very local interests within a highly centralised organisational structure allowed the principles of pricing structures to be developed and explained at the centre, and then, with this imprimatur, applied across the country. This ability of EDF tariff designers like Boiteux to disperse the marginalist approach from the centre offered a sharp contrast with the experience of the electricity supply industry in Britain during the 1940s and 1950s. That contrast was only heightened by the efforts which were made in early post-war Britain to secure tariff and pricing reform.

Almost immediately after the nationalisation of the electricity supply industry in Britain in 1948, attempts were made to change the level and structure of electricity prices. Relative fuel prices were subject to persistent criticism by economists, notably by Ian Little in *The Price of Fuel*, while the structure of electricity prices attracted the attention of economic-literate ministers like Hugh Gaitskell (Little, 1953). In the UK, the ratio of industrial:domestic electricity prices had, as in France, become distorted during the war, as increases in coal prices had only been passed on in 'coal-clause' contracts to industrial consumers. Thus, by January 1948, domestic supplies were cheaper on average than they had been in 1938. While the average price per unit for power units had risen by 0.22d, that for lighting, heating and cooking had fallen by 0.138d (TNA, 1948). Yet concerned at the impact of electricity price increases on lower-income families, not least those living in the all-electric pre-fabs, the immediate post-war Attlee government rejected proposals that it should rectify the industrial:domestic electricity price ratio. Yet coincidentally, there was also growing concern with the investment implications of the level of peak demand during the early post-war years. The section of peak demand which was subject to closest scrutiny was the heating load of domestic consumers who, subject to coal rationing until 1958, had snapped up and switched on electric fires costing £1–10 shillings each. However, the low diversity of use among the 10 million individual consumers each accounting for 0.4 kW, meant that their aggregate peak-hour use cost £20 in additional investment require-ments, as space heating accounted for one-fifth of domestic sales but three-fifths of the peak by the mid-1950s (TNA, 1954, 1955b). At the same time, the nationalised electricity industry competed aggressively with the nation-alised gas industry for the thermal load (cooking, water heating and electric fires). Commercially successful in terms of increasing domestic electricity customers from 9.7 million in 1948 to 14.3 million in 1958, this strategy raised serious economic doubts concerning the peak-hour costs of supply-ing such a load.

As Minister of Fuel and Power, Gaitskell attempted to persuade the elec-tricity industry to introduce some form of time-of-use tariff so as to price away some of the peak demand. Establishing the Clow Committee in 1948, Gaitskell's efforts to chivvy the industry into tariff reform ran into the sand as the industry exploited asymmetries of information arising from its monopoly structure. At nationalisation, not only had the industry been transferred into public ownership but it had also seen all competition extin-guished in the generation section of the industry. Exploiting its new state-approved monopoly status, the industry simply refused to release information concerning the price elasticity of peak-hour demand, in the same way as the sales-maximising area boards suppressed information on the costs of supplying different components of demand. After 1948 the post-war research reports of Paul Schiller in the BEA's (British Electricity Association) commercial department on such topics were no longer being published as they had been in the pre-war Electrical Research Association (Schiller, 1946, 1948). Only grudgingly did the industry agree to a seasonal, rather than a time-of-day, differential and even then the differential was much narrower than that sought by Gaitskell. Where Gaitskell sought a winter–summer split of 1.25d–0.5d/kWh, the industry hung out for 1.0d–0.7d. Eventually a compromise of 1.1d–0.65d was negotiated (Chick, 1998, p. 94). The industry then proceeded to advertise the new seasonal tariff in a desultory fashion, so that quarterly customers were only made aware retrospectively of the higher winter charges, thereby allowing the industry to claim their consumption pattern as indicative of the low price elasticity of peak-hour demand. The seasonal tariff was withdrawn in 1949 even in the nearly 50 areas such as the London and Home Counties Joint

Electricity Authority where pre-nationalisation seasonal tariffs covering around 750,000 customers had been operating (TNA, 1965a, p. 371; Chick, 1990, p. 120).

Quite apart from the agency problems affecting relations between government and a monopoly nationalised industry, the difficulties of introducing marginal-cost tariffs were exacerbated both by the decentralised structure of the industry and by the personnel and outlook of the area boards. As Paul Schiller observed:

> One of the principal defects seems to me that a not inconsiderable number of those responsible for framing and carrying out policy, especially within the Area Boards, are men who are proud to have learnt the trade the practical way – by trial and error – who do not believe in 'theorists', economists, etc., and who have not been able to realise that as servants of a nationalised industry their approach to problems of development and commercial policy must be governed by considerations of the national interest, and not by the parochial interests of an industry or an individual supply organisation . . . Tariff making is still largely regarded as an art, the 'know-how' of which is automatically – and exclusively – acquired by long practical service in the industry, and which is not amenable to theoretical treatment. (TNA, 1954)

One means of weakening the independence of the area boards was to move towards a more centralised structure. Yet, even within the later Herbert Committee, Ronald Edwards, Professor of Economics at the London School of Economics and a keen supporter of tariff reform, expressed an overriding concern at the inefficiencies which were likely to be hidden within a centralised monopoly of some 200,000 employees. Edwards viewed the area boards as an essential check against centralised inefficiencies, regarding it as 'an axiom of organisation in nationalised industry that the onus of proof must rest on those who favour larger rather than smaller statutory areas of organisation' (TNA, 1955a). None the less, for much of the 1950s, area boards set retail tariffs which underpriced peak-hour demand, supplied electricity prices at below long-run marginal cost, increased the forecast capacity requirements of the industry and provided an obvious and serious likely source of resource misallocation within the economy.

Ultimately, it was the Treasury which was to make the greatest progress in pushing the electricity industry towards pricing at long-run marginal cost by means of applying pressure, not so much directly on tariff structures, but on the test discount rate used by the industry in its process of investment appraisal. Even the initial Treasury emphasis on opportunity cost and the need to earn required rates of return in its 1961 White Paper on the nationalised industries was sufficient to prompt some changes to tariff structures. In 1962/63, the basis of assessment of the fixed charge was shifted from the area boards' chargeable maximum demand to national simultaneous demand. At the same time a day and night differential was introduced into the running charge, with the expressed aim of helping area boards to improve night rates to consumers for block storage, underfloor heating and water heating. Meek considered the reforms of 1962/63 to mark a major turning point in the history of electricity tariffs as the basis of assessment of the fixed charge was radically changed from being based on the chargeable maximum demand of an area board to its demand at the time of the national simultaneous demand (Meek, 1968). By 1963, the Cabinet Economic Section was reasonably happy with the tariffs offered for industrial load, but was as ever concerned that domestic consumers' tariffs failed to differentiate sufficiently between peak and off-peak on both a seasonal and time-of-day basis (TNA, 1963h, 1965g). While progress was made in bringing area board prices more into line with the BST, Ronald Edwards continued to press the CEGB for greater tariff differentials according to time and season and experiments with the price sensitivity of different demand continued to be undertaken (TNA, 1960d, 1960e, 1964f). Roughly coinciding with the 1967 White Paper on Nationalised Industries, the further adjustments to the BST pushed the tariff closer to marginalist principles (TNA, 1967a). The Treasury's approach to pricing issues by means of the test discount rate will be discussed at length in the next chapter, but the investment-side approach was always accompanied by Treasury exhortations to the electricity industry to reform its tariff structures along marginalist lines. While it was not until 1967 that the White Paper on nationalised industries prescribed pricing at long-run marginal cost, for much of the decade before that the Treasury had made increasing use of marginalist microeconomists and in particular of Ralph Turvey (Turvey, 1968). Although seconded to the Electricity Council, Turvey was in close and frequent correspondence with the Treasury during the long run-up to the 1967 White Paper (TNA 1966g, para. 12). As in his academic publications, so too in his papers for the Treasury, Turvey urged the benefits for economic efficiency of setting prices equal to long-run marginal (social) costs, and these in turn for investment purposes, being equal to the marginal social rate of discount (TNA, 1966b, para. 2). If this twin approach should be applied anywhere, then it was in the capital-hungry, capital-intensive electricity industry. As Turvey noted: 'It ought not to be a hopeless task. Books have been written about marginal cost pricing in electricity, and if the concept is viable anywhere it is here. At least there is a relatively simple concept, and not a whole variety of costs on different parts of a system like railways' (TNA, 1966g, para. 11).

Prompted and badgered by the Treasury, the Ministry of Power also began scouting around for economists with an interest in marginalist energy matters. Among those trawled up were R.L. Meek at the University of Leicester, and Ian Little at Oxford. While the ministry noted that since writing *The Price of Fuel* Little had 'taken no overt interest in the subject', he was still of interest to them as 'an expert and authority on the theory of welfare economics, which has relevance to pricing issues'. The ministry also cast around for relevant reading and the Economic Research Unit at the Treasury sent a list of 17 articles on marginal-cost pricing. However the ministry's view of the list was 'there appears to be little in it that merits special attention' (TNA, 1966e). Nor was it much taken with a selection of articles by Boiteux, Massé and Dessus which, at Debreu's suggestion, James Nelson had translated and gathered together in a book entitled *Marginal Cost Pricing in Practice* (1964) when both he and Debreu were in the economics department at Yale University (TNA, 1966e). That Nelson had gathered translations of these French articles together did, of course, reflect the growing interest outside of the Ministry of Power in marginalist approaches to pricing and investment (Morlat and Bessière, 1971). Needless to say, influential mandarins at the Treasury were familiar with much of this literature, and some, like John Laurie Carr, were even contributing articles to the *Economic Journal* on approaches towards investment appraisal, the happy bedfellow of marginal-cost pricing. Eventually the Ministry of Power employed the Cambridge economist, Michael Posner, to help them through the marginalist thickets. Not the least of Posner's labours was to write a clear and accessible paper on marginal-cost pricing for officials which began with Dupuit and his bridge, and then proceeded to explain two-part tariffs in terms of the subscription and dining costs of London clubs (see Appendix A2).

That the 1967 White Paper prescribed nationalised industry pricing at long-run marginal cost is noteworthy, not least as establishing a clear measure of the progress which had been made from the guidance of the legislation nationalising major utilities, and also as a testimony to the Treasury's assumption of responsibility for establishing the economic criteria for the behaviour of nationalised industries. That a politician like Richard Crossman chose to deride the 1967 White Paper as only of interest to a 'few dons and experts' and more seriously that in the turmoil of the early 1970s the government imposed price controls on nationalised industries which thwarted most strivings towards economic rationality was clearly unfortunate (Millward, 1976; Chick, 1998, p. 136). None the less, the journey to the 1967 White Paper with its prescriptive setting of price at long-run marginal cost had been instructive, and in many ways prophetic of what was to come decades later when regulators would require utilities to price at long-run marginal cost. In exposing some fundamental problems of information asymmetries besetting principal–agent relations between government and the nationalised industries, the early post-war decades had grappled with problems which were to be given a more formal theoretical exposition during the 1970s by the likes of Akerlof and Stiglitz (Akerlof, 1970; Rothschild and Stiglitz, 1976).

In the United States during the 1970s, the established regulatory consensus which had existed since the war increasingly came under critical scrutiny. Part of this arose as a result of OPEC oil price hikes and the development of fears of shortages of energy in the future. Allied to these concerns was the growth of environmental groups urging greater efficiency in the use of energy (Acton, 1976, p. 4; Joskow, 1976, pp. 204–5). Specific problems also arose in the electricity industry centring on what Richard Hirsh has termed 'technological stasis' and which had direct consequences for the viability of traditional tariff structures (Hirsh, 1989). For much of the 1950s and 1960s, the declining-block rate structure had been the most widely used residential electricity tariff in the United States, although the actual levels of rates varied across the country reflecting differences in the average cost of supply (Mitchell et al., 1978, pp. 7, 15). On the basis of increasing economies of scale and technological progress, electricity utilities had offered promotional rates for the all-electric home, encouraging the use of air-conditioning in the summer and home heating in the winter (Kahn, 1970, p. 64). In expectation of rising peak demand, new plant was built, bringing with it productivity improvements which caused the industry's average costs and rates to fall (Joskow, 1979b). So, for example, in Los Angeles from 1927 to 1970, the Department of Water and Power had 14 rate decreases and only two rate increases. In the nation as a whole, the average price of electricity fell from the 1920s until 1950 and remained fairly constant in nominal terms until about 1970. Of course, in real (constant dollar) terms, the price continued to fall even until the early 1970s. With costs following this favourable trend no one worried about the exact details of electricity pricing. However, price rises were particularly intense either side of the 1973 oil crisis. Nationwide, rates rose 90 per cent in the five years after 1970. In New York the increase was even sharper: some customers were paying nearly twice as much per kilowatt-hour in 1974 as they had been in 1972. People who had been induced to buy 'all electric' homes were especially hard hit. Consolidated Edison, New York's giant utility, reported that the typical monthly bill for residential electric heating in Westchester County was about $250 in March 1974, which was up from about $130 one year earlier (Anderson, 1981, p. 69).

As rates rose, so too were the traditional regulation and rate-setting practices of utilities subject to greater critical scrutiny. As far as short-run marginal costs were concerned, the promotion of demand under the declining-block structure was criticised as inducing a careless use of oil, which was seen to be expensive and viewed by some as worryingly finite. Yet, as well as predictable efforts to use fuel more efficiently, there was also a burgeoning interest in using capital more efficiently by addressing the peak-hour demand. While generic hearings on electricity pricing were held in a number of states, including Wisconsin, New York, California and Massachusetts, some public utility commissions went as far as to require electric utilities to devise peak-load tariffs (Joskow, 1976, p. 197; Mitchell et al., 1978, pp. 7, 15). In 1974, the National Association of Regulatory Utility Commissioners called on the Edison Electric Institute and Electric Power Research Institute to undertake a far-reaching 'study of the technology and costs of time-of-day metering and electronic methods of controlling the peak-hour usage of electricity, and also a study of the feasibility and cost of shifting various types of usage from peak to off-peak periods'. Their findings were produced in a mammoth *Electric Utility Rate Design Study*, which ultimately ran to some 95 reports (Kahn, 1988, p. xxviii).

Rate reform was most actively pursued in the two largest states of California and New York, as well as in other states like Wisconsin. Both California and New York had a large regulatory staff, although they were to follow different routes to rate reform. In California, both lifeline and time-of-day rates were adopted. Lifeline tariffs were characterised by an inverted-block rate structure in which a price below average cost was set for the first block of kilowatt-hours used per month, with a higher rate for subsequent blocks. Lifeline tariffs were intended to subsidise low-income households or reduce rates below costs for consumers who used small quantities of electricity. New York eschewed lifeline in favour of peak-load pricing. On 29 January 1975, the New York State Public Service Commission (NYSPSC) issued orders instituting a 'generic' rate investigation 'to inquire into the merits of, and to develop principles and methodology for, the revision of electric rate schedules'. The conclusion reached was that 'marginal costs . . . provide a reasonable basis for electric rate structures' and each of the electric utilities within the Commission's jurisdiction was ordered to develop 'studies sufficient to translate marginal cost analysis into rates'. Within six months the Commission had examined and found reasonable the state's first mandatory time-of-day rate based on marginal cost (Anderson, 1981, pp. 81, 89–90). In some parts of the United States, at least, the marginalist approach began to move to centre stage.

One of the driving forces behind the commission's work was Alfred Kahn. Kahn had been appointed chairman of the NYSPSC in July 1974 and he would later serve under President Carter as chairman of both the Civil Aeronautics Board and the Council on Wage and Price Stability. Yet even this committed marginalist, Cornell Professor of Political Economy and author of the major two-volume *The Economics of*

Regulation: Principles and Institutions had to allow pragmatic compromise in the implementation of marginalist tariffs. In 1975, the Commission's first petition for permission to restructure electricity rates along marginalist lines came from the Long Island Lighting Company (LILCO). Saddled with an exceptionally poor load factor, a rapidly rising summer peak, and struggling to service its large capital needs, LILCO looked to peak-hour pricing for some relief from its woes. The tariff proposed by LILCO claimed to follow a methodology developed by Ralph Turvey, in which demand was divided into three periods: peak; intermediate or shoulder peak; and off-peak. No capacity charge was assigned to the off-peak, and initially a request was made for a ratio between peak and intermediate periods of between 18:1 and 20:1. Subsequently, this was modified to an 8:1 differential. Even then, in approving the new rate structure for the utility's 175 largest commercial and industrial customers only, the Commission authorised a differential of 4:1, some way from what arose from a strict marginal-cost assessment. The rates became effective on 1 February 1977 and a year later preliminary studies seemed to support earlier assurances given by Kahn to industrial users. Of the 173 accounts for which the NYSPSC staff had figures, only 11 had paid more under the new rate structure than they would have paid under the traditional one. All of the increases were less than 2 per cent whereas, among those who had received decreases, savings had ranged up to 21.3 per cent. As a class, the 173 large users had saved over $1.5 million, about 4 per cent (Anderson, 1981, pp. 89–90, 115, 129–30; McCraw, 1984, ch. 7).

In their promotion of the marginalist approach to rate setting, economists in the United States both acknowledged their debt to the earlier work of EDF and drew on newer theoretical developments arising out of the broader interest in the deregulation of utilities. Reflecting this interest in the earlier French work, William Baumol and David Bradford, in the economics department at the University of Princeton, took the time to translate and get published Boiteux's 1956 article 'On the management of public monopolies subject to budgetary constraints' (Boiteux, 1971). Looking back, Paul Joskow acknowledged that: 'The French have developed a theoretical methodology which encompasses both the American approaches to peak-load pricing – with its recognition of demand elasticity and the possibility of shifting peaks – and the British approach – with its explicit emphasis on the technical possibilities for generating electricity' (Joskow, 1976, p. 199). Indeed, the structure of the time-of-day tariff that went into effect in early 1977 for the 120 largest customers served by the Pacific Gas & Electric Company (PG&E) in California closely resembled that of the French industrial tariff (Mitchell et al., 1978, p. 164). More generally, the European experience was also now of use to American economists as a source of empirical data on the effects of marginal-cost-based tariffs, in particular in the largely thermal systems of England and Wales, France and West Germany, rather than those of Norway (99 per cent hydro in 1976) and Sweden (56 per cent thermal, 33 per cent steam and turbine, 11 per cent nuclear) (British Electricity Council, 1974; Joskow, 1976, pp. 204–5).

To this European store of experience could be added the fruits of a renewed interest in utility pricing. A return to the familiar ground of multi-part tariffs was allied to a greater interest in viewing utilities as multi-product industries. Such an approach also coincided with a diminishing sympathy for the redistributive ambitions which had strongly influenced pricing policy from the 1940s. In the United States, the practice of fully distributed cost pricing, dominated by average-cost pricing, in the postal service, railroad and telecommunications, came under increasing attack. Coinciding with this was an increasing preference for specific marginal-cost pricing over the, by now, more traditional uniform inverse elasticity pricing of Ramsey. The efficiency gains likely to accrue from switching from Ramsey pricing to marginal-cost pricing (optimal non-uniform pricing) were seductive. Estimated at around 2–3 per cent of revenue, these efficiency gains from Ramsey pricing paled into insignificance compared with estimated gains of 65 per cent of revenue resulting from the use of marginal-cost pricing (Ramsey, 1927; Baumol and Bradford, 1970; Brown and Sibley, 1986, pp. 3, 51, 60). While Ramsey prices had tended to be uniform (or 'linear') for particular services or classes of service, the use of multi-part or non-linear tariffs allowed marginal consumption to be priced closer to marginal cost, with the revenue deficiency (or surplus) made up in the infra-marginal price – the fixed fee or the price for the initial usage or blocks (Willig, 1978; Goldman et al., 1984). In this context there was renewed interest in Coase's suggestions, made in 1946, for two-part electricity tariffs in which the entry fee covered the firm's total costs with the marginal price being equal to the firm's marginal costs (Brown and Sibley, 1986, pp. 2, 3, 66, 129). To this was added more recent work on such problems as the 'shifting peak'. There was also a renewed interest in the consumers' surplus which could be traced back to Dupuit's work in the 1840s, particularly after work by Willig emphasised its practicality as a suitable measure of welfare, not least as the requisite data were typically available to both utilities and regulators (Willig, 1978). In France, Allais returned to Dupuit afresh, claiming in fact that it was not until November 1973 that he had been able to get his own (photo)copies of Dupuit's articles. While it was true that in the immediate post-war years there had been no published collection of Dupuit's articles, his work was taught and written about at length by the likes of François Divisia with whom Allais had been in correspondence at the time. Allais's fresh reading of Dupuit's work with his interest in different, not uniquely marginal, prices existing once surpluses had been exhausted was part of his wider revision of his earlier important contributions to neo-Walrasian economics (Allais, [1981] 1989; Baumstark and Bonnafous, 2000).

By the start of the 1980s, peak-load pricing was required in almost half of the states. This was principally for industrial and commercial, rather than residential, users and perhaps as much to fill the valleys as to reduce the peaks. Peak-hour pricing was not adopted for its own merits, but as a response to the combined problems caused by inflation, the energy crisis, the environmental movement and the consequent searching for cost-cutting and capacity-saving devices (Stelzer, 1970; Joskow, 1979a; Breyer, 1982, pp. 57–8). None the less, by 1987 electric utilities in 25 states were using marginal costs explicitly in setting retail rates and the 1978 Public Utility Regulatory Practices Act (PURPA) employed a marginalist avoided-cost approach to rate setting for environmentally-friendly new entrants. In general, the increasing electricity rates which had prompted interest in peak-hour pricing reflected the fact that marginal cost was more often above average cost than had been usual. However, by the mid-1980s, the more usual relationship between average and marginal cost had reasserted itself and with the appearance of excess capacity there was again a case for short-run promotional tariffs. Progress to marginal-cost pricing had been significant during the 1970s but by no means complete. A notable feature of the later Californian electricity crisis was the absence of metered time-of-day tariffs. This reflected not only continued political interference with prices but also the persistence of the issue of the costs of metering residential consumers in relation to any anticipated benefits. This had certainly been the case at the time of the introduction of the *Tarif Vert*. Although the cost of metering was not itself that high, it did form a high proportion of the total charges to the mainly smaller domestic consumers, whose annual consumption of 550 kWh of electricity for lighting and domestic purposes compared with 2,000 kWh per annum used by the average domestic consumer in England. That the use of marginal-cost pricing should have made significant but not complete progress in shaping electricity tariffs, that utility prices continued to be subject to political interference, and that many households did not have time-of-day meters is not surprising to students of the development of electricity pricing since 1945 (and before). Even in France, the marginalist message was not followed in its purest form within EDF, and outside of the nationalised electricity industry it fell on stony ground. Although in 1952, at the industry's request, Maurice Allais had written a long exposition on the application of the marginal-cost concept in the French coal-mining industry, his advice had been politely ignored by the industry until the emergence of coal surpluses at the end of the 1950s led the Fifth Republic's new Minister of Industry, Jean-Marcel Jeanneney, to exploit Allais's marginalist thinking as a means of reshaping French post-war energy policy (Allais, 1952a, 1952b; Morsel, 1996, p. 32, footnote 6). On the railways, the disregard of the marginal-cost evangelists had been even greater. While Allais had made repeated calls for the strict marginal costing of each type of service (sleepers, off-peak and peak hours), little had happened. Instead, Allais increasingly cited the railways as a prime instance of the anarchy caused by coalitions of personal interests, while Boiteux persistently criticised the continued pricing of rail according to the value of the service provided, with this mispricing forcing too much freight off the tracks and onto the roads (Allais, 1949; Boiteux, 1956b).

Just as the reception of the marginalist message varied between utilities, so too was there variety in the nature and motivations of those who sought to implement marginal-cost pricing. In France it was a small and remarkable group of *ingénieurs-économistes* who deployed the marginalist approach as a guiding principle in an industry which was subject to rapidly increasing demand, a changing technological base, a proportionately strong industrial demand, and an environment in which strong connections were made between the strength and efficiency of such crucial industries and national efficiency and security. In Britain, it was the Treasury which, motivated by a growing concern with public expenditure and public finance issues, used marginalist economists both within its own ranks and, more often, drawn from outside, as one means of obtaining greater influence over public utility investment but without being drawn into the nitty-gritty and second-guessing of decision making in the industry. In the United States it was the coincidence of oil crises and inflation, allied to productivity problems in the electricity industry, which provided the catalyst for reviving the traditional approach to electricity pricing. In looking over the experience of all three countries, it is the variety of those experiences which is striking, but throughout which, whether in France from the 1950s, Britain from the 1960s, or in the United States from the 1970s, microeconomists came to play an increasingly important role in shaping electricity pricing, bringing with them an approach to pricing in which, as Kahn had observed, the margin was central.

5. Electricity investment: rewarding the past, discounting the future

L'acte d'investir est un transfert dans le temp qu'accompagne nécessairement un pari car il n y a de certitude que le présent. (Paul Langevin)[1]

Not only was the electricity industry the largest single industrial area of fixed capital investment in the economies of France, Britain and the United States, but its capital:labour and capital:output ratios also made it one of the most intensive and potentially productive capital investment sections of those economies. As seen in the previous chapter on pricing, it was in part concern with the size and use of the investment resources absorbed by the electricity supply industry which had motivated many economists to advocate the use of marginal-cost and peak-hour pricing in this industry. Yet alongside efforts to influence the size and character of electricity investment by restructuring tariffs, there also sat the more direct route of regulating and appraising the fixed capital investment undertaken by the electricity supply industry in each economy. Regulation and investment appraisal essentially viewed fixed capital investment from different points in time. Regulation, as practised in the United States, allowed rates of return to be earned on plant once it was up and running. As such, this form of regulated return constituted a judgement on past investment decisions, allowing those that passed a test of prudence to earn a 'fair and just' rate of return. In so doing, it sought to influence investment decisions in the future by suggesting that they too would probably be able to earn a 'fair' regulated return on investment deemed to be reasonable. An implicit contract might be said to have existed between the regulator and the investor, especially if while the investment was being undertaken the regulator did not rule it to be imprudent.

In contrast to this form of regulation based on the outcome of past fixed-capital investment decisions, investment appraisal looked forward in time to *ex ante* rather than *ex post* decision making. Commonly it selected a rate at which to discount the proposed project back to its present value, this 'test' discount rate then forming an important consideration in deciding whether to proceed with the project. Such an approach to investment appraisal was formally adopted by the Treasury in Britain in its 1967

White Paper, *Nationalised Industries: A Review of Economic and Financial Objectives*, although it had in fact been in use for some time before that (Cmnd. 3437, 1967). The issues of the level and type of discount rate to be adopted will be discussed in some detail in this chapter. However, the larger importance of the Treasury's adoption of this form of investment appraisal was that it represented a significant contribution to its efforts to circumvent the agency problems affecting government–nationalised industry relations. In embracing, albeit more in theory than practice, this approach towards investment appraisal in electricity and the other nationalised industries, the Treasury was influenced significantly by the experience of EDF and its development of methods of appraising and comparing proposed marginal additions of thermal- and hydro-generating plant to the French electricity system. In France, methods and approaches developed within EDF were later to spread out into the wider machinery of national economic planning as criteria were sought for the allocation of resources. In Britain, the developments in EDF were initially applied to stop the construction of any new hydroelectricity sites in Scotland, and were then applied by the Treasury to all nationalised industries as an important instrument in its efforts to contain the growth of public expenditure. As such, approaches to investment appraisal were of much greater relevance in Britain as an important aspect of the public finance constraints which were imposed on nationalised industries from on high by the Treasury, rather than, as in the case of EDF, developing from within the industry and then working their way out into the wider machinery of economic planning.

As with the nationalised industries in Britain and France, so too with the investor-owned utilities in the United States, regulation had developed to strike a balance between public and private concerns relating to investment and pricing in industries, most of which were deemed to contain a significant element of monopoly and/or public interest. Unlike in France and Britain, in the United States at both state and federal levels, law courts had played a fundamental role in determining the scope and basis of regulation. In textbook tradition, the practice of what we now recognise as regulation is traced back to the 1877 *Munn v. Illinois* Supreme Court decision that, given the 'public interest' in the prices shared by grain elevators and warehouses, the State of Illinois could set these rates (or prices) (Hunter, 1917; Phillips, 1984, p. 80; Viscusi et al., 2005, p. 363). Municipal and town councils could also offer rate regulation with an associated period of protection during which utility companies could recover and earn an adequate return on their sunk investments. In Britain, legislation such as the 1882 Electric Lighting Act provided 21 years in which returns could be earned, but with town councils then having the right to take over ownership of the investment. The regulatory regime was even tougher in France.

In Paris, by 1889, the six *concessionaire* companies in Paris were on 18-year leases, but the French regulatory regime often offered much shorter leases (Millward, 2005, p. 82).

Even if such assurances of an ability to recoup investment and earn an adequate return had not been made, once the natural monopoly network had been constructed then the familiar problems of safeguarding against the abuse of its monopoly position while also safeguarding the investor an adequate return on the investment arose. So it was that in the United States, the 1898 *Smyth v. Ames* ruling judged that the Union Pacific Railroad Company was entitled to earn a 'fair' rate of return on its assets, the determination of what constituted 'fair' being made by the regulator. Regulated asset-based rates of return effectively gave rise to regulated prices which were presumably below those which might otherwise have obtained in the market. As to '*quis custodiet ipsos custodies?*', later rulings moved to protect companies from regulators setting rates which were unduly favourable to voters or powerful interest groups. As was affirmed by the New York State Court of Appeals in 1908, while the new regulatory commissions had the authority to establish maximum prices, they also had to grant higher rates to utility companies when justified. For both investors and customers, such certainty of returns and prices was attractive. Regulation offered greater certainty and protection. Customers were protected from high rates and monopoly power; companies were protected from municipal ownership, competition and local political abuse of their rates and returns. As Anderson remarks, such regulatory functions were largely negative in intent, designed to prevent the worst of abuses rather than to promote the optimal use of economic resources (Anderson, 1981, pp. 56, 61; Hirsh, 1999, pp. 27–9). As such they proved attractive in railways and in that other major area of large lumpy investment, electricity. In electricity, the first modern public utility commissions were established in 1907 in New York and Wisconsin, followed by: Vermont (1908); Maryland (1910); California, Connecticut, Georgia, Kansas, Nevada, New Hampshire, New Jersey, Oregon and Washington (1911); Arizona (1912); and Colorado, Idaho, Illinois, Indiana, Maine, Massachusetts, Missouri, Montana, North Carolina, Ohio, Oklahoma, Pennsylvania, Rhode Island, Virginia and West Virginia (1913). Between 1907 and 1913, nearly two-thirds of states established such public utility commissions (Blackford, 1970; Anderson, 1981, pp. 42, 55–6).

Establishing that utilities were entitled to a 'reasonable' or 'fair' rate of return on their assets did not, of course, provide any precise guidance as to what constituted 'fair' (Phillips, 1984; Crew and Kleindorfer, 1986, p. 98; Vietor, 1994, p. 103). Almost ever after, generations of accountants, lawyers, utility managers and regulatory commissioners were to make a good living arguing this issue, but essentially a mix of administrative practicality, technological progress and political common sense eased their discussions. For administrative reasons, the assets selected as the basis for rate setting were valued at their historic, rather than replacement, cost, minus depreciation and excluding variable expenses. Technological progress and increasing economies of scale in industries like electricity allowed unit costs to fall, allowing profits to be increased in the regulatory lags between rate settings, while leaving the monthly electricity bills of customers largely undisturbed. And political common sense of the 'if it ain't broke, don't fix it' type, left the regulators and the regulated alone so long as political interest groups and voters did not complain. The main concern of this mix of cost-of-service and cost-plus regulation was with preventing abuse rather than promoting efficiency. So efforts were made to deter undue padding of the rate base, gold-plating of capital equipment and other means of raising the rate base, but, not, until the 1970s, to reassess the basis of this form of regulation (Breyer, 1982, p. 38; McCraw, 1984, pp. 31, 59–60). Indeed, the combination of the Supreme Court's 1934 ruling in *Nebbia v. New York*, that an industry need not have a monopolistic structure to be regulated, and the politically protecting response to the economic depression of the early 1930s, widened the scope of regulation to cover at federal level, surface-freight transport including trucks, water barges and oil pipelines, broadcasting, telecommunications; at state level, oil production; and at interstate level, electricity and natural gas commerce (Viscusi et al., 2005, pp. 364–5). Thus, in the immediate post-war period, as the French and British governments moved to nationalise their gas, coal and electricity industries, in the United States the mainly private investor-owned utilities continued to be subject to a variety of regulation at federal, state and interstate levels (Joskow and Schmalensee, 1986; Hirsh, 1999, p. 28). In 1944, the Supreme Court ruling in the *Hope Natural Gas* case left to the state commissions the determination of the rate base and the rate of return (Phillips, 1984, p. 162).

Such regulatory concern to set 'just and reasonable' rates of return on a 'fair market value' of assets contrasted with the initially vaguer guidelines for the treatment of capital investment in the nationalising legislation in both Britain and France. In Britain, the legislative guidance that costs be covered taking one year with another was generally taken to sanction prices based on average costs without any particular imperative that specified returns be earned on capital assets. It was only gradually that first, required rates of return (RRR) on existing assets, and then, test discount rates (TDRs) on proposed investment projects were applied in British nationalised industries. The legislative guidelines were no more precise in France, but, as with pricing, EDF conspicuously developed a marginalist approach to investment appraisal. Not only was this of interest in itself, but it was of particular importance given that the French marginalist approach came to exercise a significant influence on the development of the investment appraisal techniques applied by the Treasury to the nationalised industries.

In France, the main spur to the development of electricity investment appraisal came from the need to make a technological choice between investing in thermal (coal or oil-burning) or hydro generation. In the post-war Monnet Plan (1947–52), the electricity industry was selected as a priority area to which resources should be directed, not least so as to ease *le goulot de l'énergie* (the energy bottleneck) (Gaspard and Massé, 1952). EDF received the bulk of the FME (Fonds de Modernisation d'Équipement) funds in 1949, and well into the 1960s French governments were willing to extend capital grants to the industry on favourable terms (Straus, 1994; Morsel, 1996, p. 101). Aspirations to strengthen future national security through economic modernisation led to ambitious output targets being set in the Monnet Plan, the target of 35.5 billion kWh compared with 21 billion kWh in 1938, shocking managers at EDF (Fourquet, 1980; Kuisel, 1984; Lynch, 1984). Investment more than trebled between 1950 and 1964 and electricity output grew by 7 per cent p.a., thereby doubling every nine years in conformity with Ailleret's Law (Ailleret, 1955; FONT, 1963).[2] By 1960, EDF was expecting to construct generating capacity over the succeeding nine years equal to that required since the birth of the industry (Boiteux, 1964; Morsel, 1996, p. 368).

In the immediate post-war years this investment in new generating capacity was split roughly equally between thermal and hydro forms of generation. Hydroelectricity remained an important and traditional source of electricity in France, providing around half of French electricity output in the early post-war period compared with one-quarter in the United States, and barely more than 2 per cent in the UK. It had long been used in areas of France unconnected to the emerging national grid network, and in post-war conditions of coal shortage, being able to generate power from rain and melted snow had an obvious appeal (FONT, 1951; Massé, 1967, p. 347; Frost, 1991, p. 137). While hydroelectricity was accorded an important place in Monnet's Plan, its relative inferiority compared with thermal generation was increasingly emphasised by the supporters of thermal generation, whose ranks included the Economic Co-operation Administration (ECA) which oversaw the distribution of American aid to Europe (Morsel, 1996, p. 103). Many of these criticisms of the proportionate size of the hydro programme were gathered together in July 1952 by Gabriel Taïx, adviser to the Ministry of Industry, a member of the EDF board and of the government advisory Economic and Social Council (ESC), in his report *Le plan Monnet est-il une réussite?* (The Monnet Plan is it a success?).

Given the declining marginal efficiency of new hydro sites, the improving absolute and relative efficiency of thermal generation, and the growing extent and rate of interconnection, Taïx asked whether greater priority should not now be given to thermal over hydroelectric investments. Indeed, was there not a case for reducing hydro investment? While in the past in the absence of interconnection, French hydros had tended to overinvest so as to have adequate capacity at times of low water, the spread of interconnection allowed hydros to sell beyond their former areas, to make a particular contribution to easing peak demand, and equally to import thermal power during low-water periods. For asking sensible questions in an awkward manner, Taïx was thrown off the EDF Board in November 1952 by Jean-Mare Louvel, the Minister of Industry, being accused of having represented his own views as those of EDF at an ESC meeting.

However uncomfortable, Taïx's questions needed answering, and in 1953, the formal EDF response came initially from Pierre Massé (1898–1987), EDF's Assistant Director-General, and Roger Gaspard, EDF's Director-General, in an article on investment choices in the *Revue Française de l'Énergie* of October 1952 and then subsequently in the seminal work, commonly known after its cover colour as *La Note Bleue* co-authored by Massé, Jean Ricard and Jacques Tissier.[3] Developed between 1949 and 1953, *La Note Bleue* was a procedural blueprint for the future appraisal and ranking of new projects, by which each addition to existing generating capacity, whether thermal or hydro, was to be assessed according to its marginal contribution to the entire system. The value of a project would be expressed in comparative terms when set against a *projet de référence* having the same ability to supply the grid. Thus the value of a proposed hydro project would be compared with an equivalently rated thermal station and this comparison would be projected across the future expected life of each plant. Such a marginalist, systems-based approach to the appraisal of proposed investment formed a highly compatible bedfellow for the development of the EDF marginalist pricing tariffs which were to culminate in the industrial *Tarif Vert* of 1958 (Chick, 2002). Together, the combined marginalist approach to investment appraisal and pricing would help to overcome distortions arising from applying average-cost pricing across the industry, not least when existing hydros with their capital debt burden eased by inflation had average costs of around 2F/kWh, while for new hydros, carrying the full financial charges on capital invested, the equivalent was 3.50F/kWh (Boiteux, 1956b, p. 114). There was a distinct risk that simply charging average costs across all hydro capacity, both old and new, would distort the comparison between thermal and hydro, and cause too many resources to be sunk, literally, into new reservoirs.

As well as shifting EDF's appraisal of investment onto a clear marginal, systems-based approach, Massé also brought to the debate about the comparative merits of hydro- and thermal-based generation, his long-standing interest in the accommodation of time and obsolescence in the appraisal of new investment. In 1945, in *Les Réserves et la Régulation de l'Avenir*, and again in 1959 in *Le Choix des Investissements*, Massé urged the growing need to distinguish between

> economic and physical time, which has become evermore marked in recent years, [in which] the physical life-span of the things we build is tending to outlast their economic usefulness. Obsolescence anticipates wear and tear . . . Every investment is, to a certain extent, a fossilising process . . . in the real world, the passage of time is inseparable from the appearance of risk. An investment is not simply a transfer of funds; it is a gamble. (Massé, 1959 [1962], pp. xi–xii)

In the light of *La Note Bleue*'s emphasis on the marginal analysis of additions to the existing system, such an approach advocating the discounting of time, effectively turned the traditional view of hydroelectricity on its head. While hydroelectricity had higher initial capital costs than thermal generators, the traditional defence had been that its subsequent greater longevity provided more than sufficient time for the initial costs to be recouped while the benefits of its low operating costs were enjoyed. Now, longevity was regarded as a source of risk, heightening the chances of technological obsolescence, and therefore no longer guaranteeing a comfortably long period in which to achieve payback. That such risks should attach to hydro, whose initial capital costs were so much higher than those of conventional thermal-generating plant, painted a bleak future for the prospects of new hydroelectric plant being installed in an increasingly interconnected national electricity system.

These developments in investment appraisal were watched with increasing interest by the UK Treasury. The Treasury's interest was born of considerations of political economy, rather than from any intrinsic interest in the respective merits of hydro and thermal generation. The broad political context was one of growing concern with the level and growth rate of public expenditure. In 1958 the issue had been given a sharper political edge by the resignation from Prime Minister Harold Macmillan's Conservative government of Peter Thorneycroft (Chancellor of the Exchequer), Nigel Birch (Economic Secretary to the Treasury) and Enoch Powell (Financial Secretary) in protest at the Cabinet's refusal to sanction large cuts in public expenditure. As might be noted from Appendix Table A1.6, as a share of GNP public expenditure was lower in the UK than in France but, even with the growing interest in Britain in French economic planning, this comparison was unlikely to impress the likes of Enoch Powell. It was also unlikely to carry much weight with the Treasury which was becoming increasingly concerned with the financial performance of nationalised industries like coal mining and railways, and the heavy fixed-capital investment requirements of the electricity industry. If the Treasury held a dim memory of the failure of the Clow Committee to introduce peak-hour pricing for electricity, the cost of the recent decision to treble the size of the nuclear power investment programme was still fresh in its mind. Inasmuch as nationalised industries formed part of any public expenditure problem, Macmillan established the Nationalised Industries Committee in January 1959 to review the organisation and performance of these industries. It was on this committee that Treasury sought to address the financial problems of the nationalised industries and to begin to unpick some of the public corporation locks protecting such industries. Richard 'Otto' Clarke of the Treasury quickly set the tone by suggesting that the committee members set about answering 'the wrong exam paper' and devote time to examining the financial and productivity performance of the nationalised industries, rather than worrying about their organisational structure (Clarke, 1978, p. 14). Before long the Nationalised Industries Committee had moved quickly both 'to the view that financial problems were of the first importance' and to a working assumption that nationalised industries should move from current efforts to meet the statutory requirement that they 'break even taking one year with another' to a future requirement that they earn rates of return on assets similar to those earned in comparable privately-owned industries (TNA, 1959f, para. 2). This 'opportunity cost' approach lay at the heart of the principal fruit of the Committee's discussions, the Treasury's 1961 White Paper on the nationalised industries (Cmnd. 1337, 1961). Reporting gross yields on net assets for a highly aggregated private manufacturing and distribution industrial sector of 19.3 per cent in 1957, and of 20.3 per cent for iron and steel, the White Paper compared these unfavourably with the selected nationalised industries' returns of 10.9 per cent for coal, 8.8 per cent for gas, 9.6 per cent for electricity (England and Wales), 10.1 per cent for the South of Scotland Electricity Board (SSEB), 4.9 per cent for the North of Scotland Hydroelectric Board (NSHEB), and 2.4 per cent for the British Transport Commission. As to what any such future RRR should be, whether they should all be the same, and by what criteria they should be determined, the 1961 White Paper remained relatively quiet, leaving these for subsequent negotiation. In fact a variety of RRR targets was to be set for the nationalised industries, the average target set for the electricity industry being 12.5 per cent gross (Bates and Webb, 1968).

The 1961 White Paper did mark an important shift in the returns expected from nationalised industry investments. It marked a prescriptive break with the original statutory encouragement simply to cover costs over a period. It did prompt some changes to the BST. Yet it remained essentially a retrospective judgement on existing assets, and one directly at odds with any marginalist inclination to view bygones as bygones. The interest of the work of Massé and others at EDF was that their marginalist approach bore directly on future additions to capacity, assessed in relation to the entire system. Such an application of a TDR was of increasing interest to the Treasury, but it was not clear how this could be applied to nationalised industries while respecting the arm's-length protective principles of the public corporation. Quite by chance, the solution to this problem arose out of a comparison of thermal and hydroelectric forms of electricity generation, not in France but in the Highlands of Scotland.

Compared with France, hydroelectric output was insignificant in the UK. While French hydroelectricity provided half of French electricity output, at its height UK hydroelectricity generation concentrated in the NSHEB was never to contribute more than 2.5 per cent of total electricity output. Yet it was precisely this low relative contribution to total output compared with the NSHEB's share of total electricity investment which brought it to the Treasury's attention in the first place. In the first decade of the nationalised electricity supply industry's existence in Britain, the NSHEB absorbed 9 per cent of the industry's total capital expenditure, but contributed only minimally to total generated output (Hannah, 1982, p. 154). Given its high initial capital costs and long construction times, some lag between project starts and output flows was to be expected, but it was not clear that Britain would ever want all of the hydroelectricity which the construction boom of the 1950s was likely to produce. In addition, in an interconnected electricity system such as that in the UK, it was difficult to see why a stand-alone hydro-generating capability was required at all. Traditionally, a major attraction of hydroelectricity stations was their ability to be built in often outlying areas where no other source of electricity was available. In France, hydroelectric schemes had proved valuable in geographically challenging areas such as the Alps, especially if the ability to position them on rivers or downhill streams obviated the need to build expensive reservoirs as was unfortunately the case in Scotland (Lévy-Leboyer and Morsel, 1994, pp. 733–5). Yet in the interconnected British system much of this justification disappeared, and it was political sentiment rather than economic rationale which allowed the NSHEB to retain responsibility for generating its own electricity.

Established in 1943 to help regenerate the Scottish Highlands, the Board had always enjoyed strong political support both in Scotland and England. Its first chairman was the former Scottish Secretary of State, Tom Johnston, and he in turn received support from his former Parliamentary

Secretary and successor as Scottish Secretary, Joseph Westwood. In London, the post-war Labour Lord President Herbert Morrison and Emanuel Shinwell, the Minister of Fuel and Power, had returned from visits to the Pitlochry and Sloy hydro schemes in Scotland suitably impressed with the potential of this long-term coal-free source of energy. With such backing, the NSHEB embarked upon a capital investment programme, which even the Board's official historian described as 'frenzied', as between 1953 and 1958 the Board never spent less than £11 million p.a., or over 75 per cent of their total capital investment, on new hydro schemes. At one stage in 1953, 14 power stations were simultaneously under construction, and major new stations were commissioned at a rate of nearly four a year throughout the decade (SRO, 1961; Payne, 1988; Chick, 2003). The NSHEB's own financial contribution to this investment frenzy was minimal, offering only £1 million from internal resources to finance an investment programme of £21.5 million in 1957 (TNA, 1957c, 1959e; SRO, 1960, para. 2). Its financial performance was sufficiently dismal for the Treasury to express the view in 1959 that: '[this] most social-service-minded of all the power nationalised industries seems to be wedded to the idea that it is doing all right if it just scrapes home in good years and makes a loss in bad ones' (TNA, 1959d). Yet, any suggestion that it increase prices so as to make a greater contribution to its own investment costs was greeted as an affront to Scottish dignity. Anyway, given the political sensitivity of increasing prices and the fact that the NSHEB's high capital:output ratio meant that a price increase of 10 per cent was required to raise a 1 per cent return on investment, the Treasury's scope for improving NSHEB self-financing ratios through price increases was always fairly limited.

What might have looked attractive in the 1940s when interest rates and coal stocks were low, looked decreasingly less so as coal surpluses grew from 1958 and interest rates climbed steadily higher. Even the gap between the much-vaunted low operating cost of hydro and of thermal generation had begun to narrow. While between 1951 and 1958 the NSHEB's average hydro-generating costs more than doubled from 0.3647d to 0.7267d per unit generated, those of thermal generators in England and Wales rose by just a third from 0.6617d to 0.8931d. Those of the thermal-generating SSEB were even lower at 0.844d in 1958, begging the question of why electricity might not be thermally (coal) generated in the south of Scotland and transmitted to the north, thereby avoiding the large capital cost of constructing new hydro reservoirs and plant (SRO, 1963b; TNA, 1964e). Existing hydro works could be used to help cover the peaks in the SSEB's demand, thereby reducing its new peak-hour thermal capacity build.

Coincidentally and separately from the Treasury's concerns, the Mackenzie Committee was established on 21 March 1961 by the Secretary of State for Scotland and charged with reviewing the availability and cost of hydroelectric power. This issue of comparative efficiency quickly resolved itself into the old, longer-running issue of whether a hydro-dominated NSHEB should be merged with the thermal-dominated SSEB. Invited to give evidence to the Committee, the Treasury's Under-Secretary Matthew Stevenson, like Clarke on the 1959 Nationalised Industries Committee, took his chance to divert the Committee's gaze away from what the Treasury regarded as secondary issues of organisational structure. Instead, he pressed the Committee's members to focus on the Treasury's central concern, namely the dubious value of much NSHEB generating investment. In doing so, he regaled the Committee with his own rendition of Massé's concerns regarding technological obsolescence. Underlining the risk of technological obsolescence, whether from a continued relative improvement in thermal efficiency, breakthroughs in fuel cell technology, a shift in relative primary fuel prices, or the depopulation of the Scottish Highlands, he promoted the value of EDF's work in evaluating the comparative merits of thermal- and hydroelectric-generating investment and incorporating time-related risk in the application of TDRs to projects (Payne, 1988, p. 214). While the Mackenzie Committee remained resistant to the application of TDRs to proposed projects, preferring instead to employ the long-term cost of borrowing, the Committee's report of November 1962 more than delivered the means of securing the Treasury's main objective. The Committee's recommendation of the merger of the generation operations of the North and South of Scotland Boards would mean that with the SSEB accounting for three-quarters of electricity output in Scotland, its increasingly efficient thermal generators would become the dominant generating technology for the whole of Scotland. However, in the face of strong opposition from the NSHEB and sufficient of the Scottish public, in the long run-up to the 1964 General Election, the British Cabinet rejected the recommended merger on 10 July 1963.

For the NSHEB, the victory was to prove brief and pyrrhic. In the subsequent political horse-trading between ministers and an outraged Treasury, the Treasury secured agreement from the Secretary of State for Scotland, Michael Noble, that as new schemes in Glen Nevis, Fada-Fionn and Laidon, which had waited upon Mackenzie's recommendations, came forward, there would be a strict 'assessment of the economics of these projects'. Comparisons would be made between the proposed hydro schemes and a large coal-burning station planned for partial operation by 1969 (TNA, 1963e, para. 6). The first such assessment, by means of an Inquiry in 1964, was initially limited to Fada-Fionn but then enlarged to include the Laidon project. The Inquiry's Reporters were J.A. Dick, QC, and the economist Professor A.D. Campbell, but crucially the 'economic test' for the proposed schemes was set, not internally by the Inquiry, but externally by the Treasury. A test rate of 8 per cent was chosen, a rate at which Laidon and Fada-Fionn were left dead in the water. From henceforth discount rates were to displace borrowing costs as the prime financial measure of the viability of hydro projects. The higher the discount rate, the less likely it was that long-term hydro projects would be sanctioned.

The Treasury was keenly alive to the wider political significance of this victory. In terms of the historical development of government (Treasury)–nationalised industry relations, it marked the definite exchange of the post-war role foreseen for the Treasury by some advocates of nationalisation as a lender of low-cost funds, for its new self-perceived role as an investor of scarce resources on behalf of the public. As such, the Treasury would need to subject proposed investments to an 'economic appraisal . . . based on calculations of the relative opportunities, risks, returns and costs of different courses of investment action' (SRO, 1962). Now a public interest, opportunity cost-based, *ex ante* TDR could be set for all nationalised industries, in place of the *ex post* RRR setting. As the Cabinet mulled over the Mackenzie Report, the Treasury stepped up its evangelisation of the gospel of TDRs and systems-based marginal analysis. In November 1962, as Mackenzie reported, so too did the Treasury circulate to all departments a paper on 'The Profitability of Nationalised Industries' which offered a simple explanation of how to calculate the 'present value' of an investment by discounting each year's receipts and expenditures back to the starting date (TNA, 1959g; SRO, 1962, para. 21). Departments were informed that such calculations should be applied to the whole of the undertaking and not simply to the individual project under examination, thereby following the systems analysis approach embodied in EDF's *La Note Bleue*. At the same time, letting bygones be bygones, any appraisal was to concern the effects of new decisions, rather than being a post mortem on old decisions. In May 1963, as the Cabinet equivocated over Mackenzie's recommendations, the Treasury sent out a further paper, this time on 'Investment Criteria for Public Enterprises', which reiterated the discounted message and offered keen civil servants a short further reading list of Pierre Massé's *Le Choix des Investissements* (1959); Stephen Marglin's *Approaches to Dynamic Investment* (1963a); and Harold Bierman and Seymour Smidt's *The Capital Budgetting Decision* (1960) (SRO, 1963a). In recommending the work of Bierman and Smidt, along with Massé and Marglin, the Treasury not only tapped into earlier work in accounting (Bierman) and managerial economics (Smidt), but also into the earlier research of Eugen Böhm-Bawerk, Knut Wicksell and Irving Fisher as well as the more recent contributions of Dean, Lorie, Savage, Solomon and Hirshleifer (Fisher,

1930; Dean, 1951, 1954; Lorie and Savage, 1955; Solomon, 1956, 1959; Hirshleifer, 1958b; Marglin, 1963b).[4]

This quickening of academic and public sector interest in the use of discount rates from the 1950s is of interest, not least because in the United States it also often focused on water, this time on the practical problem of water management. Unlike many utilities in the United States, water was a rising-cost utility often to be found under public ownership and management. Although lacking strict equivalents to the French and British nationalised industries, the issue of the public management of water resources in the United States had many resonances with European concerns in social discounting and welfare economics. Early attempts to compare costs and benefits, thereby admitting the social nature of a public investment decision, were seen in the 1936 US Flood Control Act and the later codification of practices in the *Green Book* of 1950, produced by the Federal Inter-Agency River Basin Committee. This was quickly followed by another attempt at formalisation in the Bureau of Budget's Circular A-47 of 1952. It was no coincidence that the major breakthroughs in cost–benefit analysis approaches related to water, with the simultaneous publication of works by Eckstein, Krutilla and Eckstein, and McKean (Eckstein, 1958; Krutilla and Eckstein, 1958; McKean, 1958; see also Pearce, 1971). The significance of these publications lay in their attempt to formalise public investment criteria in relation to the established criteria of welfare economics. Thus benefits were related back to the consumers' surplus criterion of Dupuit, Marshall and others, and ranking in terms of net social benefits was justified in terms of Paretian criteria for welfare maximisation. These links were strengthened further in 1962 when the Harvard Water Resource Programme published a monumental volume on the use of cost–benefit analysis in relation to water resource development. Many of the contributors had previously assisted with the President's Consultants' Report which had also provided detailed rules for the guidance of US agencies and had forged further links between the formal theory of welfare economics and cost–benefit (Maass, 1962). While these developments in cost–benefit analysis did not influence the Treasury's discussions of setting a TDR for the nationalised industries, the work of economists in the United States like Hirshleifer and later Baumol who favoured an opportunity-cost-based discount rate was read. The Treasury drew particular comfort after the publication of its 1967 White Paper, *Nationalised Industries: A Review of Economic and Financial Objectives*, from William J. Baumol's 1968 article 'On the social rate of discount' in the *American Economic Review*. As the Treasury's Peter Mountfield noted in his covering note to colleagues to whom the article was circulated, it was 'well worth glancing at – it confirms, broadly speaking, our approach to t.d.r.' (TNA, 1968g).

In the long run-up to its 1967 White Paper on nationalised industries, the Treasury's promotion of the application of TDRs to proposed investment projects reflected its growing interest in the marginalist approach to pricing and investment which had been applied in EDF. (TNA, 1966a). This interest was not born of some major intellectual revolution within the Treasury, but rather the straightforward adoption of an economic approach which neatly matched its wish to exercise greater influence over aspects of nationalised industries' investment, while respecting the public corporation model and avoiding detailed involvement in the day-to-day decision making in the industries. The marginalist emphasis on the future rather than the past suited the Treasury's purposes, and in a sense meant that during the 1960s it developed beyond the essentially retrospective rate-setting regulation practised in the United States. To some extent, it also chimed with developments occurring in some private industries in the UK, as well as at the CEGB. From 1959, while not evaluating capital expenditure statutorily required to meet demand, the CEGB had moved to the discounted cash flow (DCF) appraisal of 'optional' expenditure (for example, the choice of generating technique, or expenditure designed to lower costs) requiring them in theory to make a 10 per cent net (16 per cent gross) return (Hirshleifer et al., 1960). From 1964, both as a partial result of pressure emanating from the RRRs set in the 1961 White Paper, and reflecting the wish of the CEGB to pass on a truer cost structure to the area boards, the Board began to apply a discount rate of 7.5 per cent in all investment appraisal calculations (Webb, 1966).

Yet, if the future was to be discounted back to present value, what still remained to be resolved was the rationale for, and level of, rate setting. Before setting off into this tangled wood of ideas, the Treasury consulted Pierre Massé. Given their growing interest in the activities of the NSHEB and general preoccupation with the growth of public expenditure, the Treasury's Matthew Stevenson arranged a brief meeting with Massé in 1957. Stevenson wondered what rate EDF were using. While *La Note Bleue* had insisted that the rate be higher than the long-term cost of borrowing and approximate to some opportunity cost of capital, that is, the minimum acceptable return on the use of the resources in an alternative project, it had necessarily not specified what that essentially changeable rate should be. Asked by Stevenson what rate EDF was actually using, Massé replied: 'Well, we adopt a planning rate of 7 per cent', although when Stevenson 'asked why 7 per cent, the conversation then degenerated into somewhat obscure French' (SRO, 1961). Yet whatever criteria had helped to shape EDF's choice of discount rate, the perspective framing Massé's criteria was about to change. In February 1959, Massé moved from EDF to become head of the Commissariat Général du Plan (CGP) where, beginning with the third French Plan, he gave a major impulse to the use of marginalist techniques and discount rates in French economic planning. In assuming ultimate responsibility for the Third Economic Plan (1958–61), Massé's role was now even closer to that of the UK Treasury's in that he was now deciding on a rate for the entire economy and not just for the electricity industry alone (Morsel, 1996, pp. 352, 392). In doing so, Massé drew on advice from colleagues at EDF such as Marcel Boiteux, French economists such as Edmond Malinvaud and Maurice Allais, and the internationally known work of the likes of John von Neumann, Oskar Morgenstern and Paul Samuelson. In particular, Massé's friend James Tobin, when not acting as economic adviser to President John F. Kennedy, offered suggestions on rate setting for the Third Economic Plan. Not that Tobin's ideas were always accepted. While Tobin urged Massé to move to a rate in the 9–10 per cent, rather than 7–8 per cent, range, Massé's political antennae cautioned him to temper economic advice with political pragmatism. As Massé recalled: 'I did not dare – for fear of the outcry, and therefore I went for a compromise', settling for 8 per cent (Massé, 1965, p. 275; see also Tobin, 1963; FONT, 1973). None the less, this marked a significant step up from the 4 per cent employed in the first two French economic plans. For the Fourth and Fifth Plans (1962–70) this rate was to fall to 7 per cent before rising again to 10 per cent in the Sixth Plan (Picard et al., 1985, p. 152).

If the Treasury was to use opportunity cost as the conceptual basis for setting a TDR, it needed to discover at what level such a rate should be set. For help in resolving this issue, the Treasury turned to private companies in Britain. Prominent among those consulted was Courtaulds, the textiles producer. Arthur Knight, Courtaulds' Finance Director, supplied the Treasury with confidential memos outlining the company's methods of investment appraisal and Treasury officials attached great weight to articles written by Courtaulds' Chief Economist, A.M. Alfred. Indeed, one article in December 1963 by Alfred on discounted cash flow and the choice of a test rate was cited by the Treasury as the best single reference to date on the subject. To Alfred's work, the Treasury also added that of Anthony Merrett and Allen Sykes who, before becoming better known as academics, worked for Esso and Rio Tinto Zinc, respectively (Merrett and Sykes, 1962a, 1962b). From their position in private industry, Alfred, Merrett and Sykes all paid particular attention to the cost of obtaining risk capital as a guide to the level at which a test rate should be set. Alfred thought the cost of equity capital to be 6 per cent after tax, which, erring on the side of caution, the Treasury interpreted as indicating a 7 per cent minimum rate of return (TNA, 1963f). Slightly higher returns were reported by Merrett and Sykes but their view that the supply price of risk capital had to be sufficient to give equity investors average returns of the order of 7–8 per cent in real terms after tax was questioned by J.L. Carr of the Treasury (TNA, 1964b). Indeed, on the basis of Merrett and Sykes's two articles in the *District Bank Review* for September and December 1963, Carr launched an attack on their 7 per cent thesis.

Without descending into the interstices of Carr's arguments, his central concern was that while the arithmetic average of net returns, including untaxed capital gains, over eight successive (overlapping) 11-year periods between 1945 and 1963 was 11.6 per cent in money terms and 7.6 per cent in real terms, returns over the several periods differed considerably, varying between 6.0 per cent in money (1.5 per cent real) terms between 1947 and 1958, and 17.0 per cent in money (13.2 per cent real) terms between 1949 and 1960. All the returns exceeding 10.4 per cent in money (5.2 per cent real) terms covered 11-year periods embracing the Stock Exchange boom, when a very rapid rise in capital values came about with a fall in earnings and dividend yields and the appearance of the reverse yield gap. While Merrett rejected the view that this boom was a once-for-all adjustment on the grounds that there was no reason to think that any basic structural change had taken place, Carr thought that the appearance of the reverse yield gap implied just such a fundamental change in investors' attitudes; that in short there was no evidence to support the view that risk capital would only be forthcoming if investors received real net returns of 7 per cent or more (Merrett and Sykes, 1963a, 1963b, 1966; TNA, 1966c; NEDO, 1971, p. 17). Yet, despite this, and the fact that recent Stock Exchange experience offered little support for the view that investors could expect to get real net-of-tax returns of 7 per cent or more on well-spread equity portfolios, Carr accepted that Merrett's thesis had gained wide acceptance (TNA, 1966c). Or as Carr's Treasury colleague, Lawrence Airey put it in 1965:

> As regards the TDR, there is, of course, some difference of view whether 8 per cent is exactly right, but there is not much doubt that the marginal rate of return in the private sector, properly calculated on an equally risk free project, would be something of this order. Most of the independent calculations of other economists point to the same conclusion (Alfred, Merrett and Sykes). (TNA, 1965f)

This preference for 8 per cent was reiterated to departmental representatives and nationalised industry chairmen in meetings held under the Treasury's chairmanship (TNA, 1968d).

It was 8 per cent which was chosen for the White Paper on nationalised industries of April 1967. This 1967 White Paper marked the theoretical highpoint of a marginalist, welfare-economic approach to the management of the nationalised industries, combining as it did the application of a TDR to future investment with pricing at long-run marginal cost. That its moment of intellectual purity was soiled, and its fundamental baser public expenditure concerns revealed, by the Treasury's attaching of financial targets to the sufficient twin mechanisms of the TDR and long-run marginal-cost pricing only reflected the persistent public finance and public expenditure motors which had driven the Treasury along the marginalist route (Cmnd. 3437, 1967, paras 10 and 34; TNA, 1968i, para. 11). As hoped, the White Paper stimulated further reforms to the electricity BST in 1967/68 and greater disaggregating of investment in a 'total system' for full appraisal purposes (Meek, 1968). However, many of the wider problems of application which were to beset the 1967 White Paper were apparent in electricity too. TDRs were applied to only a limited proportion of investment, because much of the nationalised industries' investment was regarded as part of an existing, usually grid network, system or as necessary in terms of requirement for, say, safety standards or security of supply (Cmnd. 7131, 1978, paras 59, 66).

A useful comparison can be drawn between the origins, provisions and effects of the 1967 White Paper in the UK and the Report of the Nora Committee in France. Both were published in 1967 and both were driven in large part by public expenditure concerns. In France, the upward shift in public expenditure as a percentage of GDP occurred a little later than in the UK, but in the same year, 1959, as Prime Minister Macmillan established the Nationalised Industries Committee, so too was the Armand–Rueff Committee echoing the recommendations of its UK counterpart in calling for greater '*vérité des prix*', and self-financing by nationalised industries (Rueff and Armand, 1960; Buzelay, 1971; Quennouëlle-Corre, 2000). During the 1960s, as the British Treasury prepared the 1967 White Paper, the French Prime Minister Georges Pompidou on 4 April 1966 charged a committee headed by Simon Nora (1921–2006), a senior civil servant and brother of the historian Pierre Nora, with undertaking a fundamental review of government–nationalised industries relations in France. EDF exercised a significant influence on the committee's proceedings, both because of its reputation as one of the highest areas of total factor productivity (TFP) in the French economy and the presence on the committee of EDF employees like Boiteux, the newly installed Director-General of EDF in which post he was to remain until 1979. Massé, who was to leave the CGP in that same year, 1966, to return to EDF and serve as its President until 1969 was also an important *éminence grise*. With Boiteux heading up Nora's sub-committee on tariffs, with EDF's TFP performance making it a leading sector of the economy, and with EDF highlighting its promotion of rational marginalist approaches to pricing and investment, EDF was able to negotiate for itself a measure of contractual independence from the government and an acceptance that it should be dealt with separately from other nationalised industries (Chick, 2003). With an intervening delay occasioned by the '*événements*' of May 1968, the *Contrat de Progrès* was negotiated by 1969 and the five-year *Contrat de Programme* was signed on 23 December 1970. Commercially, the contract gave EDF greater freedom of action in pricing, where marginal-cost tariffs were to be continued in monopoly conditions, while allowing a more competitive pricing strategy to be pursued in competitive markets (FONT, 1967; Estrin and Holmes, 1983, p. 68). EDF was given greater freedom to raise its own finance, subject to meeting targets of a return on capital investment of 8 per cent in 1971 and 8.3 per cent in 1972 (Monnier, 1983, pp. 125, 144–5). However, on the assumption that EDF's TFP would rise by at least 4.85 per cent p.a., total price increases (high and low tension) were not to exceed an average of 1.85 per cent p.a. for each general price increase of 2.5 per cent. Inflation indexing could only apply when inflation was between 1 and 4 per cent (Monnier, 1983, p. 144; Picard et al., 1985, p. 219).

The greater commercial independence gained by EDF in the contract in the years following the Nora Report contrasted with the British government's treatment of the nationalised electricity industry during the 1970s. In one sense, matters improved. The political agency problems which had dogged government–nationalised industry relations since the days of the Clow Committee and the arguments over peak-hour pricing were at last formally addressed, if not solved, in a chain of reports from the Select Committee on Nationalised Industries (SCNI) in December 1973, from Lord Rothschild's Central Policy Review Staff (CPRS), and from the National Economic Development Office (NEDO) in 1976 (Cmnd. 7131, 1978, paras 1, 6–8). However, against this and in sharp contrast to the French government's treatment of EDF, the nationalised electricity industry tended to be lumped in with all the other nationalised industries and subject to the same price controls and discount rates. Increasingly, approaches towards the nationalised industries became dominated by the overriding concern with public expenditure, as the PSBR:GDP (public sector borrowing requirement:gross domestic product) ratio rose from 2.3 per cent in 1971 to 6.4 per cent in 1979, through a peak of 9.6 per cent in 1975 (Pratten, 1990, p. 170; Middleton, 1996, p. 580). The price controls imposed as part of the Heath (1970–74) government's anti-inflation policies scrambled many of the principles and potential benefits arising out of the 1967 White Paper (Millward, 1976). Also subject to interference in the professed interests of wider macroeconomic stability were the various discount rates applied to the nationalised industries during the 1970s. Beginning with the TDR, soon after the publication of the 1967 White Paper and in the wake of the 1967 devaluation of sterling, UK government economists like Alec Cairncross and Michael Posner had to fight off efforts to raise the TDR from 8 to 10 per cent, preferring instead to achieve the stated aim of releasing resources for export by means of budgetary deflation (TNA, 1968a, 1968b, 1968c, 1968f). When in 1969 the TDR was increased from 8 to 10 per cent this was in response to evidence, much of it from A.M. Alfred of Courtaulds, that the minimum rate of return being sought on investments in the private sector had risen substantially above 8 per cent, not least as the recent 2.5 per cent increase in corporation tax had increased by 1 per cent the minimum return expected by industry (TNA, 1967f, 1968h, 1972).

With the continued economic difficulties of the Heath government, pressure switched from using the TDR to reduce demand to attempting to use it as a means of stimulating economic activity by increasing fixed capital formation (GES, 1979, paras 1.5, 3.8). Blocked from changing the level of the rate, supporters of increased public investment pushed for a change in the type of rate used, urging the theoretical benefits of the social time preference rate (STPR) over the allegedly inhibiting 'opportunity cost'-based TDR. What the STPR expressed was the government's choice of an interest rate which reflected its own weighting of the balance between the present and the future. While the TDR could be presented as reflecting an 'opportunity cost' concern with the returns forgone in using resources in one project rather than another, the advocates of the STPR questioned whether TDRs reflecting market returns were still likely to privilege current over future satisfaction. That in Arthur Pigou's terms, man's 'telescopic faculty is defective, and that we, therefore, see future pleasures, as it were, on a diminished scale' (Millward, 1971, pp. 195, 197). Essentially the argument for using an STPR was that a social discount rate should reflect society's preference for present benefits over future benefits, and that an STPR would overcome any selfish disinclination by the present generation to forgo current consumption in favour of investment for the benefit of themselves and others to come. Again, this use by government of an STPR was widely discussed by economists, particularly in the United States (Feldstein, 1964; Arrow, 1966; Arrow and Kurz, 1970; Arrow and Lind, 1970; Solow, 1974). These arguments revolved around the issue of risk and the extent to which the risk of public sector projects was distributed and diversified over the entire population.

Within the Treasury in the 1960s, the STPR was dismissed by Carr as a 'red herring', although he did give a more considered, if still sceptical, consideration of the concept in a note in the *Economic Journal* in 1966 (Carr, 1966; TNA, 1968d). Carr remained sceptical as to any government's ability, outside of war, to decide from first principles on an 'appropriate' STPR, his view being that something more than a 10 per cent return would be needed to persuade people voluntarily to revert to the living standards which they had enjoyed a decade ago, and that to speak as though they might well be willing to sacrifice some of their current consumption in return for returns of the order of 4 per cent was absurd. More generally within the Treasury, concern also existed as to whether even if a known STPR different from the TDR existed, it could be demonstrated that an economy would be better off selecting investments with returns less than the opportunity cost of capital in preference to those yielding returns equal to or above the opportunity cost of capital (TNA, 1968e). None the less, during the 1970s the use of STPRs was increasingly advocated, and eventually a compromise was worked out and published in 1978 as the White Paper, *The Nationalised Industries*, a step backwards in terms of welfare economics from the 1967 White Paper (Cmnd. 7131, 1978; Posner, 1973). Now, the TDR was effectively reformulated as an RRR on total investment, with the choice of appraisal method and discount rates necessary to achieve the RRR being left for the industries and their sponsoring departments to decide. The definition of the 'opportunity cost of capital' was widened with STPR considerations being reflected in the RRR for public investment being compared with the alternative use of resources for investment or consumption. It was explicitly recognised by the Treasury that sanctioning public projects with an STPR of, say, 5 per cent, when private projects were subject to 10 per cent would provide a means of raising total national investment, as well as palliating the discouragement given by a high TDR to longer-term projects with high initial capital costs. In this context, the RRR for nationalised industries, while still nominally reflecting the 'opportunity cost of capital', would be applied to industries' investment programmes as a whole, with government and nationalised industries negotiating a more direct way of relating the opportunity cost of capital to their financial performance in order to reinforce the principles of Cmnd. 3437 (Cmnd. 7131, 1978, paras 60, 64). Finally, the rate chosen in the 1978 White Paper on nationalised industries was 5 per cent, rather than the interdepartmental review committee's 1976 recommendation of 7 per cent, as the mid-point of its suggested range of 6–8 per cent (GES, 1979, paras 1.2, 3.12, 3.3, 3.14). What remained constant was the abiding presence of concern with public expenditure. Industries would be subject to external financial limits (EFLs) which had initially been introduced in 1976 as cash limits. While, in the medium term, investment would be subject to an RRR set over projects as a whole rather than individually, since the calculation of a 5 per cent RRR on medium-term investment proved 'too difficult' for the Department of Energy, the EFL came to play a dominant role in limiting total expenditure (Heald, 1980; Helm, 2003, p. 34).

This twisting and elaborating of the use of the rate of discount by British governments during the 1970s reflected wider problems in national and international economic management as many of the assumptions under-pinning the operation of the economy during the Golden Age suddenly seemed to fall away. This was as true of the generation economics of the electricity industry as it was at a macroeconomic level of the perceived inverse relationship between shifts in the rate of unemployment and inflation, or of the ability of the dollar to act as the Pole Star in a system of fixed exchange rates. In the United States, for much of the Golden Age, the regulation of utilities like electricity had settled down into a state of qui-escent stability. Applications for rate review were infrequent and prices were stable as much of the 43 per cent fall in the real price of electricity between 1951 and 1971was not passed on to consumers. Politicians had quickly lost interest in utility affairs, managers had enjoyed the certainties of life in a protected regulated utility and in the words of the chairman of one of New England's commissions, 'regulation during the 1960s was non-existent' (Anderson, 1981, pp. 65, 69; Hirsh, 1999, p. 3).

However, by 1967, the economies of scale and technological advances which had caused electricity unit output costs and prices to fall began to dry up. Thermal efficiency gains in traditional steam turbine-generator technology reached a new plateau, and economies of scale in building power plants ceased accruing. Thermodynamic theory limited steam systems to a maximum efficiency of about 48 per cent, while in practice, metallurgical problems appeared in boilers and turbines when efficiency reached 40 per cent (ibid., p. 56). With their costs rising, companies were forced to approach state utility commissions for rate reviews (Joskow, 1974; Joskow et al., 1989; McCraw, 1984, p. 242; Hirsh, 1989). This con-trasted sharply with the small number of applications for rate review during the Golden Age. While some 'voluntary' rate decreases were made, and prices were raised between 1949 and 1952, and between 1957 and 1961 when fuel (especially natural gas) prices rose, much of the 1950s and most of the 1960s until 1969 saw little formal regulatory hearing activity. From 1969, the rate of filing for increases picked up. Whereas in 1963 only three cases were being reviewed nationwide, in 1969 the number had increased to 19, and by 1975 it had shot up to 114. Rates to the average residential consumer more than doubled from 2.1 cents per kWh (in unad-justed terms) in 1969 to 4.4 cents in 1979. In the same period, rates for industrial customers increased from 0.9 to 2.6 cents per kWh. As rates rose, so price elasticity of demand slowly kicked in. In place of the virtu-ous circle of increasing demand, economies of scale and technological progress, came the vicious circle of rising prices, slowing demand growth, excess capacity and falling profits. For the first time since 1946, post-war total sales of electricity fell 0.1 per cent between 1973 and 1974 as resi-dential rates surged almost 19 per cent, from 1973 to 1974. Sales rose

1.9 per cent in 1975 and fluctuated wildly thereafter. As income growth slowed and costs grew, the fall in profits caused financial analysts to downgrade the bonds of many electric utilities, thereby increasing their future costs of raising capital. To all of this could be added the effects of the inflation of the 1970s. A second hike in oil prices in 1979–81 simply sent further 'rate shocks' down the wires to consumers. In 1981 regulators approved rate increases which added $8 billion to customers' bills, four times the amount granted in 1977, 1978 and 1979 (Anderson, 1981, pp. 70, 73; Hirsh, 1999, pp. 61, 172).

Quite apart from these electricity rate shocks, it was difficult to find any section of the fuel and power sector which appeared to be performing well. Even as the 1960s ended, delays and backlogs in plant manufacture caused capacity shortages in some East Coast utilities, resulting in peak-time 'brownouts' (reduced voltage) in the summers of 1967, 1968 and 1969, with persistently rising demand intensifying the problem in 1970 and 1971. The natural gas industry also failed to maintain a reliable supply of gas as the long-term effects of the decision to regulate wellhead, rather than just pipeline, rates made themselves felt. The coal industry also struggled to meet demand, coal producers having opened few new mines in expectation of an increased use of nuclear power by utilities (MacAvoy and Pindyck, 1975; Hirsh, 1999, p. 59).

In the nuclear industry itself, technological and construction problems bedevilled the industry such that, rather than being too cheap to meter as had been hoped in the 1960s, from 1972 to 1975 the cost per kilowatt of new nuclear capacity rose 80 per cent while the cost of new coal-fired power plants doubled (Anderson, 1981, p. 70; Hirsh, 1999, p. 5). As the issue arose as to who should bear the rising capital cost of nuclear power, the traditional regulatory assumptions came under increasing strain. While inflation triggered a lively discussion on whether the original or replacement costs of assets should form the basis of rate setting in the future, at the heart of the debate lay the regulators' difficulties in squaring their traditional obligation to provide utilities with a 'fair' return with their reluctance to visit sharp price rises upon utility customers (Averch and Johnson, 1962; Stigler and Friedland, 1962; Stigler, 1971; Kahn, 1988, pp. xxvi–xxviii). As Kahn remarked, echoing Horace Gray's article of 1940, it was precisely the unbridgeability of that gap between what appeared to be fair to the company under original cost principles and what appeared to be fair to consumers in these circumstances that produced institutional breakdown, and opened up the possibility of a true 'passing of the public utility concept' (ibid., pp. xxvi–xxviii). In the wake of the Three Mile Island accident, the imposition of increased safety requirements imposed unwanted higher costs on the nuclear industry, not least as load factor fell as plant stayed out of service for longer, but this was not the main cause of the industry's difficulties.

With voters complaining of sharp price increases, and with the regulated fuel and power industries struggling to meet some of the most basic public assumptions concerning supply and performance, political interest in energy regulation revived. Unusual relationships were struck up, politically between the likes of Edward Kennedy and Ralph Nader, and in a wider political–economic market between politicians and academic economists. The economists could be divided crudely into three groups. First, there were those who were long-standing critics of regulation, among whose ranks could be commonly counted Averch and Johnson with their concern that asset-based regulation was encouraging over- (and sometimes gold-plated-) investment and the likes of Stigler and Posner who drew attention to the problems of regulatory capture (Laffont and Tirole, 1991). Then there were economists who, excited by the possibilities offered by new technology whether in telecommunications, electricity or airlines, revisited the traditional drawing of natural monopoly boundaries and injected new life into such concepts as the consumers' surplus, contestable markets and marginal-cost pricing, while also questioning the use of public utilities for redistributive purposes. Notable among this group of economists were Vickrey, Baumol and Willig and this burgeoning of fresh interest in matters regulatory can be followed with ease in the pages of the *Bell Journal of Economics and Management Science*, which was established in 1970 and later renamed the *Rand Journal of Economics* (Baumol, 1977; Crew and Kleindorfer, 1986, pp. 4, 26). The final group of academic economists comprised those who actively participated in the business of (de-)regulation itself. Pre-eminent in this group was Alfred Kahn. In 1977, President Jimmy Carter appointed Kahn as chairman of the Civil Aeronautics Board. Ignoring the issues of hub airports and access to airport stands, the airline industry was free of the natural monopoly issues which complicated the regulation of utilities. With Kahn evangelising the marginal-cost message, to the point of memorably referring to aircraft as marginal costs with wings, the deregulation of the airline industry produced startling and some-times brutal results.

As national governments struggled to demonstrate economic com-petence and purpose at a macroeconomic level, such benefits to voting con-sumers of deregulatory microeconomics had obvious political attractions. Funding was provided to investigate the scope for policies promoting com-petition. Between 1967 and 1975 the Ford Foundation granted $1.8 million to the Brookings Institution, a Washington-based public policy research organisation, for research on the regulation of economic activity. Political support for deregulation cut across party lines with Gerald Ford, Jimmy

Carter and Edward Kennedy among its high-profile backers. Kennedy was chair of the Subcommittee on Administrative Practice and Procedure of the Judiciary Committee, in which capacity he met Stephen Breyer, special counsel to the Subcommittee and an ardent advocate of regulatory reform. Breyer was a professor of administrative and antitrust law at Harvard and had worked in the Justice Department's Antitrust Division in the late 1960s when it was beginning to get involved in regulatory proceedings. It was Breyer who, on joining the subcommittee staff in the spring of 1974, urged Kennedy to consider airline regulation as a subject for investigative hearings. In such conditions, and given its earlier supply failures, it was difficult for the gas industry to avoid the regulatory eye. It certainly did not help the industry that Breyer had co-authored work with the economist Paul MacAvoy arguing for the deregulation of natural gas (Breyer and MacAvoy, 1974; Derthick and Quirk, 1985, pp. 35–40).

With political backing, and advised by lawyers and economists, the programme of deregulation began to roll forward. In the same year, 1984, that AT&T was dismantled, so too was access to gas pipelines liberalised and natural gas wellhead prices significantly decontrolled. A year later airline rates were completely deregulated with the abolition of the Civil Aeronautics Board on 1 January 1985. It was in this deregulatory context that the effects of the Public Utility Regulatory Policies Act (PURPA) worked themselves out. In 1978 the passage of the PURPA legislation had reflected the contemporary concern with the efficiency of fuel and energy use, not least as evidenced in the growth of such environmental groups as the Sierra Club and the Environmental Defense Fund, who were particularly critical of the environmental impact of the electricity industry and of its pro-growth and pricing policies (Hirsh, 1999, p. 1). PURPA used a marginalist approach to future rate setting inasmuch as new providers of electricity could charge a rate reflecting the cost avoided by the utility in not producing. This pursuit of environmental improvement through the use of the marginalist approach had been seen a few years earlier when Alfred Kahn had persuaded groups like the Environmental Defense Fund of their common interest in marginal-cost pricing (McCraw, 1984, p. 249). Yet almost unintentionally, PURPA also initiated the deregulation of the electricity industry by allowing new, environmentally friendly, entrants into the generation section of the industry with regulatory-enforced requirements that utilities buy from these qualifying facilities (Hirsh, 1999, p. 6).

Amidst the increased uncertainties which accompanied the slowdown in international economic growth from the late 1960s, many governments sought, or were forced, to reappraise their relationship with nationalised and regulated utility industries. In this process of negotiated change, perceptions of the past performance of the industries, and of their role within the economy, were particularly important. In France, in the reassessment of the role of the nationalised industries conducted by the Nora Committee, the political strength and physical presence on the committee of EDF leaders, its ability to present itself as a source of rational, best practice within the economy, allied to the association in the public mind of EDF with modernisation and national security, all combined to allow EDF to negotiate its way to a new, contractual future. In Britain, the electricity industry could present a case that, in response to the 1961 and 1967 White Papers on the nationalised industries, it had taken considerable steps to ensure that both its pricing and investment decisions followed much more economically rational guidelines than had been the case in the 1940s and 1950s. However, it was the nationalised electricity industry's misfortune that the dominant voice in reshaping government–nationalised industry relations was the Treasury. Pre-eminently concerned with public finance issues, the Treasury's instinct was to treat nationalised industries as a group, in contrast to the greater contractual independence extended to EDF in France. It was also unfortunate that it was against the electricity industry that the Treasury had often directed its public finance-driven promotion of investment appraisal techniques incorporating TDRs. What is noteworthy is the surprising importance in the early development of this Treasury approach to investment appraisal of the French lessons offered by EDF. The technologically-driven system-based approach of EDF to investment appraisal was to move out of this most modern of nationalised industries and spray out over the major industries in France under Pierre Massé's direction as *Commissaire au Plan*. This organic growth, from the bottom up, contrasted with the prescriptive, top-down, almost teleological approach of the Treasury. Both the French and British cases contrasted with the experience of the United States. While British and French officials and engineers had become increasingly engrossed in the techniques and philosophical underpinnings of investment appraisal, in the United States for much of the Golden Age, regulation remained quiescently becalmed. Those arguments which did occur were more often about the regulatory rate base rather than the broader, economic basis of that rate. When the mix of oil crisis and technological stasis in the electricity industry stirred up calls for a review of the regulatory basis, there was almost an inadvertent drift in the PURPA towards a reconsideration of the regulated structure of the industry, or, more precisely, of its market. By so doing, by admitting new entrants, the basis of regulation began to shift in its emphasis towards an *ex ante* perspective, in which utilities could no longer rely on the assumption that an implicit contract existed between them and the regulators. As some of the regulatory practices of the Golden Age unwound, new attitudes towards market and industrial structures began to emerge. It is to a consideration of that changed world of deregulation, privatisation and liberalisation that we now turn.

NOTES

1. Quoted in P. Massé, 'Quelques problèmes d'optimum économique', in *Stratégies et Décisions Économiques Études Théoriques et Applications aux Entreprises*, CNRS, Paris, 1954 (Weart, 1979). Paul Langevin (1872–1942) was a French physicist whose research included work on the electric charges of electrons in atoms.
2. Ailleret's Law was a statistical observation commonly referred to as showing electricity demand doubling every 10 years in this period; nine years is more accurate. Pierre Ailleret was Director-General of Studies and Research at EDF.
3. Its full and formal title was *Essai de détermination d'un critérium pour le choix des équipements hydrauliques et thermiques*. Jean Ricard was an expert on thermal generation and Jacques Tissier was in charge of the service for energy studies.
4. The works of Fisher and Böhm-Bawerk, with their interest in discounted investment appraisal, were both known in France, Fisher's *The Rate of Interest* (1907) being translated into French in 1909 and his *Theory of Interest* (1930) in 1934.

6. Deregulation, privatisation and liberalisation

In 1978, Congress passed the Airline Deregulation Act, the Natural Gas Policy Act and the Public Utility Regulatory Policies Act (PURPA). In terms of the contribution of each piece of legislation to what might be viewed as a programme of deregulation in the United States, the first opened the skies to airline competition, the second decontrolled the most expensive sources of new gas and established a schedule for future deregulation, and the third almost unintentionally pushed the electricity supply industry down the first few steps towards the deregulation and attempted liberalisation of the industry and its markets. With its origins in the anxieties concerning the future supply and current efficiency of energy use, PURPA encouraged electricity generation by environmentally-friendly, new entrant generators. Full, federal efforts to promote competition and the liberalisation of the wholesale market were not to be made until the 1992 Energy Policy Act and the subsequent Federal Energy Regulatory Commission (FERC) rulings. During the intervening decade of the 1980s, the British government initiated its programme of privatisation. Among the large public utilities, first British Telecom and then British Gas were privatised in November 1984 and December 1986, respectively. With these two major privatisations privileging the transfer of ownership over the promotion of competition, it was not until the 1989 Electricity Act that an act of British privatisation deliberately and firmly pursued both the restructuring and privatisation of a nationalised industry with the specific intent of liberalising its wholesale and, eventually, retail markets. Throughout these developments in deregulation and partial liberalisation in the United States, and of privatisation, restructuring and liberalisation in Britain, the French government and EDF sought to protect its existing nationalised monopoly status. In this chapter, the often strongly contrasting development of each of these approaches towards the electricity supply industry in each country will be examined. Initially, a chronological approach is adopted inasmuch as PURPA in 1978, the Electricity Act of 1989, and then the Energy Policy Act of 1992 are discussed in order. The chapter will then examine the trading arrangements adopted in the United States and

British electricity markets and the problems arising from the existence of stranded costs and assets, as well as analysing the tensions between federal legislation, regulatory rulings and state-based responses to competition in the United States. The Californian débâcle is discussed, as is, at the other end of the competitive spectrum, the French resistance to privatisation and liberalisation.

The 1978 PURPA, fashionably embracing the marginal concept, required utilities to purchase power from certain types of approved independent power producers called qualifying facilities (QFs) at the utility's avoided cost. The subsequent QF output was not subject to price regulation. Avoided cost was taken as being the cost which the utility 'avoided' by not having to build its own plants, although that avoided cost could be set sufficiently high by state regulators so as to make these contracts highly lucrative for their owners (Hunt, 2002, p. 257). QFs qualified on the grounds of their environmental friendliness, with co-generators and renewable energy facilities being the most favoured forms of production. Co-generators used a small version of a utility's turbine generator, and while lacking economies of scale, they benefited from the mass production of several of its key components. Their capital costs were between $800 and $1,200 per kW in 1986, which compared favourably with fossil-fuel turbine generators, and were generally lower than the cost of nuclear units which ranged from anywhere between $932 and $5,192 per kW at the beginning of 1984 (Hirsh, 1999, pp. 102–3). At such a cost, with prices unregulated, and utilities required to buy from QFs, the maths proved attractive. By 1992, 60 per cent of new capacity in the United States was being built by independent power producers (IPPs) using mainly co-generation and renewable energy facilities. Nowhere were IPPs more active than in California, where by 1990, of about 56,000 MW of Californian capacity, 9,412 MW came from QFs. In 1991, non-utility companies in the Golden State provided one-third of the state's electricity, and 21 per cent of all of the electricity produced by IPPs in the United States (Joskow and Jones, 1983; Hirsh, 1999, pp. 6, 93; Joskow, 2005). Yet while this marked a significant break with the traditional, regulated, vertically-integrated industry supplying a captive market and subject to cost-of-service regulation, it was not, nor was it ever intended to be, the spearhead for a fundamental restructuring of the industry and its markets. The impact of the IPPs remained at the level of the state, and then varied between states, and they sold on long-term contracts to the utilities (Crew and Kleindorfer, 1986, p. 205). Not that liberalisation was unknown in the United States. In 1984, the same year in which AT&T was deregulated and long-distance calls made competitive, access to natural gas pipelines was liberalised. As part of the shift from coal gas to natural gas, interconnecting pipelines had been built across state boundaries. As such they fell under federal rather than state jurisdiction and were thereby more amenable to national reforming legislation and rulings. Most of the electricity supply industry remained fairly ensconced within its state boundary and protected, from outside at least, from liberalisation. For their first view of a deliberate effort to introduce competition into this technically complex industry, electricity-industry watchers in the United States needed to turn their gaze towards Britain.

The privatisation of the electricity supply industry in England and Wales by means of the 1989 Electricity Act was neither the first privatisation of a utility nor the first attempt to liberalise a fuel and power market. In 1984 British Telecom had been privatised, and British Gas in 1986. In 1982, in the Oil and Gas (Enterprise) Act and in 1983 in the Energy Act, efforts had been made to encourage competition in the relevant markets. Both pieces of legislation reflected the outlook of the new Energy Secretary, Nigel Lawson, whose arrival in the Department of Energy in September 1981 marked a sharp break with its past practices. The outcome of these thwarted efforts to promote competition and to change ownership were instructive and influential in shaping the privatisation of the electricity supply industry. They demonstrated the difficulty of promoting competition in markets dominated by an incumbent publicly-owned monopoly. Both these issues, of public ownership and monopoly, were subsequently tackled, although the former more easily and quickly than the latter. While both the privatisations of British Telecom and British Gas proved to be politically popular, they disappointed economists in passing up the opportunity to introduce much more competition into each industry. British Telecom was privatised in 1984 as a vertically-integrated monopoly owning the entire existing network to which Mercury as its sole licensed competitor was granted a time-limited access. Notoriously, British Gas was privatised as a licensed monopoly. Any aspirant entrants were left to negotiate access terms with British Gas and unsurprisingly none of the 10 attempts to secure access between 1982 and 1990 proved to be successful (Newbery, 1999, p. 193). Entry only occurred in 1990 after the Office of Fair Trading had forced British Gas to contract for no more than 90 per cent of new gas supply in 1989. Thus, the privatisation of these two major utilities disappointed those who along with John Moore, the Financial Secretary to the Treasury in 1983, expected that privatisation would not only be of benefit in exposing those industries to the disciplines of the capital markets, but that it would also be accompanied by the restructuring of these industries into a genuinely competitive form (Moore, 1986). As it happened, information asymmetries and electoral time constraints made their influence felt, and the transfer of ownership took priority over the introduction of competition (Kay and Thompson, 1986; Chick, 1994, 2004; Newbery, 1999, p. 176).

Fundamentally, any restructuring of the electricity supply industry so as to encourage or provide for competition required the grid network to be separated out from the rest of the industry and placed under independent control. In itself, this interest in separating out the grid reflected a change in the general view as to where the boundaries of natural monopoly lay within the industry. When in the mid-twentieth century the utilities had been nationalised in France and Britain, and regulated in the United States, the general tendency was to view the entire industry as constituting a natural monopoly. At the time there had been critics of this approach, but the political decision makers had greater faith in their ability to control monopoly abuse than to live with the uncertainties of the competitive market (Gray, 1940; Chick, 1991, 1998; Foreman-Peck and Millward, 1994; Hirsh, 1999, pp. 120–21). As dissatisfaction with the performance of nationalised and regulated utilities intensified during the 1970s, a new generation of economists found a more receptive audience for their questioning of the extent to which these industries constituted natural monopolies. A punchy questioning of the extent and incidence of natural monopoly came from Alfred Kahn, while the work of Baumol and Sharkey on defining the boundaries of natural monopoly in what were increasingly viewed as multi-product utilities such as telecommunications, and as such to distinguish between sustainable and contestable markets, received considerable attention, as did their work on utility pricing theory (Baumol, 1977; Baumol et al., 1982; Crew and Kleindorfer, 1986, p. 26; Kahn, [1970] 1988, pp. 11–12; Sharkey, 1982). In this light there was no reason why the electricity supply industry should not be separated into its natural or necessary monopoly components (transmission, distribution and system operations) and its contestable sections, notably generation. After all, as the interwar experience of the construction and operation of the electricity grid in Britain had shown, the natural monopoly network component could be used to promote competition in the generation section of the industry (Hannah, 1979, ch. 4). Separating out the grid component was a necessary but not sufficient condition for the promotion of competition to supply across the grid. The incumbent's power to influence access to the grid also had to be weakened. In the Oil and Gas (Enterprise) Act of 1982, while British Gas's statutory monopoly on the pipeline system had been removed, it had been left free thereby to deter and exclude entrants by setting uneconomic access charges. Similarly, in the 1983 Energy Act, the CEGB had been left able to restructure tariffs so as to deter entry into potentially competitive markets (Newbery, 1999, pp. 178, 193). As Cecil Parkinson, appointed Secretary of State for Energy in 1987, recalled:

> Although I had no firm idea about the privatisation of electricity, I was deter-
> mined that we would not follow the pattern set by British Gas and British
> Telecom and take it to the market as a highly regulated monopoly. I wanted to
> introduce competition where possible and regulation where it was not. (Henney,
> 1994, p. 50; Parkinson, 1992)

Given the difficulties of restructuring and liberalising after its privatisation, the government resolved to effect the industrial restructuring required
to introduce competition in the electricity supply industry before, rather
than after, privatising the industry. The barebones of such a restructuring
required the competitive sections of the industry (for example, generation,
marketing and retail supply) to be separated from the regulated sections
(distribution, transmission, system operation) and access to the grid to be
allowed on a fair basis for all (Joskow, 2005, p. 38). Arrangements also
needed to be made for an independent system operator (ISO) to manage
the operation of the entire network. Competition would occur through a
mix of long-term contracts and wholesale spot market trades, with retail
tariffs unbundled to separate the price of retail power from the price for the
use of distribution and transmission services. New entry would be encouraged in generation and retail supply (Newbery, 2005b).

Such restructuring necessarily involved informed, technical rearrange-
ments being made in the industry. In contrast to the political mood at the
time of the privatisation of British Telecom and British Gas, during the
negotiations leading to the privatisation of the electricity supply industry,
there seemed to be an acceptance that privatisation was more likely to
occur, than to slink away in the face of determined resistance by the industry. Indeed, trade union officials spent more time negotiating the future
pension rights, shareholdings and job security of their members in a privatised industry than in staging public protests at any presumed affront to one
of the major nationalised creations of the post-war Attlee government.
Again, among the industry's management, there was no solid show of
opposition to privatisation, but instead the emergence of old tensions
between the CEGB and the area boards. Among the most zealous of
opponents of privatisation was the chairman of the CEGB, Walter
Marshall, who feared for the future of the nuclear power programme in a
privatised industry. His concerns for the future of the nuclear power
programme, though not his opposition to the privatisation of the electricity supply industry, were shared by the Prime Minister, Margaret
Thatcher. The accommodation of the nuclear programme in a restructured
privatised industry was to have a fundamental influence on both the process

of privatisation and on the immediate structure of the privatised industry (Henney, 1994, pp. 52, 57).

An early proposal for restructuring the CEGB was that generation should be split between five fossil fuel companies which together would jointly own a nuclear company. However, the government had misgivings over the practicability of being able to split the CEGB in this manner, and especially of being able to do so before the summer of 1991, the likely date of the next general election. The government was also resistant to a substantial break-up of the CEGB since it wished to privatise the nuclear power stations and to complete four pressurised water reactors (PWRs). As such, it decided to group the 12 nuclear stations with a large fossil generation company, National Power. However, prospective shareholders were concerned about the future, unknown costs of decommissioning and fuel reprocessing as well as the apportioning of risks in the construction of Sizewell B and three further PWRs. To finance the construction of the nuclear stations, very long contracts would need to be negotiated between National Power and the regional electricity companies (RECs) and both the cost and allocation of risk were uncertain (ibid., pp. 54, 59 63, 141; Green, 2005). Unable to sell such a nuclear pig in a poke, the government was forced to withdraw the nuclear power component from the privatisation issue, but without then altering the structure of the industry which no longer had to support the nuclear programme. In the Electricity Act of 1989, National Power accounted for 60 per cent and PowerGen for 40 per cent of conventional generation capacity in the newly privatised industry. The high-tension grid was transferred to the National Grid Company (NGC) which in turn was transferred to the joint ownership of the RECs and these in their turn were sold to the public in December 1990. Sixty per cent of National Power and PowerGen were subsequently sold to the public in March 1991, with the balance sold in March 1995 (Newbery, 1999, pp. 202–3). At privatisation, all 12 nuclear stations were placed in Nuclear Electric. Subsequently in 1996 the five newer advanced gas-cooled reactors were privatised as British Energy. The seven old Magnox reactors were moved to the publicly-owned British Nuclear Fuels plc, the fuel reprocessing company. The government had used public ownership to absorb the nuclear reactors which the market would not accept (Gilbert and Kahn, 1996b, pp. 185–6; Gilbert et al., 1996, p. 18; Newbery, 1999, pp. 153, 260; Hunt, 2002, pp. 39, 264). This use of public funds and ownership to overcome what was a stranded asset problem provided a neat point of comparison with the attempts in the United States to introduce competition into the electricity supply industry.

In the United States, following the encouragement given to new entrants at state level by the PURPA of 1978, the next major legislative encouragement to competition was not given until 1992 in the Energy Policy Act. This and the subsequent orders issued by the FERC constituted the major efforts at a federal legislative and regulatory level to promote the liberalisation of electricity markets in the United States. In among all of the debates over trading arrangements and the appropriate balance between state and federal influence, a persistent problem which arose out of PURPA in 1978, the Energy Policy Act of 1992 and the FERC rulings was that of stranded assets and stranded costs. The problem of stranded assets and stranded contracts can be said to arise when investments or contracts are no longer likely to recover their costs and earn their expected return because market conditions differ from those which had been expected when the original decisions to invest or contract were made (Baumol and Sidak, 1995b, ch. 8). Classic instances of stranded assets are nuclear power stations, all of whose higher-than-expected construction costs the regulator is no longer willing to pass on to customers and/or where changes to market structure, notably through encouraging new entrants, make it extremely difficult for the nuclear power stations to recover their capital costs. To a lesser extent, stranded contracts could be said to have emerged in the wake of the implementation of the PURPA. The contracts signed with QFs based on what the states and their utility commissions judged to be the utility's avoided costs locked the utilities into taking higher-cost power than they would have done left to their own devices. Nowhere was this more so than in California, where in the post-1978 PURPA period, most of the early dealings with the QF new entrants centred on long-term contracts along the lines of what the European Commission was later to dub as the single-buyer model. Under this arrangement, the existing integrated area monopoly bought from competing generators under life-of-plant contracts, the length of contract offering a safeguard against the potential monopsony power of the utility to manipulate its purchase price from the independent generator. Prices were decided and then regulated through a form of auction so as to determine the lowest cost offering. These contract prices were then passed on to the final customers as part of bundled tariffs and in general this limited form of competition kept risk with the customer. The risk borne by the QF was that while free of rate-of-return regulation and therefore offered the incentive of retaining profits arising from cost-reducing innovation, the outcome of new technology was uncertain and its costs less recoverable than in the case of regulated firms. While PURPA legislation applied to all states, nowhere were its possibilities relished more than in California. Yet the risks borne by customers of the early post-PURPA contracts signed with QFs became evident as many of these contracts were themselves revealed as stranded costs, as prices dropped well below the exaggerated estimates of future avoided costs originally made by state regulators (Gilbert and Kahn, 1996b, pp. 201, 204; Newbery, 1999, p. 260; Hunt, 2002, pp. 42, 257).

The most contentious instances of stranded assets were those which arose from the active encouragement of competition in the Energy Policy Act of 1992 and subsequent FERC rulings, in which new entrant competition using new gas turbine technology was able to undercut existing nuclear plant, leaving utilities to reminisce of a time when it had been possible to charge the average total cost of expensive nuclear power (Baumol and Sidak, 1995a and 1995b; Brennan and Boyd, 1996, p. 2). By 1993 in California, the new gas-fired plant was competitive at one-quarter of the price of the older Diabolo Canyon nuclear power plant (Newbery, 1999, p. 259). Nuclear plant had already often proved more expensive to build than anticipated, and the imposition of increased safety requirements after the 1979 Three Mile Island accident lengthened down times, thereby causing plant load factors to fall and operating costs to rise (Crew and Kleindorfer, 1986, p. 203; Kahn, 1988, pp. xxvi–xxvii; Gilbert and Kahn, 1996b, pp. 185–6). The most infamous case of a nuclear station which had taken longer and cost more to build than anticipated and had then proved uncompetitive was the Shoreham nuclear plant in Long Island. Originally proposed for less than $100 million in the 1960s and eventually costing about $6 billion, it never produced a single kilowatt-hour of commercial power (Hunt, 2002, p. 260). In the light of overcapacity in the 1970s and the shift in attitude towards new entrants suggested by PURPA, some utilities began to cancel orders for nuclear plant. Those that did not, or the construction of whose plant was too well-advanced to be cancelled, would seek compensation for stranded assets arising from alleged breach of implicit contract. Whereas in Britain, the state had absorbed the costs of an expensive and unwanted old nuclear programme, such a use of public funds was not an option available in the US. Stranded assets had to be recovered either through new contracts or through the law courts. In 1996, estimates of the stranded costs in the electricity industry ranged as high as $200 billion, which exceeded the value of the equity in electric utilities (Hirst and Baxter, 1995).

The irony was that those states in which the potentially stranded costs and contracts contributed strongly to their electricity prices being higher than in other states, were the very same states who were interested in exploiting the reforming opportunities offered by the Energy Policy Act of 1992, which were in turn to throw up yet more problems of stranded costs and assets. In 1995, while the average price of electricity in the United States was 6.9 cents/kWh, it was 9.9 cents/kWh in California, 10.3 cents/kWh in Massachusetts, and 10.5 cents/kWh in Connecticut.

Residential prices in those three states were 11.6, 11.4 and 12 cents, exceeded only by New York at 14 cents/kWh, compared to the US average of 8.4 cents/kWh (Newbery, 1999, p. 260; Hunt, 2002, p. 257). As the level of national average real retail electricity prices had fallen between 1985 and 2000–01 on the back of falling fossil fuel prices, interest rates and inflation, in states like California, New York and New England prices had risen. These states could now add the high cost of QF contracts to the expense of nuclear power station assets, with both holding prices up. As such, these contracts and assets contributed to the emergence of large disparities between regulated retail electricity prices in different states and the apparent market value of electric generation services in the regional wholesale-power markets. In the northeast, California, Illinois and a few other states, the large gap between the regulated price of generation service and the wholesale-market value of these electric generation services, led industrial consumers to view regulated utilities as representing a barrier to obtaining lower-priced power available in the wholesale market. In states such as California, Massachusetts, Rhode Island, New York, New Jersey, Maine and Pennsylvania, industrial customers, independent power producers, and aspirant electricity marketers with experience in the natural gas industry, notably Enron, lobbied for reform and in particular for retail competition. Tempted by the prospect of a significant fall in retail prices on the back of introducing competition and tapping the wholesale market, state regulators, governors and legislators all proved ready listeners. Quite how lower prices were to be squared with the recovery of stranded costs was never entirely clear (Joskow, 2005, pp. 35–6).

The progress in restructuring the electricity supply industry in the United States and in liberalising markets provides some useful points of comparison with the slightly earlier privatisation, restructuring and attempted liberalisation of the electricity supply industry and markets in Britain. In the United States, even though reforming legislation and rulings were initiated at the congressional and federal levels, the major influences on the success of reforms remained mainly at the level of the individual state. Even in the 1992 Energy Policy Act, while Congress gave the FERC power to open access for wholesale transactions, it was specifically prohibited from ordering access for final customers. Unlike the UK, where privatisation was by parliamentary legislation, in the United States, ultimately, only the states could deregulate. The decision on opening retail access remained with the state. While the 1992 Energy Policy Act encouraged independent generators by exempting them from some of the onerous provisions of the 1935 Public Utility Holding Company Act, the buyers from independents had to be co-operatives, municipalities or utilities; no retail customer could choose its supplier, until and if this change was agreed at state level. This did not please the industrialists and their potential independent suppliers, who began lobbying the state to give them retail access. Similarly, as responsibility for metering and tariff design remained with the states, there was an awkward split between the FERC concern for trading and transmission arrangements and the states' sway over the metering necessary to get competitive wholesale markets working well (Hunt, 2002, pp. 10, 265).

For a long time the FERC, which administered the 1935 Federal Power Act, had had relatively little to do with the electricity industry. Since its federal jurisdiction had only concerned the wholesale prices and transmission charges arising from interstate transactions, and since for all practical purposes there had been few wholesale sales, the industry remained overwhelmingly regulated at state level. There was a sharp contrast between the FERC's role in the gas and electricity industries. In gas, the industry's move from coal-based 'town gas' to natural gas had significantly expanded the interstate pipeline system and the transactions through it, thereby bringing it under FERC jurisdiction. Although retail sales continued to be regulated by the states, the FERC was able to use its jurisdiction over wholesale gas sales to deregulate gas production and to establish a regulatory regime for the pipelines. The 1992 Energy Policy Act expanded the responsibilities of the FERC, although without any commensurate increase in its authority and budget. While the Energy Policy Act was the only piece of federal legislation passed by Congress to affect the electricity supply industry during the 1990s, the FERC itself did issue a series of rules affecting the wholesale-market institutions. Initially, following the 1992 Energy Policy Act, the FERC had settled access requests on a case-by-case basis between 1992 and 1996. However, in 1996 it issued Order No. 888 and a companion Order No. 889, in which it codified its previous individual decisions on access into general rules. Order No. 888 ordered all the investor-owned utilities subject to its authority to provide open access to their transmission systems to third parties, it set out the rules for trading arrangements and for the provision of balancing and operating reserve services, and it required the separation of the trading and system operations. Order No. 888 also ruled that stranded costs due to lost wholesale sales could be recouped from the departing wholesale customer, provided that efforts had been made to mitigate the effects. This rule-making on the hoof by the FERC betrayed the absence of any well-thought-through blueprint for the introduction of competition into the electricity supply industry, whether affecting any or all of its wholesale markets, transmission institutions, and existing vertical and horizontal structuring. There was no equivalent to the legislation privatising the electricity supply industry in England and Wales, or for that matter to the arrangements made in advance of reform in Norway, Sweden, Spain, New Zealand and Australia. While it was true that Scotland had ducked out of the initial British-wide plans for reform, none the less the privatisation of the electricity supply industry in England and Wales, and in particular the restructuring of the CEGB, was a remarkable, ambitious and centrally-planned effort to introduce competition into the bulk of a long-standing vertically-integrated national monopoly (Joskow and Schmalensee, 1983, 1986; Baumol et al., 1994; Newbery and Green, 1996; Hunt, 2002; Joskow, 2005).

That in the United States much discretion remained with the states as to the extent to which they accepted the federal invitation to extend competition into their jurisdiction, reflected both the distribution of government powers within the United States and also the technologically disparate nature of the electricity system. Unlike in Britain and France, there was no national transmission system in the United States. Instead, transmission was geographically fragmented, with its boundaries paying more attention to franchise territories and state boundaries than to what constituted the efficient size for an electricity market. The transmission system was owned by more than 200 public and private entities with over 140 local system operators. There was interconnection between states, but this varied in its extent. Interstate transmission had improved from its minimal level in 1935, not least after the 1965 blackouts in the northeast had encouraged neighbours to interconnect, but this interconnection was undertaken to improve reliability rather than efficiency of supply. Even by the 1990s there were three broad areas of interconnection: most of Texas (known as ERCOT, or Electric Reliability Council of Texas), the Eastern interconnection, and the Western interconnection. Standing alone, Texas was never interconnected with the rest of the United States. New England only had 1,500 MW of transmission capacity connecting this six-state region with the rest of the US. While the Pennsylvania, New Jersey, Maryland, Delaware and Washington DC area, in which the major utilities had participated in the PJM (Pennsylvania, New Jersey, and Maryland) power pool since the 1920s had a strong internal transmission network, it only had about 3,500 MW of firm simultaneous transmission capacity with neighbouring states. The nature and extent of the transmission networks represented a potentially serious constraint on the level of effective competition which was likely to occur even if wholesale electricity markets were thoroughly deregulated. Again, an obvious contrast was with the unbundling and deregulation of the gas industry by the FERC during the 1970s and 1980s and the wider, earlier development of an interstate natural gas pipeline network (Hunt, 2002, pp. 9, 254, 263, 268, 275, 286, 333; Joskow, 2005, p. 44).

In the longer term, if a centralised transmission/dispatch pooling system was to be developed in the United States, then regional systems would need to be merged. However, without public ownership or compulsion, it was far from clear that this would be achieved by voluntary association. Even after Order No. 2000 in 1999 in which the FERC ordered investor-owned utilities to join up in regional transmission organisations and report back, they did so with more than a dozen different plans for trading arrangements and the organisation of the transmission business. Since the FERC could not order private utilities to divest themselves of transmission into a new regulated regional Transco, it continued to rely on persuading them into improved arrangements. In this it was not helped by a regulatory system which required efficiency gains to be passed on in lower prices, while also reducing the reserve capacity and hence capital base on which rates of return were calculated, thereby diminishing the attraction of moving to Pool arrangements. In general, most states seemed likely to continue to strike bilateral contracts with each other for the sale and purchase of power. The lack of a national transmission system continued to increase the chance of congestion and to reduce the effective size of markets as well as increasing the incidence of stacked 'pancaked' fees as electricity crossed between transmission systems, each of which asked its own fee (Gilbert and Kahn, 1996b, pp. 201, 204, 210; Joskow and Tirole, 2000; Hunt, 2002, pp. 98–9, 196).

Inevitably perhaps, in an electricity system in which responsibilities were split between the FERC and the individual states, and in which interstate transmission systems were highly variable in extent and strength, there was considerable variety in the trading arrangements adopted by states, with California's bilateral market and the Midwest's wheeling model being only some among a range of models. There was also variety in the stages in which competition was introduced, with retail access preceding the establishment of a competitive wholesale generation market in Arizona, Ohio, Montana, Illinois, Virginia and Michigan. Some states which implemented retail competition programmes also encouraged or required the affected utilities to separate their regulated transmission and distribution businesses from their wholesale generation and marketing activities. Some, usually the first states to implement retail competition programmes, also required their utilities to divest substantially all of their generating capacity through an auction process (for example, California, Massachusetts, New York, Maine and Rhode Island). Others allowed the utilities under their jurisdiction to retain the bulk of their generating assets and to move them into separate unregulated wholesale power affiliates within a holding company structure (for example, Pennsylvania, Illinois, Maryland, Ohio, Texas and New Jersey). Whether the generating assets were divested or transferred to affiliates, the utilities affected typically retained some type of transition or 'default service' obligation to continue to supply retail customers who had not chosen a competitive retail supplier at prices determined through some type of regulatory transition contract (ibid., pp. 127, 270, 276; Joskow, 2005, pp. 44–5).

In choosing trading models, the dominant up-and-running example was that of the Pool in England and Wales. These pool arrangements were themselves partially modelled on the 'tight' pools operated in New York, PJM and New England in the United States. The Pool operated as a daily, day-ahead, sealed-bid auction with the bids for each of the following day's 48 half hours being submitted by 10 a.m. each morning. Generators declared their plant availability and their guaranteed prices for the start-up cost in pounds sterling, the no-load cost (£/h), and three-generation costs (£/MWh) for three ranges of output reflecting differences in thermal efficiency at differing rates of utilisation. On this basis, and acting commercially rather than using the technical details of station performance, the NGC established a merit-order now using bids rather than costs as in the CEGB days, so as to minimise the financial operating costs over the next day. In this manner the system marginal price (SMP) was set by the bid of the most expensive station in normal operation, with the gap between this price and the short-run marginal cost (SRMC) of lower-bidding generators providing a contribution to fixed costs. Specific payments were also made for making capacity available, these being based on the estimated loss of load probability (LOLP) multiplied by the value of that lost load. So, for all but the marginal set in operation, the sum of the SMP and the capacity elements gave the pool purchasing price (PPP) for those operating sets. Companies buying from the Pool would pay a pool selling price (PSP), which was the PPP plus what was called an 'uplift', which covered a variety of other payments made to generators. Just as capacity payments smoothed out some of the capacity costs, so too could some of the uncertainties of operating in the Pool be reduced by hedging activities. Using contracts for differences, between 80 and 90 per cent of electricity trades through the Pool were hedged by buyers and sellers of electricity (Henney, 1994, p. 53; Newbery, 1999, pp. 208–10; Hunt, 2002, pp. 10, 136, 164, 188; Green, 2005, pp. 105–6).

Given the initial structure of the generation section of the electricity industry after privatisation, the principal problem affecting the operation of the Pool was the market power of the two generators, National Power and PowerGen. This market power potentially allowed them to exploit the low price elasticity of demand and to influence the SMP, such that by raising the price of marginal plant, the revenue earned by inframarginal plant could also be raised. During the first three years of the operation of the Pool, the two fossil generators set the pool price 90 per cent of the time and as contracts expired they raised pool prices even though fuel costs were falling. Ultimately, in April 1993, following a sharp increase in pool prices as the final vesting contracts ended, the generators were threatened with a reference to the Monopolies and Mergers Commission to investigate their alleged abuse of market power. Preferring to choose their own medicine, the generators agreed to a price cap on pool prices during the 1994–95 and 1995–96 financial years, and to divest 6,000 MW of plant. National Power divested 4,000 MW of its 26,000 MW capacity, and PowerGen, 2,000 MW of its 20,000 MW. This was sold (strictly, leased) to Eastern Group, the largest REC, which thereby became a major generator with significant distribution assets while the duopolists' share of generation fell from 54 per cent in 1995–96 to 39 per cent in 1998–99. Further divestiture of 8,000 MW took place in 1999, again under regulatory pressure, in response to a further bout of high prices. There were also moves to bolster efforts to increase competition with a greater degree of regulatory oversight of generators' conduct (Green and Newbery, 1992; Newbery, 1999, pp. 203, 210, 226; Hunt, 2002, p. 97; Jamasb and Pollitt, 2005, p. 14).

Ultimately the Pool was replaced, after persistent complaints from the coal-mining industry and some large industrial consumers of electricity of high prices resulting from gaming activity and an alleged bias towards nuclear and combined-cycle gas turbine (CCGT) stations which could bid zero but still receive the PPP, or a contract price which might be even higher, thereby keeping prices higher than they might otherwise have been. There was also a fundamental, if misjudged, liberal objection to the compulsory nature of the Pool. In place of the Pool a series of bilateral contracts were developed in the new electricity trading arrangements (NETA) which became operational in 2001. Generators, suppliers and customers were left to strike contracts as and when they wished. Shortfalls could be made up in a balancing market, but at a cost. NETA did not provide an opportunity for all generators to participate in a real-time market, because the balancing process was only used to adjust for imbalances between aggregate supply and demand and transmission constraints, and it violated the law of one price. The shift to bilateral contracts favoured generators with predictable outputs who could strike longer-term contracts, but worked against co-generators and wind generators whose output was not predictable. What was also lost was the transparency that had characterised the Pool, although it was this very transparency and its repeated auction structure which allowed collusion when there were fewer than four or five comparable generation companies. Under NETA, new entry became more difficult than under the Pool, and it encouraged vertical integration as one means of reducing the transaction costs imposed by the new market structure (Newbery, 1999, pp. 278–9; 2005a, p. 5; Hunt, 2002, p. 172; Green, 2005, p. 127).

For all of its variety and kaleidoscopic state-based initiatives in comparison with the unitary approach in England and Wales, nevertheless progress was being made in reforming parts of the electricity supply industry and its markets in the United States. In the wake of the Energy Policy Act of 1992, California was the first state to announce retail access. In 1994 the Californian Public Utilities Commission (CPUC) issued the 'Blue Book' with proposals to form a regional transmission grid under a systems operator from the four (interconnected) grids which up till then had been vertically integrated with their local utilities. Larger customers would be allowed to buy from any supplier, both inside and even outside the state, and the CPUC invited comments on whether this should be achieved through an English-type compulsory pool or through bilateral contracting, with a voluntary balancing pool. California's example of opening access was soon followed by Massachusetts and Rhode Island and states began deregulating. Encouraged by the example of the liberalisation of electricity supply in England and Wales, and emboldened by supportive rulings from the FERC concerning transmission and wholesale market transactions, California, Massachusetts and Rhode Island began operating retail competition programmes in early 1998. Generation was unbundled from transmission and distribution, and retail customers were given the opportunity to choose their power supply from among competing retail suppliers. Such programmes had spread to about a dozen states by the end of 2000 with another dozen states declaring their intention to follow suit in the near future. It even seemed that Congress might enact legislation to remove the remaining legal and policy barriers to effective wholesale and retail competition and to harmonise diverse state policies. And then came the débâcle in California and the rolling ball of deregulation was suddenly stopped, and left to gather moss for years (Hirsh, 1999, p. 8; Newbery, 1999, p. 260; Joskow, 2000, 2005, p. 32; Hunt, 2002, pp. 2, 266, 270).

The lights went out in California and on electricity reform in the United States between the two Junes of 2000 and 2001. Rolling summer blackouts of firm load began in June 2000 and were still continuing in the winter, even though the air conditioning had been switched off. Notable rolling blackouts recurred in January, March and May 2001, and those in January occurred when daily demand was near its lowest annual level. As a result of the crisis, Pacific Gas & Electric (PG&E) declared bankruptcy in 2001 and Southern California Edison (SCE) came close to doing so. The California Power Exchange (PX) went bankrupt. The State of California felt forced to intervene, and it immediately spent $8 billion on wholesale electricity between January and May 2001, and then locked itself into high-price, long-term (up to 20 years at times) contracts to the value of a further $60 billion. Edison and PG&E were re-regulated and received regulated cost-based rates for the energy and services from their remaining generating plants. All parties to the crisis became involved in refund hearings at the

FERC, with the State of California demanding $8.9 billion in refunds from generators (Joskow, 2001; Hunt, 2002, pp. 19, 385; Wolak, 2005, pp. 164, 170–71).

What then caused the crisis and did it point to fundamental problems in the approach towards electricity liberalisation in the United States? In general, the crisis was one of regulation rather than of economics. Specifically, the problems stemmed from efforts to accommodate the recovery of stranded assets. In April 1994, when the CPUC issued the Blue Book proposal requiring the utilities to open their wires for retail access, they also indicated that they would be allowed to collect their stranded costs. In August 1996, the state legislature, in response to pressure from the three state investor-owned utilities, PG&E, SCE and San Diego Gas and Electric (SDGE), provided legislative guarantees for the recovery of stranded costs between 1 April 1998 and March 2002. By the latter date it was expected that stranded cost recovery would be completed. To placate customers and to provide early evidence of the benefits of reform, retail prices were reduced by 10 per cent and then frozen. Customers could shop around, but if wholesale prices proved too volatile they could return to this retail price frozen at 90 per cent of the regulated retail price of 1996. Stranded costs were to be recovered from the gap between this frozen price and the generators' costs (Hunt, 2002, pp. 377–80; Wolak, 2005).

While such an approach to reform carried a clear element of risk, these arrangements did work for the first two years. Indeed, San Diego recovered its stranded costs. What played havoc with the Californian approach to reform was an unforeseen sharp increase in wholesale electricity prices and the pressures generated by the misalignment of rising wholesale and frozen retail prices. That wholesale prices moved sharply upwards was due to a hot summer throughout the west, a sudden increase in gas prices, and, in the heat, a fall in hydroelectricity imports in the summer of 2000, primarily from the Pacific Northwest. Since California imported between one-fifth and one-quarter of its energy needs, this was a significant marginal loss of supply. However, the effects of these unfavourable developments were heightened by some almost idiosyncratic arrangements made for electricity trading in California. Perhaps uniquely to California, utilities had not been allowed to enter into bilateral contracts for the purchase of power, such as might have helped tide them through the early years of reform, or at least until the retail prize freeze melted and price elasticity reduced demand. The CPUC imposed this purchasing requirement so as to provide a transparent mechanism for the recovery of the utilities' stranded costs. The CPUC's concern was that if it used the average wholesale price that each of the three investor-owned utilities (IOUs) paid for their power through bilateral transactions, then these firms would have an incentive to negotiate deals with their unregulated affiliates so as to increase the amount earned for stranded asset recovery (Hunt, 2002, pp. 377, 381; Wolak, 2005, pp. 152–3, 158).

The IOUs, PG&E, SCE and SDGE, had also been required to transfer about half of their fossil generation (approximately 17,000 MW) to the new entrants, Duke, Dynergy, Reliant, AES/Williams and Mirant, which, while it reduced the old incumbents' market power, also reduced their own output and made them potentially more vulnerable to the exercise of market power by others. While the three IOUs retained ownership of enough generation capacity to serve between one-third to one-half of the hourly load obligations, this left them having to find a substantial amount of their daily energy needs in the short-term markets. Moreover, as part of the transfer of assets, no provision was made for 'vesting contracts' under which the new owners agreed to sell back to the former plant owners a large fraction of their expected annual output at a fixed price for a period of at least five years. These mandatory buy-back forward 'vesting' contracts were a standard part of the restructuring process in virtually all countries, and were used in England and Wales as well as in New England. Such vesting contracts can provide an important transition period towards the development of an active forward market. Such a forward market in which the vast majority of electricity is bought and sold substantially limits the scope for suppliers to manipulate the spot market. As it was, in California the three IOUs were exposed to the spot market, and they chose not to hedge against the spot price, even though the CPUC allowed them to do so through the PX block-forward market. It appears that the IOUs simply did not believe that the wholesale price would rise and stay high for any sustained period of time. If it did do so, then they may have expected the FERC to intervene and declare the wholesale electricity prices to be unjust and unreasonable. However, there was always a tension between the FERC's statutory mandate under the Federal Power Act of 1935 to set 'just and reasonable' wholesale prices in a market regime and its decision to promote competition in wholesale electricity markets in which prices were the outcome of supply and demand decisions made by generators and users (Hunt, 2002, p. 380; Wolak, 2005, pp. 145, 148, 150, 154, 158, 166).

In not hedging, the Californian IOUs behaved differently to their counterparts in other wholesale electricity markets, such as PJM and ISO-New England who had almost all of their final load covered by forward contracts or their own plant. Estimates of the extent to which final demand was covered by forward contracts for the PJM, New York and New England markets suggest that between 85 and 90 per cent of annual demand was covered by forward financial obligations, either in the form of generation ownership or forward financial contracts. In California during the period

May 2000 to June 2001, this figure was close to 40 per cent, or around the share of total demand which the three largest IOUs could meet from their remaining generating capacity. The Californian IOUs were left exposed to a vicious circle of activity in the short-term market. As the market tightened, suppliers withdrew plant from the autumn of 2000 and into 2001. This may well have been for necessary maintenance and it may increasingly have arisen from a disinclination to supply utilities heading for bankruptcy. Either way, the effect was the same. Wholesale prices, to which the IOUs were exposed, rose (Hunt, 2002, p. 384; Wolak, 2005, pp. 157, 168–9).

The problems afflicting the Californian electricity supply industry were also exacerbated by the arrangements made for trading electricity. Initially, reform went well as the transmission systems of the three IOUs (PG&E, SCE and SDGE) were joined into one control area. The operation of this system was placed in the hands of an independent system operator, the CAISO-California ISO. This was the first of the ISOs proposed in the United States and it had been established without a major battle over the need to separate and consolidate the system operators. However, the many municipal utilities of California decided not to join the ISO, leaving significant portions of the transmission grid under the control of operators other than the California ISO. There was also disagreement over the precise role of the ISO, such that, while SCE and SDGE initially proposed an integrated form of trading arrangements with a system operator-run spot market, what emerged from the process of negotiation with the FERC was the California PX, new and separate from the ISO. As such, there were likely to be opportunities for arbitrage, as well as problems of co-ordination between the two entities. Enron helped to design this trading system and it profited from its ability to arbitrage. Lacking sufficient forward contracts, the three large IOUs were required to purchase all of their wholesale electricity needs from the California PX day-ahead market and the California ISO hour-ahead and real-time markets. Not only did the five new-entrant merchant generation companies have very limited forward contract commitments, but they limited sales in the PX block-forward market, thereby driving the three IOUs into the day-ahead PX and real-time ISO markets (Stoft, 1997; Hunt, 2002, pp. 289, 378; Wolak, 2005, p. 168).

For all of the intricacies of the trading arrangements, what was most striking about the whole Californian débâcle was the hesitancy to address the problem of excess demand and financial losses by raising prices. While criticisms were made of the lack of any approximation to time-of-use tariffs, fundamentally it was the level of electricity prices which was out of line. As it was, with their retail prices frozen, PG&E and SCE were on a very expensive hiding-to-nothing. While in the summer and autumn of 2000 the FERC declared wholesale electricity prices to be unjust and unreasonable, joined politicians in alleging abuse of market power and approved the implementation of various hard and soft price caps requiring all generators to cost-justify bids above $250/MWh and later $150/MWh, fundamental issues such as the retail price freeze were not addressed. Typically, the political and regulatory pressure was overwhelmingly exerted on supply and not demand. The crisis reflected the consequences of efforts to allow for the recovery of stranded assets, the uncertainties arising from the federal–state split, and the persistent political hesitancy to increase prices. In the face of rolling blackouts, allegations of improper conduct by Enron, and the bankruptcy of major utilities, the political appeal of deregulation waned very quickly. States stopped coming forward with plans for brave new electricity reforms, and in 2000 about nine states that had planned to implement reforms delayed, cancelled or significantly scaled back their electricity competition programmes. Blackouts in New York and Europe in 2003 kept the squib of reform damp (Borenstein et al., 2002; Joskow and Kahn, 2002; Joskow, 2005; Wolak, 2005, pp. 148, 162).

What then of France? Having a nationalised, interconnected and centralised industry, it shared with the UK many of the advantages concerning the government's ability to absorb stranded assets, and it was free of the divisive and dispersed federal-state features of the US system. As such, the French government was very well placed to privatise and restructure the French nationalised electricity industry into a multi-firm new era of competition. Well placed, but not well disposed. Throughout the 1990s, the French government persistently stated its opposition to what was pejoratively dubbed as the Anglo-Saxon idea of privatisation.[1] In this stance the government was strongly encouraged by EDF which was happy to remain as Europe's largest electricity utility, enjoying within France possession of over 90 per cent of generation capacity, 100 per cent of the transmission grid and operating approximately 95 per cent of the distribution network. Not that EDF was averse to buying cash-rich privatised electricity utilities such as London Electricity REC in 1998, perhaps in an effort at renationalisation through the back chunnel. At home, EDF exploited the long-standing perception of itself as a modern, vital French industry consistently managed along rational economic lines and free from monopoly abuse. It was just such a perception of EDF which had provided the background to the negotiation of the contract of 1970 which had increased the degree of commercial freedom enjoyed by EDF and which reflected the French government's refusal to view EDF as part of a block of nationalised industries. There was also considerable public support for the maintenance of EDF effectively as a nationalised monopoly. Books with such titles as *EDF: Chronique d'un désastre inéluctable* and *Pourquoi privatiser? EDF et l'enjeu de l'énergie* appeared in bookshops (Soult, 2003; Darmois, 2004).

EDF continued to score high approval ratings in public opinion surveys and it continued to provide France with some of the lowest electricity prices in Western Europe (Glachant and Finon, 2005, p. 193).

More threatening to EDF than any importation of Anglo-Saxon privatisation, was the growing interest of the European Commission in opening up national electricity markets to competition, and then developing a single European electricity market. In the French resistance to privatisation, nightmare visions of blackouts, price hikes and foreign ownership had been conjured up as prophetic warnings for French politicians and citizens of the dangers and uncertainties of private ownership. The débâcle in California only seemed to confirm such prophecies. The European Commission, however, did not seek change through privatisation. Rather it sought to encourage competition in the national, and then in the European, market by securing fair access to networks for new entrants. The defence of its national monopoly posed a greater challenge for the government and EDF than that of defending public ownership. None the less, the French tried, with consultants hired by the Conseil Supérieur Consultatif des Comités Mixtes à la Production d'Électricité et Gaz de France reporting that France was well served by its public monopoly, and that the English system was not a general model for the production of electricity; 'L'Angleterre n'est pas la France' (Henney, 1994, p. 8). Nor was the European Commission, but a response had to be made to its First Electricity Market Directive of December 1996 requiring governments to open their national electricity markets to competition.

Initially the European Commission seemed happy to attempt to liberalise entry into a national electricity market containing a publicly-owned integrated utility incumbent as the least disruptive approach to reform. Member countries were allowed to choose between three models of liberalisation: the single-buyer model, third-party access and a pool. The single-buyer model was similar to the arrangements struck under PURPA in which QF IPPs signed contracts with the incumbent utilities. In the single-buyer model offered by the European Commission, the vertically-integrated incumbent was required to publish transmission tariffs and to be prepared to trade with buyers and customers charging only the published tariff. Chinese walls were supposed to keep the transmission business separate from that of generation and supply. For a country wishing to retain public ownership and uncommitted to competition, the single-buyer model offered the best chance of keeping the one and seeing off the other. As Newbery has suggested, while the separate financial accounting for transmission might make it harder to cross-subsidise the competitive parts of the company, this could be continued by revaluing assets, writing down those in the competitive divisions and revaluing those in the core networks.

Interestingly, Newbery also notes that this might be justifiable as one means of recovering stranded assets in generation (Newbery, 1999, pp. 180, 430).

Rather surprisingly, the French did not opt for the single-buyer model, but instead chose third-party access (TPA). Under TPA, transmission was transferred to a separate company to which buyers and sellers paid either a negotiated or regulated tariff. In time, while the French electricity transmission grid remained an internal department of EDF, its management and operation were separated out from EDF and placed under the direct control of the Energy Regulatory Commission which effectively ensured that the grid was run as an independent firm. That the French opted for the TPA rather than the single-buyer model may indicate that in practical terms there is little difference between them in terms of promoting liberalisation in the electricity supply industry in France.

Certainly the French opting for TPA was not accompanied by any greater enthusiasm for liberalisation of their electricity markets. The main French responses to the European directives came in legislative acts passed in February 2000, January 2003 and August 2004, but often the European Commission's approach suited the French aims. While the European Commission's Second Directive in 2003 moved towards the creation of a single European electricity market by toughening the independent regulation of access to national and cross-border transmission systems and links, the European Commission was often unable to move directly against the dominant incumbent in the national economy. It did not push privatisation as a route to restructuring and liberalisation, and while developing conditions of access to the transmission system, it did little to move against dominant incumbents in Spain, Germany, Belgium and Portugal as well as France. The relationship between the European Commission and the national electricity industries was not unlike that between the FERC and the state-based IOUs in the United States. The European Commission could encourage and cajole certain behaviour, but it could not enforce it (Glachant and Finon, 2005b, p. 181; Newbery, 2005b, p. 4). While in the 2003 Electricity Directive the European Commission was to move against the single buyer and require the regulated TPA model for access to distribution networks, the persistent presence of a dominant incumbent could act as a steady deterrent to new entrants. In France, non-EDF suppliers served about 15 per cent of the eligible market in 2004, and the 2003 Directive required that all non-household customers could freely choose their electricity supply by 1 July 2004. Full market opening to include all household customers was to follow by 1 July 2007 (Jamasb and Pollitt, 2005, pp. 23–4).

Given the strength and lack of congestion on the French transmission system, there was, in theory at least, some scope for cross-border competition for the price-sensitive French industrial customers from surrounding countries such as Germany, Spain and Britain. However, the impact of this challenge was likely to be muted by the existence of excess generating capacity in France and the lumpy presence of EDF's nuclear power stations. Nearly 80 per cent of French electricity was generated by nuclear reactors whose short-term costs were about two-thirds that of the coal- and gas-fired and combined-cycle generation technology already in operation. The low SRMCs facing new entrants was emphasised by the additional 10 per cent of French generation output coming from hydro-electricity. The effect of the threat of cross-border competition was to impose a ceiling price on the French market, but without that competition being sufficient to drive EDF prices down nearer to its generation costs. However, so long as EDF's prices in France were lower than those in most Western European countries, the position was likely to remain politically tolerable (see Appendix Table A1.7). It did not prevent EDF selling outside of France, and, using its international transmission links, EDF was the leading European exporter sending some 15 per cent of output across its national borders (about 15 per cent of its generation). As public finance temptations lead French governments to push for a very French form of quasi-privatisation, it is nevertheless unlikely that strong competition will develop in the French market so long as the nuclear presence looms with its SRMC and its lengthening life expectancy (Glachant and Finon, 2005, pp. 184–5, 201).

One effect of efforts to increase competition in electricity markets will necessarily be to increase investor uncertainty. As Alfred Kahn once noted, the corollary of increased competitive activity among public utilities was often the avoidance of sunk costs (Kahn, 1988, p. xxxvi). Viewing past investments mutating into stranded assets, and being less than certain of the credibility of government undertakings concerning the future structure of markets, investors are likely to fight shy of long-term, sunk investments, notably nuclear. Instead, short-term, comparatively low-cost investments with returns earned reasonably quickly were favoured, as illustrated by the large-scale investment in CCGTs. Equally, companies were likely to favour strategies reducing uncertainty, not least when, as in Britain, the NETA balancing arrangements made shortfalls in supply expensive. Vertical integration, as pursued by EDF, E.On and RWE in Europe, provided one such strategy, and while no large trans-European British player had appeared in the British market by 2001, five main vertically-integrated companies had emerged: PowerGen; Innogy; London/EDF; Scottish Power; and Scottish and Southern.

That both horizontal mergers and vertical integration will continue across Europe seems likely, not least because of the European Commission's rather bizarre tendency to judge the competitive impact of such activity in predominantly national terms. Thus, EDF's purchase of London Electricity in Britain, and its purchase of a stake in Énergie Baden-Württemberg were both regarded by the Commission as welcome evidence of competitive, new-entrant activity in each market, irrespective of the fact that the state-backed, domestic market-protecting EDF was a dominant player in the European market (Helm, 2003, pp. 311, 382–3). In the electricity industry, which is so characterised by lumpy, sunk investments in which investor uncertainty about the future structure of the industry and its markets requires some credible reassurance by governments and European institutions if substantial new investment is to occur, there is always likely to be a fundamental tension between reducing uncertainty and promoting competition. When competition favours the use of marginal system prices, in which the old cost-recovery guarantees of average-cost pricing are removed, then companies are likely to integrate backwards and forwards in the industry, so as to reduce their exposure to such uncertainty and to spread their risks over a wider range of production and supply stages. It is to a consideration of such persistent trade-offs among uncertainty, investment incentives, risk and the marginalist approach that we now turn in the final and concluding chapter.

NOTE

1.   For one expression of French dislike of Mrs Thatcher, listen to Renaud's 1985 song 'Miss Maggie'.

7. Conclusion

Kind Sir, I've read your paper through,
And faith, to me, 'twas really new!
How guessed ye Sir, what maist I wanted?
This monie a day I've grain'd and gaunted,
To ken what French mischief was brewin;
(Robert Burns, *To A Gentleman*, 1790)

By the early years of the twenty-first century, variety was the striking feature of any comparison of energy policy in Britain, France and the United States. While Britain and France had begun the post-war period as nationalised monopolies, by the start of the new century Britain had privatised and liberalised virtually all of its main fuel and power industries. In contrast, France had resolutely defended both the public form of ownership and the monopoly structure of her markets, only in very recent years being pushed by public finance pressures into flirting with a very French form of quasi-privatisation for EDF and Gaz de France (GDF). European Commission pressure for liberalisation was strongly resisted, not least by exploiting the entry-deterrent effects of its large investment in nuclear power stations. That programme in itself only added spice to the variety, as the size and pride of the French nuclear commitment contrasted sharply with the uncertainties attending any new nuclear investment in Britain and the United States. In the United States, following the blackouts in California and elsewhere, a long period of reflection had set in concerning the political and economic merits of liberalisation (Joskow, 2006). Yet as variety characterised the outward appearance of energy policy, so too were economic forces pushing the electricity industry in each country back towards a greater degree of vertical integration. The interaction between economics, politics and policy persisted.

In considering the changes which did occur in the national energy policies of France, Britain and the United States during the 60 years from 1945, what we might call the 'long 1970s' (1968–84) emerged as a crucial, pivotal period. It was during that long decade against a backdrop of oil price hikes, coalminers' strikes and nuclear accidents, that deregulation was initiated in the United States, denationalisation and then privatisation were embraced in Britain, and a strong defence of public ownership, a fresh round of nationalisations and a major switch into nuclear power were undertaken in

133

France. In considering how this decade of change affected the electricity industry in each country, particular emphasis was laid, almost in 'path development' fashion, on the influence of the past in shaping perceptions of the industry and the envisaging of the industry's future. In France, it was argued, EDF cleverly exploited its reputation for rational economic management, and its influence within government and economic planning, to distance itself from the other nationalised industries and negotiate for itself a contractual future. This option appears not to have been available to the electricity industry in Britain, not least because of a public-finance-minded Treasury's tendency to view nationalised industries as a group. While the Treasury sought to prescribe guidelines for the nationalised industries from on high, EDF had negotiated its future from below. In the much less centralised United States, the future for the electricity industry had often been fought out at state level, with federal regulatory orders providing some of the ground rules and field boundaries for discussions. Stranded contracts and assets loomed large over discussions of any future change, thus again bringing the expensive weight of the past to bear on the shaping of the future. While a history book such as this might be expected to emphasise the importance of understanding the past, hopefully the merits of such a view are apparent. To be cute, there is almost no time like the present, only the past acting on the future.

Amidst the changes in policy, fuel base and technology, central issues concerning the economics and security of energy policy have been of persistent, if oscillating, importance across the entire period. At the microeconomic level, particular attention has been paid to the development, transmission and application of marginalist approaches to investment and pricing. Again, it can be argued that it was during the long decade of the 1970s that microeconomists promoting the marginalist approach pushed their way to the fore of the regulation of major industries. The regulatory example of Alfred Kahn in the United States was to be followed formally by the likes of Stephen Littlechild as regulator of the electricity industry in Britain from 1989 to 1998, but Littlechild's appointment followed a fundamental reassessment in Britain of the merits of public ownership, the boundaries of any natural monopoly, and the potential for introducing competition into what were increasingly recognised as multi-product industries. While economists like John Kay and Colin Robinson now essentially promoted the marginalist approach but within the context of the introduction of competition into fuel and power industries, their espoused approaches to pricing and investment had much in common with Ralph Turvey's proposals for the use of the marginalist approach within the state-owned electricity monopoly. The line of provenance can then be traced back further, obviously through Boiteux, Massé and Allais in France, but also back to the arguments between Meade, Coase and others in the years immediately prior to the nationalisation of the industry.

In tracing the marginalist roots of approaches to pricing and investment in public industries, no-one could boast a better pedigree than the French. Increasingly, Jules Dupuit has been drawn out from the shadow cast by Alfred Marshall, and given increasing credit for originating ideas concerning utility, its use in constructing demand curves, and its superiority to David Ricardo's concentration on labour as the basis of a theory of value. Dupuit's importance was recognised by Stanley Jevons, but Marshall was less than generous in acknowledging the debt which his consumers' surplus owed to Dupuit's 'relative utility'; subsequent scholarship has corrected this oversight (Schumpeter, 1954, pp. 839, 1061; Ekelund and Hébert, 1999). However, while it is possible to point to a strong intellectual line running through the *Grandes écoles* from the mid-nineteenth century to the present, care must be taken in placing Allais and his ideas in this line. Allais's thinking in the run-up to his *À la Recherche d'une Discipline Économique* of 1943 was strongly influenced by Walras, Pareto and Fisher. It was the marginalist approach to the allocation of resources which caught his imagination. As curious as it may seem, he was not influenced at this time by Dupuit. In fact, in later recalling those years of self-education, Allais expressly lists Dupuit as one of the authors whom he did not read, largely because few others mentioned him and, according to Allais, no edition of his works was available (Allais, 1994). That he subsequently regretted this lacuna in his reading, simply reinforces the point. It was not until November 1973 that Allais was able to obtain photocopies of Dupuit's work, which then substantially affected Allais's re-evaluation of Walras and his move towards writing the series of papers appearing in 1981 in *Économies et Sociétés*, and subsequently published together as the book entitled *La Théorie générale des surplus* (Allais, 1989). As Allais remarked in the introduction to that book, he very much regretted not having seen Dupuit's work some 30 years before, as it would have helped him to have detached himself from '*l'emprise*' of the marginalist school whose dogmatism considerably slowed the development of economic thought (Allais, 1994, pp. 74, 158). That was Allais's view by the 1980s, but not in the 1940s, 1950s and 1960s. Then, it was the marginalist approach which dominated his approach to issues of resource allocation, and not the work of Dupuit (Etner, 2000, p. 182).

Whatever the niceties of the development of economic thought in France, the fact was that in the 1970s the benefits of the marginalist approach, the renewed interest in promoting competition and the vaunting of the consumers' surplus were all being advanced by economists and being listened to by politicians. In part, this reflected the loss of confidence in the established Golden Age way of doing things, as problems of public finance deficits, agency problems and technological stasis became manifest. The refreshed ideas of competition and marginal-cost pricing seemed to offer potential solutions to accumulating problems, especially when technological advances in aircraft, telecommunications and electricity generation offered exciting possibilities for attracting new entrants into these industries. What such ideas and economists had in common with their equivalents in 1950s France was a sense of excitement, of change and of satisfaction in the explicit application of economic rationality to central problems affecting major utilities and industries. The unusual overlapping of interests between politicians and economists in Britain and the United States in the 1970s and 1980s had its counterpart in the France of the 1950s and 1960s. Of the France in which Allais and Jeanneney could discuss marginalist principles on the ESC; in the attendance of the leaders of the French fuel and power industries at Allais's seminars on energy policy; in the admission by Allais and Jeanneney that there was a technocracy operating in France, technocracy being a term which Allais admitted to finding 'a little disagreeable and a little pejorative, but which without doubt corresponds to a very concrete reality' (FONT, 1960c); to the coming-and-going of Massé from EDF to the Plan and then back again; to Boiteux's presence on the Nora Committee which provided the backdrop to the contract signed between the state and EDF; and to the often one-way trade between French economists and their international brethren. Yet within France the network of economists was important, as many of them moved in and out of major industries, government committees and departments. As a completely unscientific snapshot, consider that in January 1965, Allais, Boiteux, Debreu, Massé, Rueff, Roy and Malinvaud were all Fellows of the Econometric Society. So too was James Tobin. Networks overlaid each other.

It is difficult to find an equivalent in Britain of this network of *ingénieurs-économistes* who came and went between industry, government and the plans. It is certainly difficult to think of an equivalent of an internationally recognised economist like Marcel Boiteux heading up a nationalised industry in Britain. Without descending into tales of individual acts, the influence of economists and *ingénieurs-économistes* like Allais, Massé and Boiteux in France was a vital influence on the development of government–EDF relations. Prior to the Nora Committee, it was the perceived management of EDF which allowed it to negotiate the contracts, with the state. While there were always departures from these contracts mainly on the part of successive governments, none the less they provided EDF with a position apart from the bulk of the nationalised industries from which it could negotiate the extent of any deviations. If public finance pressures applied to all nationalised industries in France from the 1970s, none the less it was EDF which, with Ministry of Finance backing, was able to raise finance for its nuclear power programme on the international capital market. For the nationalised electricity industry in Britain, it was more difficult to negotiate for a position distinct from other nationalised industries. It lacked the equivalent access to government of the leaders of the French electricity industry, an influence which was the result of French tradition, the quality of the *ingénieurs-économistes*, and the willingness of EDF leaders to come and go between the industry, the plans and the governments. That influence was to make itself felt when the 'Anglo-Saxon' ideas of privatisation and competition began to gather around France.

The most determined and widespread attempt to transfer ownership from public to private hands and to introduce competition into a previously monopolistic industry occurred in Britain, and above all in the electricity supply industry. Introducing competition proved to be much more difficult than transferring ownership, not least as managers often welcomed privatisation as providing them with an opportunity to use international capital markets as well as increasing their own salaries. Where competition was introduced, the effects were often most immediately striking in their impact on employment. In electricity, whereas in 1989 on the eve of privatisation, the CEGB employed 47,000 workers, by 1996 the four successor companies together employed just over 21,000 workers, or 44 per cent of the earlier figure, while producing about the same amount of electricity. Among the individual generators, the impact in terms of workers per kilowatt-hour generated was even more dramatic, with reductions of between 58 and 62 per cent in the 1990–96 period. During those same years, the number of workers fell by 73 per cent in National Power, by 64 per cent in PowerGen and by 39 per cent in the still-public Nuclear Electric. Even more dramatic was the loss of employment in the coal-mining industry. There were 200,000 miners at the time of the 1984–85 strike, 70,000 in 1990, 20,000 in 1993 and fewer than 10,000 by 1998. This collapse of employment in the industry was the effect of the, albeit jerky, opening up of the fuel and power markets to competition, both from imports and from coal substitutes, notably natural gas. By 1998–99 coal accounted for less than one-third of electricity generated in England and Wales, while the gas share had risen from nothing to one-third, slightly more than coal (Newbery, 1999, pp. 148, 151, 237).

While the impact of privatisation and liberalisation on employment in industries like coal and electricity was often dramatic, what was less striking were the effects on total factor productivity (TFP) in a heavy, capital-intensive industry like electricity. Indeed, the TFP data for electricity confound some popular perceptions of the industry's productivity performance both before and after privatisation. While the annual growth rate of TFP in the electricity supply industry in Britain was, at 2.54 per cent p.a., superior to that in the United States (1.85 per cent p.a.) between 1960 and 1979, the British performance slipped to 1.78 per cent p.a. for 1979–89, and 1.22 per cent p.a. in 1989–97. In contrast, in the United States, the industry's TFP improved to 2.6 per cent in 1979–89 before falling slightly to 2.55 per cent. On this basis, the TFP performance of the electricity industry in Britain was better as a nationalised than as a privatised industry, and during the period of deregulation, privatisation and liberalisation its productivity performance fell significantly below that of the industry in the United States. However in both countries, the TFP performance lagged considerably that of the French nationalised electricity monopoly. In France, the electricity supply industry experienced an annual growth rate of TFP of 3.08 per cent in 1960–79, this increasing to 4.17 per cent in 1979–89 before falling back to 3.09 per cent p.a. in 1989–97. For the entire 1960–97 period, the annual growth rate of TFP was 2.05 in Britain, 2.2 per cent in the United States and 3.38 per cent in France (O'Mahony and Vecchi, 2001; Weyman-Jones, 2003; Millward, 2005, p. 276). It was also noticeable in Britain that while fossil fuel costs fell substantially in the first half of the 1990s, electricity prices did not fall accordingly. Price reductions were offered to industrial, rather than to domestic, consumers, indicating price differentiation in relation to the competitiveness of different markets (Florio, 2004, pp. 226–7; Jamasb and Pollitt, 2005, p. 15). In part there may have been a trade-off between allowing profits to be sufficiently high to attract new entrants, notably using CCGT, and increasing the consumers' surplus. While prices did fall by 40 per cent following the full liberalisation of the electricity supply industry in 1998, they were to bounce back up by 40 per cent after 2003. While some attributed the initial fall in prices to the introduction of NETA, the relationship is one of correlation rather than causation, the price oscillations reflecting more fundamental shifts between supply and demand (Helm, 2003, p. 307).

If the persistent, if fluctuating, interest in the marginalist approach and the scope for opening up some utility output markets to greater competition reflected the abiding interests of economists, then the persistent political interest lay in security of supply. Such security worries can be divided into four broad categories: that the world is running out of fuel; that fuel supplies will be interrupted; that electricity generating capacity will be insufficient; and that the external effects of burning fuel are causing major changes to the world's environment. The first fear, that fuel is running out, is long-standing, traceable back at least as far as 1865 when Jevons was worried about the exhaustion of coal reserves. In the 1970s, similar concerns were voiced about oil reserves as there developed a conviction, not least in OPEC, that oil price rises signalled the, quite possibly premature, depletion of oil reserves. That an industry normally subject to large surpluses in producing capacity should think this was noteworthy, especially so when from the middle of the decade spot prices were falling, inventories were full to bursting, non-OPEC oil was arriving from the North Sea and Alaska, and world demand for oil was falling (Parra, 2004, pp. 217, 223). The most notable fashionable interpretation of this view of rising oil prices as consistent with the depletion of a natural resource came in the Club of Rome Report (Meadows et al., 1972). Yet this report essentially failed to distinguish between the geologically finite and the economically infinite. While geologically there was a fixed stock of oil in the world, economically oil was an inventory from which current supply was extracted but to which, through exploration and investment in new and existing oil fields, new oil could be added (Adelman, 1990, p. 9). For oil, the simplest distinction in this context was between the stock of oil in the ground and proven reserves. As price rose, so too was the rate of exploration likely to increase and more efficient means of discovery and extraction developed. Middle East oilfields had operated for most of the post-war period at a ponderous 1:100 production-to-reserves ratio, as upward revisions in reserve estimates offset production withdrawals (Parra, 2004, p. 39). While extraction would probably cease once the cost of extraction exceeded the price of oil, there might still remain considerable oil in the ground.

This was not to deny that if minerals were depleted then the cost of extraction would tend to rise, unless offset by improved technology, and that, *pace* Hotelling, the increasing scarcity of a natural resource would be reflected in net price rises over time at the rate of interest, with the optimum rates of extraction being those which generated this path price (Hotelling, 1931; Solow, 1974; Stiglitz, 1976; Dasgupta and Heal, 1979; Stevens, 2003). However, it was less clear that any such explanation applied to the oil price rises of the 1970s. The practical objection was that the oil shocks themselves had nothing whatsoever to do with the depletion of oil resources. At most, delays in investing in production capacity may have contributed to the first oil shock, when events did take place in a tight market. In addition, none of the empirical studies showed signs of the resource depletion which should have been signalled either by rising costs of production or, as a proxy, rising prices over time. The fact that oil prices fell in real terms between 1974 and 1978 was conveniently ignored although the second oil shock which saw a price rise from $13 to $34 per barrel between 1979 and 1981 was adduced as evidence that oil price rises would continue forever, even though the price hike had more to do with the effect of buyers' panic in a very imperfect market, rather than a fundamental shift between supply and demand. Moreover, the argument that producers were setting a higher discount rate for production and therefore curtailing production so as to provide for the future raised some questions about oil producers' mentality. It was in fact much more likely that they would favour a response of 'take the money and run', not least so as to pay growing debts, rather than postpone revenues into a distant future when they might not be in power or even alive. On the back of increased revenues from the first OPEC price hike, Middle East oil-producing countries sucked in imports such that the huge 1974 OPEC current-account surplus had been spent four years later, while the even larger surplus in 1980 had become a deficit by 1982 (Adelman, 1990, p. 7).

The second category of fuel-security fear, that supplies would be interrupted in their transportation, revived memories of the Suez crises of 1956, and, to a lesser extent, of 1967. However, while the fungibility of oil meant that many of those fears were exaggerated, the increasing use of gas delivered through fixed pipelines means that such fears will gain greater credibility. This is certainly evident in European, and especially German, relations with Gazprom (Stern, 2005). Yet, risk analyses of the probability and cost of interruptions to supply can be made, and precautionary action, such as stock-building, taken. Given the reluctance of companies to carry the cost of holding adequate stocks, this is an issue of public interest. As reliance on single-fuel imports such as gas rises, a precautionary response will be to seek to diversify national fuel portfolios. Such a consideration may well favour increased investment in nuclear power, although it is far from certain that private investors will be attracted to such projects. It might also be thought to cast doubt over the wisdom of running down indigenous coal industries (Glyn, 1984). Certainly in Britain, while doubts were cast over the security premium of domestic coal mining by the coalminers' strikes which contributed to the fall of the Heath government in 1974, ministers were still fighting shy of accepting the employment and security effects of the run-down of coal during the 1990s. After the expiration of the take-or-pay contracts which were maintained between British coal and the electricity industry for the three years following the privatisation of the electricity supply industry, successive Conservative and Labour governments attempted to provide protection to the industry accompanied by periodic dampening of the enthusiasm for gas. The net effect of keeping coal prices higher than they would have been was simply to increase the pace of the 'dash for gas'. By 1993, generators had signed contracts for 8.7 GW of CCGT plant, which would displace about 25 million tonnes of coal, compared with the 1992 coal burn of 60 million tonnes (Newbery, 1999, p. 147). So long as Britain could continue to exploit its North Sea oil and gas reserves the security implications of running down the coal industry after the defeat of the 1984 miners' strike could be set to one side. As North Sea oil reserves were depleted, the British government came to share with much of Western Europe a growing interest in the security of gas supplies through fixed pipelines. However, that concern was not matched by major initiatives in such areas as increasing gas storage capacity.

The third category of security worry concerns the adequacy of generating capacity and, to a lesser but important extent, of the robustness of the transmission and distribution system. One of the main arguments advanced by EDF and its supporters against privatisation was that private owners would lack adequate incentives to invest in the maintenance of the network and distribution systems. The power cuts in London in 2002 and 2003 and in the United States in 2003 were arguably due to just such a lack of investment. In addition, on the generating side for much of the late 1980s and 1990s the electricity industry had been working in conditions of excess plant capacity. With the exception of renewables and the CCGTs, much of the generating capacity dated from the 1970s. What was always uncertain was to what extent privatisation and competition would act to increase the cost of new generating investment and to heighten the uncertainties attending the expected returns. Assets could be left stranded and the scrapping of the Pool's payments for making capacity available invited potential investors to gamble in what was effectively a spot market for balancing capacity. While there had been a surge of investment in CCGTs in Britain (37 per cent of generating capacity in England and Wales by 2004) and in the United States in the wake of privatisation and PURPA, respectively, a key feature of CCGTs was their relatively low capital cost in this lumpy sunk cost industry. CCGT technology offered potential entrants a technology that could be introduced on a modest scale (300–600 MW), short construction times (24–36 months) and low capital and operating costs (Newbery, 1999, pp. 223–4; Helm, 2005a, p. 5). Potential investors in large, long-term generators are likely to seek the security of long-term contracts and to expect credible government commitments concerning future energy policy. The first sits uneasily with the rhetoric of competition and history offers little comfort that the second will be delivered. That uncertainty is only heightened by attempting to forecast how governments will respond to the threat of global warming.

The final area of security concern is with greenhouse gas emissions, the main externality of the energy industry and in particular with CO_2 emissions. In terms of reducing the rate of CO_2 emissions, one approach favoured by governments is to promote the use of 'alternative' fuels and energy sources. The energy of wind might be transferred to wind-turbine blades to produce electricity. However, the market arrangements, such as the cost-based prices of the Pool and then of NETA were never likely to provide a welcome environment for renewables, not least as renewables often carried the additional costs of being small scale and sited away from the usual areas of generation. In the absence of a direct tax on CO_2, a distortion was introduced into any comparison of renewables and fossil fuels, throwing governments back on such other incentives as obliging retail electricity companies to buy a certain proportion of electricity from renewable sources. Whether the costs of such an approach are matched or exceeded by the benefits produced is often dubious and usually not discussed by governments.

Recalling the tenor of the marginalist approach, with its according of a central position to marginal analysis and its acceptance that bygones are bygones, such an approach can usefully be applied to efforts to reduce carbon emissions. Since the CO_2 already emitted forms a stock in the atmosphere, it is the marginal additions to that stock which are of interest and relevance. While the damage caused to the environment is a function of the total size of the stock, it is the rate of marginal additions of carbon to that stock which can be altered. Hence it is the marginal cost of additions of carbon which is of interest. As the stock will rise over time, and therefore inflict increasing damage, then so should the cost of each marginal addition to the stock also rise. In acting on the flow of marginal additions, the marginal costs and benefits of ameliorative action can be compared. Where benefits exceed costs, carbon-reducing measures should be implemented and vice versa. However, such an approach is much easier to outline in theory than to implement in practice. An immediate problem is deciding on the social cost of carbon. To date, estimates of the social cost of carbon have varied widely. Some estimates put the cost at £70 per tonne of carbon (tC), an estimate which was used by the Department of Environment, Food and Rural Affairs in Britain, being consistent with the government's Kyoto target and similar to the thinking of the Royal Commission on Environmental Pollution. Other estimates, notably by the economist David Pearce, place the social cost of carbon at a much lower level, lying within a range of £4/tC to £27/tC. Yet whatever the difficulties, the central calculation is at what point the marginal cost of abatement equals the marginal costs of pollution, an issue which like much of the nascent environmental debate, stirs memories of energy issues discussed in earlier post-war decades (Helm, 2005b, p. 3; 2005c, pp. 15–16). In conducting any cost–benefit analysis, time needs to be factored in and values discounted appropriately. What discount rate should be used, and on what criteria? How, to revive the ideas of Massé, will technology change our perspectives in the future? Recalling the earlier discussions of fuel security, what is the probability of particular risks being realised and what would be their cost?

While such an approach does chime with many of the themes developed in this book, there are also issues raised by the wish to reduce CO_2 emissions which are new. One of these concerns the very international nature of the atmosphere. In assessing the cost of potential damage, do we distinguish between developed and less-developed economies? In accepting that property rights over the atmosphere do not occur naturally, how do we also distinguish between the impact of CO_2 emissions on all producers and their incentive to monitor and enforce any set limits? While the seas are a common-property resource, the fact that overfishing by one boat raises the costs of all other boats does provide some incentive to producers to enforce the quota system which serves as a proxy for property rights. The problem for the group is similar to that of OPEC in attempting to enforce production agreements. But in air pollution, the cost of overpollution by one producer is not borne by the others, thereby reducing their interest in monitoring targeted output.

Issues of enforcement and monitoring of CO_2 emission targets are likely to push governments away from a carbon tax and towards a system in which a fixed quantity of permits is traded such that the highest-cost polluters spend the most on permits. While a carbon tax sets a price on carbon and then lets quantity adjust to price, permits run in the opposite direction fixing quantity and then allowing price to be determined in the process of trading. In part this preference for tradable permits may also reflect a political dislike of raising taxes and energy prices and the preference of industrialists for postponing payment. It is also easier to negotiate, monitor and enforce international emission agreements based on quotas rather than on a carbon tax. However, in terms of reflecting the marginal costs, a carbon tax is preferable to the more fixed quantitative permits (Helm, 2003, pp. 354, 358).

What is familiar about many of these political approaches to devising effective environmental policies for the energy industries is the political reluctance to adopt what the *ingénieurs-économistes* would have recognised as a marginalist approach to pricing and investment. That politicians are allergic to sudden increases in the level of fuel prices is well known, and was confirmed by the fuel protests in Britain in 2000. That, after all the history of the post-war development of energy policy, marginalist approaches to the problem of CO_2 emissions should not spring naturally into the minds of governments is disappointing. This is particularly so given that governments, whether in economies with privatised, deregulated, liberalised or nationalised electricity industries are likely to be involved fundamentally in the development of energy policy for years to come. This is because of the time horizons and uncertainty which affect industries like electricity. To take but the most obvious example: if for reasons of concern with the security of fuel supplies, and as a contribution to reducing CO_2 emissions, governments decide to support the construction of a new round of nuclear power stations, who is to finance their construction? Certainly in Britain, anyone with an inkling of the history of nuclear power might fight shy of such temptation. Given that the viability of nuclear power stations, and indeed of all fuel energy investments, depends on future movements in relative prices, what assurances can be given to potential investors in such long-term projects as nuclear? What will happen to oil prices? High oil prices in the 1970s and pessimistic prognostications of the remaining reserves brought forth new ambitious plans for nuclear investment. The collapse of oil prices in the mid-1980s radically altered the economic prospects of such investments. The fall in electricity prices at the end of the twentieth century was reversed in the early years of the twenty-first. Given such uncertainty, investors will seek the assurance of long-term contracts but governments and regulators seeking to promote competition in the electricity market may not view such contracts kindly. Yet, sooner or later, as the existing stock of assets is worn out, new investment will be required. Not only in generation, but potentially also substantially throughout the entire system if it is decided to accommodate a much larger contribution from renewables.

Uncertainty; heavy, sunk, long-term investments; fluctuating relative prices; the challenge of internalising the externalities of CO_2 emissions; concerns with the security of fuel supplies; and the unsolved problem of what to do with nuclear waste. Mention of uncertainty and the need to calculate the probabilities and costs of risks occurring take us back at least as far as the work of Keynes and of his good friend Frank Ramsey. Even earlier, we have cited the work of Dupuit and Marshall. Many, if not all of these ideas found expression in the marginalist approach expounded by the likes of Meade, Allais, Kahn, Boiteux, Massé and many other, sometimes regulating, economists from the 1970s onwards. No-one promised to have the 'right' answers. Rather, in the face of uncertainty, all insisted on the adoption of the right approach. As seen, this marginalist approach in electricity was adopted earlier in France than in Britain and the United States by a remarkable generation of French *ingénieurs-économistes* who exploited both economic theory and national insecurity. In Britain, these ideas were cherry-picked by a Treasury driven by public finance concerns, and in the United States adopted in a context of growing disenchantment with existing regulatory practice and heightened concern at the sudden increases in oil prices. Just as there was variety in the factors allowing the marginalist ideas to be implemented, so too was there variety in the ownership and industrial structure of the industries and markets in which they were introduced. Nationalised, privatised, liberalised, deregulated industries and markets all proved receptive at various times to the marginalist approach. Extreme comparisons of the high TFP of the

French nationalised electricity monopoly with the mess of the liberalising Californian electricity markets suggests that this is a complex, sophisticated industry to which simplistic political mantra should not be applied. Since the combination of uncertainty, costly sunk investments and externalities is likely to ensure a role for governments in electricity markets for years to come, it would be encouraging if the marginalist approach could be pushed to the fore in their discussions of future energy policy.

Appendix A1

Table A1.1   *Production, trade and consumption of total industrial and public electricity (in thousand million kWh)*

Country		Production	Imports	Exports	Consumption		Installed
					Total	Per capita (in kWh)	capacity per 1,000/pop. (in kW)
USA	1950	389.640	1.935	0.150	391.425	2571	n/a
	1955	630.890	4.567	0.499	634.958	3827	816*
	1960	844.188	5.526	0.966	848.748	4697	1032
	1965	1157.583	3.565	3.687	1157.461	5957	1310
	1970	1639.771	5.634	3.380	1642.025	8015	1759
	1974	1967.289	15.420	2.726	1979.983	9344	2338
France	1950	33.025	0.6	0.36	33.265	797	284
	1955	49.627	0.743	0.811	49.559	1141	370
	1960	72.118	1.789	1.885	72.022	1576	478
	1965	101.442	3.744	2.771	102.415	2099	578
	1970	140.708	4.426	4.925	140.209	2759	764
	1974	180.402	6.400	6.588	180.214	3429	938
UK	1950	66.385		0.002	66.383	1309	376
	1955	94.076		0.002	94.074	1834	531
	1960	136.970		0.001	136.969	2601	697
	1965	196.495	0.206	0.104	196.597	3604	906
	1970	249.193	0.557	0.006	249.744	4473	1200
	1974	273.316	0.225	0.175	273.366	4873	1418

Note: * Installed capacity per 1,000/population in 1956.

Source: United Nations (1976, Table 21).

Electricity and Energy Policy since 1945

Table A1.2   Production of electricity by type (in thousand million kWh)

	Total	Thermal	% of total	Hydro	% of total	Nuclear	% of total
1950							
USA	389.6	288.6	74.1	101.0	25.9		
France	33.0	17.0	51.3	16.1	48.7		
UK	66.4	65.0	97.8	1.5	2.2		
1955							
USA	630.9	514.4	81.5	116.6	18.5		
France	49.6	24.1	48.5	25.6	51.5		
UK	94.1	92.4	98.2	1.7	1.8		
1960							
USA	844.2	694.1	82.2	149.6	17.7	0.6	0.1
France	72.1	31.6	43.9	40.3	55.9	0.1	0.2
UK	136.9	131.8	96.2	3.1	2.3	2.1	1.5
1965							
USA	1157.6	956.8	82.7	197.2	17.0	3.7	0.3
France	101.4	54.1	53.3	46.4	45.8	0.9	0.9
UK	196.5	175.5	89.3	4.6	2.4	16.3	8.3
1970							
USA	1639.8	1366.8	83.4	251.2	15.3	21.8	1.3
France	140.7	78.9	56.1	56.6	40.2	5.1	3.7
UK	249.2	217.5	87.3	5.7	2.3	26.0	10.4
1974							
USA	1967.3	1548.2	78.7	306.4	15.6	112.7	5.7
France	180.4	109.6	60.8	56.8	31.5	13.9	7.7
UK	273.3	234.9	85.9	4.8	1.8	33.6	12.3

Source: United Nations (1976, Table 20). Percentages may not compute exactly due to rounding effects.

Table A1.3 Production and consumption of primary energy (in million metric tons of coal equivalent and in kilograms per capita)

Country		Total primary energy	Production — Percentage shares of total primary energy production				Consumption — Total commercial energy	
			Coal & lignite	Crude petroleum & natural gas liquids	Natural gas	Hydro, nuclear & electricity	Aggregate	Per capita
USA	1950	1165.059	43.5	36.2	19.3	1.1	1113.988	7316
	1955	1331.845	33.3	40.4	25.2	1.1	1309.040	7889
	1960	1434.900	27.3	39.3	32.0	1.3	1476.508	8172
	1965	1711.791	27.8	37.1	33.7	1.4	1782.909	9176
	1970	2169.901	25.4	36.5	36.5	1.5	2257.878	11020
	1974	2105.807	25.8	34.6	37.1	2.4	2433.476	11485
France	1950	54.359	95.4	0.4	0.5	3.6	79.821	1912
	1955	61.380	92.2	2.2	0.6	5.1	95.110	2189
	1960	69.493	82.6	4.8	5.5	7.2	113.067	2474
	1965	71.219	74.9	7.5	9.4	8.2	150.620	3087
	1970	60.528	65.0	7.3	15.1	12.5	201.017	3956
	1974	47.164	53.7	6.3	21.5	18.5	228.174	4342
UK	1950	219.884	99.8	0.1		0.1	221.029	4358
	1955	225.886	99.8	0.1		0.1	251.767	4907
	1960	198.453	99.5	0.1	0.9	0.3	256.006	4861
	1965	194.257	98.5	0.1	0.1	1.3	277.124	5080
	1970	165.435	88.4	0.1	9.0	2.4	297.903	5336
	1974	161.689	70.0	0.4	28.7	2.9	306.486	5464

Source: United Nations (1976, Table 2).

Table A1.4 *Imports, exports and bunkering as a percentage of total primary energy production (%)*

		Imports	Exports	Bunkers
USA	1950	5.6	3.8	1.2
	1955	7.2	5.3	1.5
	1960	9.4	3.2	1.4
	1965	11.7	3.2	1.1
	1970	13.2	3.6	1.0
	1974	23.1	3.0	1.2
France	1950	64.0	12.7	3.2
	1955	87.9	23.5	4.7
	1960	93.6	16.4	4.2
	1965	152.6	21.3	5.2
	1970	295.7	24.9	11.4
	1974	499.5	37.8	18.6
UK	1950	13.0	8.1	4.0
	1955	29.0	10.0	4.7
	1960	43.6	9.7	4.6
	1965	64.8	10.5	4.3
	1970	107.4	18.1	5.5
	1974	117.7	13.5	5.2

Source: United Nations (1976, Table 2).

Table A1.5 *Use of electric appliances in selected European countries, 1953*

	Number of appliances in use per 100 subscribers in 1953			
	Electric cookers	Electric water heaters	Fridges	Washing machines
Austria (1952)	11.0	4.4	1.8	–
Belgium	4.4	1.1	2.6	30.0
France	4.8	3.5	8.5	8.0
Britain	22.0	18.6	7.2	12.5
Italy	7.8	4.0	2.2	1.0
Holland	9.0	–	–	–
Sweden	30.0	–	32.	–
Switzerland	44.0	42.0	9.9	5.0

Source: UNIMAREL, 'La consommation d'énergie électrique en basse tension en France', 17 October 1956.

Table A1.6   *Total public expenditure/GNP in France and the UK,*
              1950–1975 (%)

	France	UK
1950	28.4	30.4
1951	29.3	31.6
1952	32.1	32.9
1953	33.0	32.2
1954	32.0	31.4
1955	32.2	30.2
1956	34.3	29.8
1957	34.3	29.3
1958	33.3	30.1
1959	33.8	30.5
1960	32.5	32.2
1961	33.7	33.0
1962	35.0	33.6
1963	35.6	33.8
1964	35.6	33.5
1965	36.1	35.2
1966	36.0	36.0
1967	36.5	38.4
1968	37.6	39.0
1969	36.5	38.1
1970	38.5	38.1
1971	38.0	37.7
1972	37.8	39.4
1973	38.1	39.9
1974	38.7	44.6
1975	42.4	46.1

Note: Total public expenditure is defined as the sum of central and local government expenditures plus social security outlays. The figures are based on the series of OECD Statistics of National Accounts from 1950 to 1975. Within this framework, the public sector is broadly defined as all levels of government and the institutions of social insurance. This is a rather comprehensive definition of the consolidated public sector compared to a more narrow conception of the state excluding social security which typically prevails in budgetary statistics.

Source: J. Kohl, 'Trends and problems in postwar public expenditure in Western Europe and North America', in P. Flora and A.J. Heidenheimer (eds), *The Development of Welfare States in Europe and America*, Transaction Books, New Brunswick, NJ and London, 1981. Table 9.10, p. 338.

Table A1.7 Electricity prices for industry (in US $/kWh, using purchasing power parities)

	France	UK	USA*
1992	0.047	0.070	0.048
1993	0.048	0.073	0.049
1994	0.046	0.071	0.047
1995	0.048	0.070	0.047
1996	0.047	0.067	0.046
1997	0.047	0.063	0.045
1998	0.045	0.062	0.045
1999	0.044	0.061	0.039
2000	0.042	0.058	0.046
2001	0.043	0.057	0.050
2002	0.043	0.057	0.048
2003	0.044	0.053	0.051
2004	0.044	0.058	0.053
2005	0.044	0.075	0.056

Note: * US taxes on electricity are excluded. They are mostly general sales taxes levied by states; their rates are between 2 and 6%, but their national weighted average is unknown.

Sources: International Energy Authority, *Energy Prices and Taxes: Quarterly Statistics,* Second Quarter, 2006, OECD/IEA, Paris, 2006, Table 21. For purchasing power parities, see National Accounts of OECD countries.

Appendix A2

MARGINAL-COST PRICING

By Michael Posner, Economics Division, 2 November 1966
TNA POWE 58/57 TWP(66)5, Working Party on Tariffs

1. This note is intended to act as a background briefing for the Tariff Working Party. It suffers from three defects:

(i)   it comes after a lot of work has been done, and so most of what it tries to say will already be in people's minds in one way or another;
(ii) its author has an imperfect knowledge of past deliberations, though he believes that he has a nodding acquaintance with the main principles on which the space heating working party was based (whether this nodding acquaintance is reflected in the note which follows is for others to judge);
(iii) though brief and behind the clock, it is written in haste and without any attempt to relate it specifically to earlier documents.

2. The exposition is designed to avoid the trap of trying to teach grandmothers to suck eggs while attempting to omit none of the main analytical arguments with which we are concerned. Some of the main contentions may therefore be unsupported by argument and hence prove, in the context, to be erroneous. The aim has been to avoid excessive formality by taking the arguments discursively: the result is of course that the exposition is loose and the morals to be drawn rather lost in the jungle. But after a discussion, the paper can be redrafted in a more systematic way.

Short-run Arguments

3. We start, classically, with Dupuit's bridge. Dupuit was concerned with the construction of a bridge connecting two parts of a village separated by a river. He assumed that it was necessary to build the bridge (an assumption that later theoretical literature, and later sections of this paper, will show to be heroic: but Dupuit, like, say, the CEGB, would be inclined to

heroism regardless). Assume the bridge to have no necessary maintenance costs and to be everlasting; and assume that no congestion problems can ever arise. Nevertheless, debt was incurred by the Prefecture in construct-ing the bridge, and this debt will have to be amortised or, at the very least, 'serviced' by paying the interest charges.

Problem: how should the interest (plus amortisation) charges be financed?

4. If we charge a toll, we appear to satisfy the demands of fairness ('equity'), since those who benefit will pay for their pleasure. (This princi-ple of equity appears in many bits of this theory in many guises. Its justification has virtually nothing to do with economics, though it is some-times politically expedient to claim it as a principle of economics; no doubt sometimes politicians genuinely believe it to be an economic principle.) Moreover, it neatly hypothecates a tax for a particular purpose, and hence suggests a possible investment rule for 'public goods': make the investment if and only if you can envisage raising a toll which will service the debt arising from your investment.

5. But by charging the toll you risk discouraging a marginal user, who is either 'too poor to pay' (a vague concept which can be made a little more precise) or who prefers to spend his money otherwise: one special case of this would be the man who will wade the ford or hire a boat to row him across. Consider the effects on total utility enjoyed by this marginal indi-vidual and the resources used by the rest of the community: if he wades, he gets wet and is less happy; if he hires a rowboat, the oarsman is engaging in extra effort which could (on a full employment assumption) be used otherwise. In any case, the 'community' is less happy than it need be in the absence of a toll. This argument can be used against any toll: the optimum toll is zero.

6. Now allow for use-related maintenance costs or use-related depreciation (the two are not identical but may be assimilated to each other). Then the optimum toll equals the cost of the wear and tear imposed on the com-munity by each user. If the toll is less than this, the benefit gained by the marginal user is less than the benefit he *could* get if he refrained from making the trip and the community compensated him by paying him a sum of money representing the cost of the wear and tear that he would have imposed by crossing. If the toll is more, then the argument of paragraph 5 applies. Finally, allow other sorts of avoidable costs than wear and tear, and you get the result: optimum toll = marginal (avoidable) cost. Call this the 'short-term rule'.

The Public Finance Problem

7. But this optimum toll may yield less than the money required to service the debt. If this is so, then taxes will have to be levied to raise the money. These taxes will either be poll taxes (which public finance theory tells us are 'optimal' taxes in some sense) and may therefore hurt poor people (good chaps) more than rich people (bad chaps); or will be (? progressive) income or sales taxes, and hence disrupt optimal decisions at the margin between work and leisure. The damage to welfare or its distribution by following the short-term rule may be considerable. (Compare the Treasury gilt-edged problem of financing public sector deficit industries.) This loss through distortion caused by tax collection (together with the institutional frictions of the real world) may be of the same order of magnitude as the losses caused by failure to follow the short-term rule.

8. A possible escape route is to modify the short-term rule and to make prices (tolls) merely proportional to marginal costs – where the factor of proportionality is fixed so as to solve the public finance problem while keeping the right relationship between the prices of any two goods or services.[1]

Many Goods

9. This formulation reminds us that, while Dupuit's argument is presented for one 'good' only, it has validity only as part of the general proposition: that all prices are set according to the short-term rule (or paragraph 8's version of that rule). Economic man makes choices at the margin, and the prices set for him act as signals, relating his preferences to the costs to the community of different patterns of resource allocation. It follows that, in strict terms, the short-term rule is valid if and only if all the other $(n - 1)$ goods are priced by the same rule. If, instead, we recognise that other prices are not set optimally, we have to ask: 'Given that the best solution (the optimum) is not obtainable, what rule should I follow in pricing these goods so as to make the best of a bad world – what is the *second best solution*?'.

10. If, however, we recognise that all goods are not equally 'distant' from other goods, but that instead there are many clusters of goods that are close substitutes for each other though far from being substitutes for goods outside this 'sector', it may be that we can treat each sector (for example, the fuel sector) separately, apply paragraph 8's version of the short-term rule, and get reasonably near the right answer. (We should note

that, because only three of the four industries are directly under our control, the 'factor of proportionality' will have to be fixed by the operations of the oil industry: not all factors of proportionality are equally desirable, for reasons not here investigated, so that by letting our dog be wagged by the oil industry's tail we may be doing damage which would have to be weighed against any gain we would hope to obtain from marginal-cost pricing.) Turvey, in a formal paper, has recently argued that in such a 'partitioned sector' a form of marginal-cost pricing does in fact constitute a 'second best' solution; but many economists would have reservations on this point.

Summary on the Short-run Case

11. From this muddy pool something can be fished: if we have a small group of highly substitutable products whose marginal costs differ widely, there is a strong case for letting prices reflect these differences. I am not sure of the status of this proposition – it would make a logician squirm – but it is widely accepted and, to my mind, congenial to common sense. In this short-run case the superiority of marginal-cost pricing is that it avoids waste – capacity standing idle when it would cost the community less to allow its use than the consumer would be prepared to pay. Whereas the nationalising acts suggest 'covering costs' – a sort of average-cost pricing; and the monopolist would equate marginal cost not with price but with 'marginal revenue'; theory suggests marginal-cost pricing. But the covering of overheads, even just interest payments, may require a price in excess of marginal costs. That is the dilemma which 'proportionality' attempts to solve, but can only solve partially (see the note to paragraph 8).

Congestion and Stochastic Costing

12. In paragraph 3 we assumed there was no congestion. Relax this assumption. If we know which individuals will use the bridge (turn on their fires) at peak hours, then, at those hours those persons can be charged a fee calculated either (a) to remove congestion (necessarily so in the electricity case) or (b) to reflect the cost imposed on all users by any one user. In either case, we should have to know which individuals were concerned and their 'elasticity of demand'. But neither of these facts can be known with certainty, so we would have to estimate them – estimation which involves chance and error. But probability methods can be devised to deal with this – the *probability* of a peak at 5 p.m. justifies high prices for users at that time; or, at a further remove, the *probability* of Mr 'X' (or appliance 'Y') being a user at 5 p.m. might justify 'X' or 'Y' being charged more.

If estimation is very difficult or costly, then compulsion will have to be applied to those who happen to arrive at the bridge or to turn on their fires at the peak.

Two-part Tariffs

13. In order to follow the short-term rule while allowing for the public finance problem we have favoured the proportionality solution and hinted at a general approach in paragraph 11. But proportionality is only one possible 'solution'. Another way is to extract the capital-cost element (debt service in Dupuit's case) by a lump-sum entrance fee (compare the poll tax of paragraph 7), and then make a running charge following the short-term cost. (Some form of proportionality may have to be imposed on either component of the tariff to deal with the 'tail-wagging dog' of paragraph 10.) Now the entrance fee may 'price some consumers out of the market' – that is the disadvantage of the two-part tariff. But the proportionality solution we have previously sketched suffers by introducing distortions at the margin between work and leisure and, unless we manage to impose the same factor of proportionality fairly generally, distortions in the choice between some pairs of goods. In the context of short-term pricing there is no convincing *a priori* reason for favouring either of these two possible methods of solving Dupuit's problem.

The whole of this argument should be familiar to anyone who has tried to discuss meal pricing and subscription charges for a club. It is in that context that the short-term problem has a real content.

The Quasi-long-term Problem

14. We now relax the extreme Dupuit position that the bridge lasts for ever. Suppose that there are time-related maintenance costs necessary to the efficient working of the bridge (equivalent to an assumption that we need to make an annual payment into a sinking fund necessary to accumulate cash to finance the rebuilding of the bridge on the expiry of its natural life).[2] Recall the approach of paragraph 9, and compare two ways of crossing the river: the bridge, which we now assume to have high time-related costs but very low (or zero) marginal usage-related costs; and a ferry which lasts forever without repair, but requires much man-power to pull it across on each journey. If we follow the short-term rule in its pure form, we will charge nothing for the bridge, but a positive price for the ferry. But it may be that the annual cost of carrying all potential passengers (at a zero toll) on the ferry would be less than the annual maintenance charge necessary to maintain the bridge in working order. In general, a policy of charging

short-run marginal costs (SRMCs) may be to attract users into high capital-cost, low running-cost activities, though 'total cost' may be higher in the use they are led by our price signals to favour.

15. In this particular case, the logic of the argument would seem to favour an *average-cost price* for the bridge (still leaving Dupuit's debt servicing to be dealt with as we have already discussed) – making the consumer pay for time-related as well as for usage-related costs. But what would happen? There are two possibilities:

(a)   All users would switch to the ferry (whose capacity is assured to be adequate), and the bridge would not be maintained. On our assumptions (running cost of the ferry is less than the maintenance cost of the bridge) this would be an improvement.

(b)   Some users would stay with the bridge, because they have a preference for bridges sufficient to induce them to pay a higher price (the 'average-cost' price set for the bridge would have to take account of the statistically expected number of users, allowance made for elasticity of demand): but if the bridge were maintained, it would be running at undercapacity, and marginal users will have been choked off by a price far higher than the cost (assumed zero) that they would impose on the community by using the bridge.

16. Case 15(b) must be allowed as a possibility – perhaps a strong one. Hence the average-cost rule, designed to improve long-run allocation of resources, may damage short-run allocation.

Two-part Tariffs in the Quasi-long-run Case

17. In paragraph 13 we asserted that the argument for a two-part tariff in the short-run case was not conclusive – the potential damage would occur through the fixed charge, which might price some potential consumers out of the club altogether. But now we can consider the payment of the fixed charge as a vote by consumers on the question: 'should the maintenance charges be incurred?'. Whereas in the pure short-run case the vote was irrelevant (the bridge was already there, and there for all time), now there are annual charges which must be met if the bridge is to continue operating. Only if we get enough 'voters' in favour will we go on spending year by year. Although there is still the disadvantage that we may be underutilising a resource which we have already decided to maintain, we have now the additional advantage that we are enabled rationally to decide whether or not to maintain: the case for the two-part tariff is improved.

Pricing and Investment Policy

18. If marginal cost of a plant is systematically less than its average cost, as we are assuming, then how do we decide whether or not to build a bridge (or a second bridge, if the first is fully utilised)? The danger is that, as we saw in paragraph 14, consumers will systematically be attracted into low running-cost, high capital-cost processes. How will the public authorities conduct their investment policy? (a) They might be tempted to invest wherever congestion occurs most violently. (b) If investment policy is executed according to strict financial rules, no such loss-making capacity will ever be created. But (c), if instead a form of cost–benefit analysis is adopted, it might be possible to unite SRMC pricing with correct investment decisions. But this would imply not only the 'subsidising' of high capital-cost plants, but pouring good money after bad by building more of them! The public finance problem would be severe, as doubtless would be the political difficulties.

Excess Capacity and the Number of Plants

19. The whole point of short-term marginal costing is to avoid excess capacity. If the number of plants can be nicely adjusted to the number of consumers who would use them were *average* costs to be charged, then the short-term problem would disappear. In principle, public utilities are large capital-intensive indivisible entities which cannot be easily varied in this way – unlike the shaving soap advertisements, we have either too little or too much. But if the market is expanding through time at a rate which allows a number of new productive units to be added each 'year', then we could charge *average cost*: this would perhaps slow down the rate of increase in demand, but there is no reason to suppose that the amount of excess capacity would be greater than would occur with SRMC pricing and a faster rate of growth. It is true that, at any point of time we may have *some* excess capacity, but its amount need only be small relative both to the annual growth in capacity and of course to the total of sales. Thus at one fell-swoop the whole of the preceding discussion is made largely insignificant.[3]

20. Oddly enough there is a famous French discussion (well explained by Meek in some articles in the *Journal of Industrial Economics*) which tries to justify 'average-cost pricing' by calling it 'marginal-cost pricing'. It considers the problem of the optimum rate of investment – when to build a new plant? Suppose your existing plant is fully employed, and some of it is congested. Calculate the price which you would require to charge to choke off

the congestion. As soon as that price approaches (from below) the average cost of a new plant, decide to build the new plant. This implies that the price charged should never exceed the average cost of the new plant. Equally, suppose that, in order to utilise our existing plant we should have to charge a price below its average cost; then this implies that we should slow down our rate of investment in new plant, until we reach a balanced position where average-cost pricing leaves us without excess capacity. Assume that the new plant is identical with the old: then the marginal cost of output from new plant (its 'long-run marginal cost': LRMC) is equal to the average cost of old plant, and when we are charging (short-run) average cost we are also charging (long-run) marginal cost. Then we choose a set of plants such that we can charge this price and have neither congestion nor excess capacity.

Long-run Marginal Costs and Technical Progress

21. LRMC is then defined as the total cost of a new plant (adding in capital by taking an annuity at some reasonable rate of interest) divided by its output.[4] If technical progress is always happening, then, despite the last two paragraphs, LRMC is always below the average cost of the existing plant. Therefore, if we charge LRMC we encounter similar difficulties to those that we analysed earlier: just as SRMC implied financial losses, so will LRMC. But here the case for marginal pricing becomes stronger: whereas in the short-run case it was only *current resources* which were at risk, now it is capital investment – setting a high price to protect current assets would lead to a misallocation of resources through time. Once again, therefore, we may be tempted to seek an escape route through a two-part tariff or through a 'proportionality' rule.

22. A two-part tariff for this specific purpose would be an odd creature. Its standing charge would contain inter alia, an element designed to cover the gap between average cost of the old plant and average cost of the new plant. If the new plant actually in existence at any one time was small relative to the old plant, then the standing charge would be very large relative to the running charge. The risk, therefore, of pricing users (particularly small users) out of the market would be considerable. It does not seem a possibility worth serious attention.

23. The proportionality rule would encounter difficulties as well. If technical progress occurs simultaneously and at the same speed in two of 'our' industries, the problem is not too serious: prices can be maintained fairly high, provided they have the right relation to each other. Even on this

assumption, however, by maintaining prices we limit the attractiveness of fuel compared with other industrial inputs – we fail to achieve a 'second best' allocation. Even more difficult is the case where progress occurs in one fuel industry and not in others – proportionality will demand a drop in, for example, gas prices relative to the price of electricity, and this could be achieved without a 'public finance problem' only if electricity prices were raised!

24. It would seem that the blessings of technical progress bring with them the curses of public finance. There is no magic way out of this dilemma, even by expediting the pace of embodying technical progress (through a higher rate of investment). But a certain limited escape may be achieved by price discrimination.

Price Discrimination

25. We have hitherto assumed that all consumers pay the same price (apart from 'consumer-related costs'). But there is no reason for this to be true. Suppose there are two consumers – one with a demand curve that is completely inelastic over the relevant range, another with a partially elastic curve. Then distortion in the allocation of resources will be least if the 'overheads' (excess of average over marginal, or SRMC over LRMC) are charged to the first and not to the second. In general, on assumptions that are not too implausible, it can be shown that price should vary inversely with the arithmetic value of the elasticity of demand, to achieve the least damage with the maximum revenue. Some discrimination is in any case implicit in a two-part tariff – small users pay a higher price on average – and we will see further discrimination when we come to consider the multi-product case. Such discrimination reminds us that the price mechanism has 'distribution effects' as well as 'allocation effects' and it may be that we should be wary of deliberately varying the distribution effect already implicit in the structure of our markets and costs. But discrimination can be helpful in the particular case of technical change.

26. Natural gas will have to be sold to new industrial users, if it is all to be shifted. These users might buy only if the price per therm were substantially below the present town gas price. But some town gas (initially a lot) must continue to be sold. In these circumstances, a low price for the new gas would be matched by a higher price for the old gas users who are, after all, 'locked in' and in no position to escape. They will certainly squeal: but better that they should pay the higher price (which falls on them only as a

poll tax, inescapable and with no consequences for resource allocation) than that it should fall on the general taxpayer, the gilt-edged market, or the potential buyers of new gas.

Conclusion for the Single-product Firm

27. The whole of this discussion so far has concerned the single-product firm, allowing for technical progress but forgetting about product differentiation. The conclusions suggested are:

(a)   that in our industries the case for short-run marginal costing is slight; with the exception of off-peak electricity and gas;
(b)   that the case for long-run marginal costing is strong, and in the absence of technical progress would not cause much trouble in a growing market;
(c)   that technical progress is bound to impose a strain on any rational pricing system, and that price discrimination is a possible ameliorative device;
(d)   to the extent that price discrimination fails to supply the complete answers, the 'public finance problem' should be braved; we should therefore need to assess the size and importance of that problem;
(e)   that, between competing fuels, it is important to ensure that prices do reflect differences in long-run costs;

We must now proceed to approach a little nearer to real life.

The Multi-product Case

28. It is easiest and most appropriate to concentrate on electricity. The many products of the electricity industry are not alternative uses of the same equipment, but uses of the same equipment at different times of day. One aspect of electricity pricing which causes difficulty is the relation between the short- and long-term problems: when we price at the peak we are thinking of long-run costs; when we price off-peak, we are thinking of short-run costs. The loss incurred by not pricing at SRMC in the trough is the wastage of available capacity; the loss incurred by failing to price at LRMC at the peak is an attraction of users who may not be benefiting as much from their usage of peak electricity as it costs the economy to produce. But, as is well known, the story is complicated by the fact that the stock of equipment is never completely adjusted to known technology, so that the provision of extra plant 'for the peak' will in fact provide plant that will work throughout the day on base-load, thus lowering the cost of

trough electricity. Thus the SRMC of trough electricity is a decreasing function of the demand for peak electricity, and the LRMC of peak electricity is a decreasing function of the demand for trough electricity.

Peak Pricing

29. Let us remind ourselves of the mechanics of the calculation. We set a price for the peak equal to (the fuel cost of the worst plant) *plus* (the capital cost of a new plant divided by the number of units of peak electricity we expect to sell) *minus* (the reduction in fuel cost per unit of trough electricity multiplied by a number of trough units we expect to sell, expressed per unit of peak sales). Call this $a + b - c$. Now b must be bigger than c otherwise the new plant would be built in the absence of an increment in peak demand. The sum $(b - c)$ is the excess of LRMC over SRMC at the peak: it may or may not be of roughly the same size as an accountant's measure of a 'fair share' of the costs of an existing plant – that might be a convenience in practice, but there is no reason why it would be true. If $(b - c)$ is very large – perhaps because c is very small – the charge to the peak user may be far above his 'fair share' of the costs: it would nevertheless be the correct charge from the point of view advanced in this paper: it would set the right signal to the potential user.

Off-peak Pricing

30. On the other hand, the user in the trough would have to be charged a price far lower than a 'fair share' would suggest. If he were charged more than this, we would be outraging the principles of the short-run optimum.

Covering Average Costs

31. By a 'fair price' we mean something like the average short-run cost that we have previously defined. If theory prescribes a price above this for the peak and below it for the trough, is there (i) any reason to suppose that in total the revenue obtained will just cover costs or (ii) any reason to adjust the prices so that we force this result to come about? Save on the most special and restrictive of assumptions, the answer to (i) is 'no'. As for (ii), the public finance argument is compelling, and would lead us to suggest that any deficiency of total revenue below total costs be made good by some proportional rise in the price of all fuels – peak electricity, trough electricity *and all other fuels*. But we have already seen that this proportionality device is bound, in general, to lead industries or products into surplus if *all* products are required at least to cover costs. There would be no

difficulty in adjusting the absolute level of all electricity prices so that we fulfilled both the condition of covering total costs and the condition of maintaining proper relativity between peak and trough prices. But if we did do this, then there is no guarantee that the correct relationship between all electricity prices and the prices of other fuels would be maintained. This is the inescapable dilemma of marginal-cost pricing.

The Dilemma of Marginal-cost Pricing

32. It may be worth putting this dilemma more fully and directly. The relationship between the marginal and the average costs of different fuels is not the same for all fuels. Therefore a policy of charging marginal costs, or prices proportional to marginal costs, must lead to surpluses for some industries and deficits for others, or at any rate greater surpluses for some than for others. This is true whether we consider SRMC or LRMC. The only possible solution would be to adjust financial targets to produce the required differences in surpluses.

This dilemma is made worse by the fact that we cannot directly influence the financial target of the oil industry. And it is complicated by the existence of many products within any particular industry.

'Average Marginal Costs'

33. The principle of differentiating between peak and trough tariffs to even domestic consumers is of course accepted, though we may doubt whether the day and night differences really reflect costs sufficiently. But 'the day' has been treated in a non-discriminating way,[5] ignoring the variations in load curves during the day. This can be defended by asserting that a minute by minute variation in charging (which is what they would recommend) is in practice impossible and confusing.[6] In so far as any form of marginal-cost pricing is applied to the day, it is therefore a sort of average of a large number of different marginal costs – a device to be defended on grounds of practicability. But we have seen that the proper 'margin' at the system peak is the long-run margin – including capital costs; while the proper margin at off-peak times is the short-run margin – excluding capital costs. An average between these two is, in technical terms, a bastard concept.

34. Nevertheless, this bastard concept may be defended by considering consumer psychology. Consumers own electrical appliances intending to use them according to a certain time pattern. All they are concerned with is their total payment during a year, and they will compare that total with the cost of alternative appliances (where, as in the space heating case, such

alternative exists), bearing in mind the overall convenience of electrical appliances compared with others. Since in any case the consumer does such averaging himself, the electricity tariff might as well do it for him: a fancy tariff might well cost more to administer and meter than the community would gain from any induced shift in the time pattern of consumer demand.

35. This argument is reinforced by other practical considerations: since we do not yet know (pending the outcome in five years of present investigations by the Electricity Council) the responsiveness of consumers to changes in tariffs, why make leaps in the dark. The answer is, however, that the leaps in the dark might save a lot on money!

Time-of-day or Two-part Tariffs?

36. The last paragraphs have been concerned exclusively with time-of-day variations, and we have lost sight of the general case for two-part tariffs which we have previously stressed. For the peak, the fixed part of the tariff would reflect the maximum that the individual was permitted or expected to impose on the system, and the capital cost in extra plant[7] that this would involve; the running charge would be basically the fuel and transmission cost. At the trough, the fixed part would be zero,[8] but the running charge would also be lower than at the peak to allow for using more efficient plant. At the 'shoulder' we might also allow for a positive fixed charge to allow for the fact that, with normal growth in demand, some capital investment might be required to supply total expected demand.

37. The virtue of two-part tariffs would be that once the peak consumer 'had bought' his extra capacity, he is given the right degree of inducement to use it. The difficulty lies in the calculation (either by the consumer in the case of a subscribed maximum demand system or by the Board in the case of an imposed tariff for the use of *any* power at the peak) of the appropriate fixed charge to impose.

Relative Tariffs for All Fuels: A Warning

38. Much of this discussion has been in terms of electricity tariffs; some of it may apply *mutatis mutandis* to other fuel industries. But we must not lose sight of a primary aim: the need to maintain the right relationship between the prices of different fuels. The more it is true that 'fancy tariffs' for individual fuels are difficult or wasteful to install, the greater the need to ensure that the relative prices of different fuels reflect their LRMC. This is a truth which must not escape us.

Complications

39. This discussion had ignored many practical issues which need to be integrated with the theoretical approach. Among them are:

(i)   costs of electricity – and indeed of other fuels – contain all sorts of elements, some demand related, some appliance related, some varying with units bought, others invariant. A really fancy tariff would therefore have very many terms. Some judgement and common sense needs to be used in selecting important variables from unimportant ones;

(ii)   some of the discussions would seem to imply the desirability of dancing prices up and down – for instance, to deal with shifting peaks, and so on. As against this, we must remember that rational decisions made by consumers require some reasonable certainty about the course of future prices;

(iii) consumer rationality has been assumed in all this discussion. Alas, such an assumption is rarely true. If consumers fail to respond to small price differences, it might be desirable to exaggerate differences in costs so that 'correct' consumer decisions are induced. But this is a subject of another paper now under preparation.

Conclusions

40. The warning at the beginning of this paper – that it would be discursive – has been amply fulfilled. Conclusions have been suggested at various points, and not all of them are consistent with each other. But among the points that should have emerged are:

(a)   that where there is spare capacity, SRMCs should be charged unless the financial complications of doing so are very serious;

(b)   that in the absence of spare capacity, charges should reflect the average cost of new plants (LRMCs);

(c)   that by insisting on the correct relativity of prices rather than their absolute level we can evade some but not all of the financial problems; but to do so might require fiddling financial targets;

(d)   that where load factors vary widely between different uses, and where load factors are on average low, severe differentiation between prices is desirable;

(e)   that some 'fudging' or averaging of tariffs is inevitable, and judgement is needed to decide the degree of fudging we should practice.

These are very small mice to come from elephantine labours!

Notes

1. This proportionality rule is not the 'average cost' defined in paragraph 15 below. Suppose that there are two competing fuels, whose (short-run) marginal costs are identical, but whose capital or time-related maintenance costs differ. Then price can exceed marginal cost for both fuels, but by the same proportion: the price of one fuel may then cover its marginal cost plus capital cost (that is, price will equal average cost); but in general, the price charged for the other fuel will be greater or less than its average cost.
2. I call this the *quasi*-long-term problem because in many people's minds maintenance charges occur even in the short run. In this section we are really dealing with all those costs which have to be paid as we go along, but these are time related rather than use related.
3. This argument applies only to rapidly growing industries, and only to those where the number of plants added per 'year' is relatively large. For the Channel Tunnel, for instance, the earlier discussion retains a considerable relevance; so it does for natural gas pricing; for steel pricing; and other issues. In particular it will be seen to be of great importance for off-peak electricity (paragraph 30).
4. If it is used progressively less as time goes on so this cost could be said to increase with time. But in any case, to annuitise the capital cost is an arbitrary device. A new power station today has a shorter expected life and a low expected life-time load factor because of expected technical progress. A consumer faced with the choice of fuel should be offered either:

   (a) a time-profile of prices (neglecting general inflation) into the future: these prices would get lower as time went on, and he would be paying a high price today in return for the promise of a lower price in the future; or
   (b) a price for this power station, which he would be committed to pay in the future (for a finite time) even if this power station were prematurely scrapped. The initial price on scheme (a) would be above the fixed price on scheme (b), the relation between them depending on the rate of technical progress and the time discount rate applied.

   CEGB practice is to offer alternative (a) only. Because their customers' view of the future may not coincide with CEGB's own, alternative (b) should be offered as well.
5. Apart from the two-hour period which most boards allow to replenish night storage heaters.
6. Mr Norris's recent invention makes this argument difficult to maintain. But see below, paragraph 36, for one objection to this approach.
7. Corrected as usual from savings associated with the installation of a more modern plant.
8. But might in practice be greater than zero because of other elements not here considered.

Bibliography

PRIMARY SOURCES

British Electricity Council (1974), 'Domestic tariffs experiment', Load and Market Research Report, No. 121.

Cmd. 647 (1952), *Report of the (Ridley) Committee on National Policy for the Use of Fuel and Power Resources*, London: HMSO.

Cmd. 9346 (1954), *UK-European Coal and Steel Community: Agreement concerning relations*, London, HMSO, December.

Cmd. 9389 (1955), *A Programme of Nuclear Power*, London: HMSO.

Cmnd. 1337 (1961), *The Financial and Economic Obligations of the Nationalised Industries*, London: HMSO.

Cmnd. 2798 (1965), *Fuel Policy*, London: HMSO.

Cmnd. 3437 (1967), *Nationalised Industries: A Review of Economic and Financial Objectives*, London: HMSO.

Cmnd. 7131 (1978), *The Nationalised Industries*, London: HMSO.

Commissariat Général du Plan d'Équipement et de la Productivité (CGP) (1961), *Rapport Général de la Commission de l'Énergie: IV Plan*, Paris: Imprimerie Nationale.

Commissariat Général du Plan d'Équipement et de la Productivité (CGP) (1965), *Rapport Général de la Commission de l'Energie: V Plan*, Paris: Imprimerie Nationale.

FONT (Ministry of Industry archives at Centre des Archives Contemporaines, Fontainebleau, henceforth FONT) (1948), V770314/ I 21292, Boiteux, budgetary equilibrium and communication to société d'économétrie à la Haye, August.

FONT (1949), V770314/21292, Dessus, 'Les principes généraux de la tarification dans les services publics', Union Internationale des Producteurs et Distributeurs d'Énergie Électrique, September.

FONT (1951), V771417/I 03558, CGP, 'Programme complémentaire d'équipement électrique de 1951'.

FONT (1952), V770314/ I 21292, Union Internationale des Producteurs et Distributeurs d'Energie Électrique, Congrès de Rome, Comité d'études de la tarification, Boiteux and Stasi, 'Sur la détermination des prix de revient de développement dans un système interconnecté de production-distribution', September.

FONT (1953), V770314/I21292, Direction du gaz et de l'électricité, Commissariat du Gouvernement, 'Note', 24 November.

FONT (1956), V770314/I21292, M. Boiteux, 'La vente au coût marginal', Comité d'études de tarification de l'UNIPEDE, 8th Congress of the l'Institut d'Économie Énergétique de l'Université de Cologne, 27 August.

FONT (1959a), 80AJ205/930275, 'Note préliminaire sur une politique de l'énergie', 29 July.

FONT (1959b), 920430/42, oral evidence of Jeanneney, Conseil Économique et Social (CES), 24 September.

FONT (1959c), 920430/42, CES, Energy Section, 'Étude des problèmes posés par la coordination des diverses formes d'énergie; projet de rapport', presented by E. Mayolle, President of the Section, 13 October.

FONT (1960a), 80AJ164/ V930275, M. Gouni, 'Diffusion des méthodes de calcul économique; note sur la mise au point des procedures conduisant à un examen décentralisé des choix techniques', 10 January.

FONT (1960b), 80AJ205/930275, CGP, 'Principaux événements survenus depuis 18 mois dans le domaine de l'énergie', February.

FONT (1960c), V920430, no. 46, CES, Section de l'Énergie, 'Annexe au procès-verbal de la séance', 28 April.

FONT (1961), 80AJ206/930275/46, Commissariat Général du Plan, Quatrième Plan (1962–1965), *Rapport Général de la Commission de Énergie*, Paris: Imprimerie Nationale.

FONT (1962), 770383/21349, OECD, Comité de l'énergie, 'Action sur le plan national dans le domaine de l'énergie; memorandum du Royaume-Uni', 24 November.

FONT (1963), V770603/I22223, Ministère des Finances et des Affaires Économiques, 'Rapport relatif au prix de l'électricité'.

FONT (1965), V770603/I22223, FNCCR, Association Nationale des Syndicats de Communes, 'Révision des cahiers des charges de distribution publique d'énergie électrique', 18–21 October.

FONT (1967), 920626/52, Commissariat Général du Plan, note B3, 'Sur les problèmes de tarification', May.

FONT (1973), 80AJ178/930278/Pièce 18, Pierre Massé, *Croissance et Plan; Différents aspects de l'œuvre*, Paris.

GES (Government Economic Service) (1979), *The Test Discount Rate and the Required Rate of Return on Investment*, Government Economic Service, Working paper, No. 22 (Treasury Working Paper No. 9), January. 'The Test Discount Rate' by G.P. Smith.

Giraud, A. (1968), 'La Politique Pétrolière Française', speech before the CES, 8 August.

JMJ (Jean-Marcel Jeanneney) (1960) (Archive of Jean-Marcel Jeanneney, Sciences Po, Paris), French Senate, 'Situation de l'industrie chabonnière française; d'une question oral avec débat', pp. 1119–20, col. 443, 21 June.

LPA (1967), Re. 209, Fuel Study Group, 'Is British Petroleum compatible with British Socialism?', paper by Peter Odell, November.

LPA (1968), Re. 393 Fuel Study Group, 'Where is the BP group headed?', paper by A.A. Grennard, December.

Ministry of Power (1958), *Statistical Digest 1957*, London: HMSO.

National Economic Development Office (NEDO) (1971), *Investment Appraisal*, London: HMSO.

SAV (1957), B52.203, Ministère des Finances. Direction du Trésor, Service des Études Économiques et Financières, 'Quelques bases théoriques de la tarification des Services Publics', June.

Schiller, P. (1946), *Characteristics of the Domestic Load*, London: British Electrical and Allied Industries Association.

Schiller, P. (1948), *A Large-Scale Sampling-Survey of Domestic Consumers*, London: British Electrical and Allied Industries Association.

SRO (Scottish Record Office, henceforth SRO) (1960), SEP 14/1413, Treasury, 'Borrowings by nationalised industries for capital purposes', May.

SRO (1961), SEP 14/1457, Treasury evidence to the Mackenzie Committee, 17 October.

SRO (1962), SEP 14/1514, 'Profitability of new investment by nationalised industries', 9 November.

SRO (1963a), SEP 14/1513, 'Investment criteria for public enterprises', 3 May.

SRO (1963b), SEP 14/1420, 'Economics of electricity supply', 9 May.

TNA (The National Archives, London, henceforth TNA) (1942), CAB 87/4, R.P.(42)37, War Cabinet: Committee on Reconstruction Problems; 'Report on the electricity industry by the Paymaster General', 7 August.

TNA (1946), CAB 21/2208, S.I.M.(46) 9th meeting, Lord President's Office, minutes, 22 May.

TNA (1948), T228/308, memorandum on 'Electricity policy', Gaitskell to Cripps, 23 January.

TNA (1950a), POWE 41/59, 'Dual pricing of coal', note by Ministry of Fuel and Power submitted to the OEEC by the UK Delegation, 20 January.

TNA (1950b), POWE 41/59, C(50)24, OEEC, Council, 'Extract from report by the trade committee on dual pricing', 23 January.

TNA (1950c), T234/68, 'Extracts from report by the OEEC trade committee on dual pricing', 23 January.

TNA (1950d), CAB 134/293, FG(WP)(50)38, Working Party on Proposed Franco-German Coal and Steel Authority, 16 June.

TNA (1951a), T230/372, S.I.(O)(51)2, 'Control of prices in socialized industries', note by J.C.R. Dow.

TNA (1951b), POWE 41/33, F.G.(W.P.)(51)43, Report by a Working Party of Officials on The Treaty Constituting the European Coal and Steel Community (Schuman Plan), 31 December.

TNA (1952), POWE 41/33, F.G.(W.P.)(52)1, Cabinet, Working Party on the Proposed Franco-German Coal and Steel Authority, 'The Schuman Plan: Some considerations for the United Kingdom', note, 29 February.

TNA (1953a), CAB 134/1177, S.P.C.E 0(53)4, Cabinet, Official Committee on Relations with the Schuman Plan High Authority, 'Implications on entering the common market for coal of the European Coal and Steel Community', note, Ministry of Fuel and Power.

TNA (1953b), CAB 134/1176, S.P.C.E29, Report, Working Party, 'The economic implications of an association between the UK and the ECSC', 22nd July.

TNA (1954), POWE 24/12, letter to Eric Sharp, Ministry of Fuel and Power from P. Schiller, no date, probably 12 November.

TNA (1955a), POWE 24/13, Ministry of Fuel and Power, Committee of Inquiry into the Electricity Supply Industry; a commentary by Professor Edwards on the evidence of Area Board Chairmen, 23 March.

TNA (1955b), POWE 24/12, OE 51, Ministry of Fuel and Power, Committee of Inquiry into the Electricity Supply Industry; additional evidence received from Mr P. Schiller, 18 July.

TNA (1955c), CAB 134/1220, visit of the President of the High Authority of the ECSC to London, 20 September.

TNA (1955d), CAB 134/1220, ECS(O)(55)12, Cabinet, Official Committee on relations with the ECSC, background to the agreement, note by Cabinet Office, 2 November.

TNA (1956), T234/605, letter, Aubrey Jones to Chancellor of the Exchequer, 7 December.

TNA (1957a), CAB 134/1529, The 1957 Energy Protocol to the ECSC Treaty, draft brief by the Ministry of Power.

TNA (1957b), CAB 134/1675, Cabinet, Economic Policy Committee, 'Effects of the oil shortage', 22 March.

TNA (1957c), CAB 134/1675, 'Fuel and power industries; prices and the provision of capital finance', 26 March.

TNA (1957d), CAB 134/1675, EA(57)37, National Oil Reserve, Report of Sub-Committee on a National Oil Reserve, 12 April.

TNA (1957e), CAB 134/1677, EA(57)102, Economic Policy Committee, 'National Oil Reserve', memorandum by Minister of Power, 26 July.

TNA (1958), CAB 134/1680, E.A.(58)86, Cabinet, Economic Policy Committee, 'Fuel Problems', memorandum by the Minister of Power, 17 November.

TNA (1959a), AB7/8528, UKAEA, 'Nuclear projects of EDF'.

TNA (1959b), CAB 134/1577, CA(59)3, Council of Association between the United Kingdom Government and the High Authority of the European Coal and Steel Community, Fifth Report of the Trade Relations Committee, February.

TNA (1959c), CAB 134/1577, 'Brief on the fifth report of the Trade Relations Committee of the Council of Association', 20 February.

TNA (1959d), T234/593, 'Borrowings from the Exchequer: SSEB and NSHEB', 23 February.

TNA (1959e), CAB134/2251, 'Financial performance and obligations of nationalised bodies', 12 March.

TNA (1959f), CAB 134/2263, Committee on Nationalised Industries, report, 18 June.

TNA (1959g), T24/598, 'Radcliffe Report and the nationalised industries', 21 September.

TNA (1960a), T299/55, C. De Peyer (Ministry of Power) to R.L. Workman (Treasury), 25 April.

TNA (1960b), T299/55, Daniel (Ministry of Power) to Workman (Treasury), 6 May.

TNA (1960c), T299/55, Rome to Foreign Office, telegram, 7 May.

TNA (1960d), T319/250, Cabinet, Economic Policy Committee, 'Electricity prices; memorandum by the Minister of Power', 24 November.

TNA (1960e), T319/250, 'Electricity tariffs', J. Mark to M. Stevenson, 9 December.

TNA (1961a), CAB 134/2058, I.C.(61)1 and 2, 'Coal imports and the future of the coal industry', 5 June.

TNA (1961b), CAB 134/1520, C.M.N.(O)(61)26, Cabinet, Common Market Negotiations (Official) Committee, 'Oil and the Common Market', note by the Ministry of Power, 23 October.

TNA (1962a), CAB 134/1529, statement by Marjolin to the European Parliamentary Assembly, January.

TNA (1962b), CAB134/1528, CMN(O)(62)62, Cabinet, Common Market Negotiations Committee, 'Application of the pricing rules in the Treaty of Paris to the coal trade between the UK and the rest of the Community', note by the Ministry of Power, 27 February.

TNA (1962c), CAB 134/1527, C.M.N.(O)(62)51, Cabinet, Common Market Negotiations (Official) Committee, 'Restrictions on coal trade with the rest of the Community', note by the Ministry of Power, 20 February.

TNA (1962d), CAB 134/1529, CMN(O)(62)81, The 1957 Energy Protocol to the ECSC Treaty, draft brief by the Ministry of Power, 9 March.

TNA (1962e), CAB 134/1529, C.M.N.(O)(62)100, draft general brief for the ECSC negotiations, note by the Ministry of Power, 27 March.

TNA (1962f), T312/431, telegram to Foreign Office, Dixon, 28 March.

TNA (1962g), CAB 134/1695, EA(62)49, Economic Policy Committee, 'National Oil Reserve', memorandum by Minister of Power, 29 March.

TNA (1962h), CAB 134/1695, E.A.(62)62, Cabinet, Economic Policy Committee, 'Possible imports of Russian fuel oil', note, 4 May.

TNA (1962i), CAB 134/1696, Coal Reappraisal Group, 'Report', 13 June.

TNA (1962j), T319/250, 'Electricity tariffs', paper by J.L. Carr, 22 August.

TNA (1962k), CAB 134/1696, E.A.(62)115, Cabinet, Economic Policy Committee, 'Possible imports of Russian fuel oil', 2 November.

TNA (1962l), T312/428, K.L. Stock, 'Conversation with Monsieur Morin', 15 November.

TNA (1962m), T312/428, K.L. Stock, UK delegation to the EEC conference, Luxembourg, reported notes of conversation with M. Brondel of the European Commission, 21 November.

TNA (1962n), T312/428, K.L. Stock, 'Conversation with Monsieur Simon', 29 November.

TNA (1962o), CAB 134/1696, EA(62)127, Economic Policy Committee, 'Policy for Primary Fuels', memorandum by the Minister of Power, 7 December.

TNA (1962p), CAB 134/1696, Policy for Primary Fuels, December.

TNA (1963a), T312/433, 'Report on the conference for the accession of the UK to the ECSC, Luxembourg, September 1962–January 1963.

TNA (1963b), T312/428, Lucas to Owen, 1 February.

TNA (1963c), T312/431, letter D. Proctor (Ministry of Power) to W. Armstrong (Treasury), 27 February.

TNA (1963d), CAB 134/2269, N.P.(63)1, Report of the Working Party on Choice of Investment in Generating Stations, March.

TNA (1963e), CAB 134/1700, 'Electricity in Scotland', 20 June.

TNA (1963f), T319/15, contains an offprint of A.M. Alfred, 'Discounted cash flow; the proper assessment of investment projects', reprinted from *Investment Analyst*, no. 7, December 1963.

TNA (1963g), T312/710, UK Energy Policy, meeting, 31 December.

TNA (1963h), T319/250, E.C.(S)(63)4, Economic Section Discussion paper, 'Gas and Electricity Prices'.

TNA (1964a), T312/710, European Energy Policy, note, Carr to Clark, 10 January.

TNA (1964b), T319/8, notes, J.L. Carr, 6 April.

TNA (1964c), T312/710, UK delegation, telegram, 28 April.

TNA (1964d), POWE 58/76, 'Electricity', summary brief for Minister, 2 October.

TNA (1964e), T319/254, Report to the Secretary of State for Scotland, J.A. Dick, and A.D. Campbell, October.

TNA (1964f), T319/251, 'CEGB Bulk Supply Tariff Increases', Carr to Sargent.

TNA (1965a), T319/251, D.J. Bolton, 'A seasonal tariff for domestic supplies', PROC. IEE, 112 (2), February.

TNA (1965b), T319/253, 'Prices of secondary fuels', paper, J.L. Carr, 23 June.

TNA (1965c), POWE 58/38, 'Fuel policy review', memorandum, 6 July.

TNA (1965d), POWE 58/38, FPR 4(Final), Fuel Policy Review, memorandum on fuel policy, 14 July.

TNA (1965e), T230/744, Treasury press cutting, Duncan Burn, 'America's Lead in Nuclear Power', 27 July.

TNA (1965f), T319/34, 'Nationalised industries; control of investment programmes', 2 August.

TNA (1965g), T319/252, 'Electricity costs and prices', note to Mr Airey from J.L. Carr, 17 November.

TNA (1966a), T319/47, notes on the draft White Paper on Nationalised Industries.

TNA (1966b), T319/57, 'Financial targets, prices and investment policy of state enterprise', paper by R. Turvey, 28 January.

TNA (1966c), T319/47, 'Return on investment in private industry', 18 February.

TNA (1966d), POWE 58/43, FCC(66)10, Fuel Co-ordinating Committee, 'Tariffs', paper, 15 March.

TNA (1966e), POWE 58/57, 'University work on pricing policies', paper, Ministry of Power, 4 April.

TNA (1966f), CAB 134/1219, 'Economic Implications of UK membership of the European Communities; interim report by officials', July.

TNA (1966g), T319/57, 'Marginal cost of electricity generation', paper, P.V. Dixon, 21 July.

TNA (1967a), POWE 58/45, MCC 1/67.

TNA (1967b), POWE 58/45, note, Tucker to Bell, 2 February.

TNA (1967c), POWE 58/70, SOS(67)1, Interdepartmental Working Party on security of oil supplies, note of a meeting, 10 July.

TNA (1967d), POWE 58/71 MCC3/67, Ministerial Co-ordinating Committee, notes of a meeting, 10 October.

TNA (1967e), POWE 58/70, SOS(67)28, 'Security of Oil Supplies: Transport', paper, Ministry of Power, 16 November.

TNA (1967f), T319/789, letter, Middleton to Airey, 15 December.

TNA (1968a), T319/789, Posner to Vinter, 15 January.

TNA (1968b), T319/789, 'Test rate of discount', note, 17 January.

TNA (1968c), T319/789, note, Carr to Airey, 17 January.

TNA (1968d), T319/943, 'History', March.

TNA (1968e), T319/939, 'Public sector discount rates', 16 May 1968 and 23 April 1969.

TNA (1968f), T319/937, 'Test discount rate', meeting, 3 December.

TNA (1968g), T319/937, note, P. Mountfield, 5 December.

TNA (1968h), T319/937, note, Cairncross to Vinter, 18 December.

TNA (1968i), T319/937, note, M.V. Posner to W. Godley, 19 December.

TNA (1969), POWE 68/15, OECD Energy Committee, 'French Energy Policy', 8 May.

TNA (1970), CAB 184/10, 'Oil Policy: Report by a Working Party of Officials', 5 August.

TNA (1971), CAB 164/870, Interdepartmental Working Group on International Oil Questions, October.

TNA (1972), T319/1619, note, Price to Smith, 15 March.

Treasury, Government Economic Service (1979), *The Test Discount Rate and the Required Rate of Return on Investment*, Working Paper, No. 22 (Treasury Working Paper no. 9), January. 'The Test Discount Rate' by G.P. Smith (Treasury) *Test Discount Rate*, Treasury Working paper no. 9.

United Nations (1948), *Post-War Shortages of Food and Coal*, New York: Department of Economic Affairs.

United Nations (1976), *World Energy Supplies 1950–1974: Statistical Papers*, Series J, No. 19, New York: UN Statistical Office.

SECONDARY SOURCES

Acton, J.-P. (1976), 'The move towards marginal cost pricing in electricity', *Rand Paper Series*, P-5673.

Adelman, M. (1962), *The Supply and Price of Natural Gas*, Oxford: Blackwell.

Adelman, M. (1972), *The World Petroleum Market*, Baltimore, MD and London: Resources for the Future, Johns Hopkins University Press.

Adelman, M. (1982), 'Coping with supply insecurity', *The Energy Journal*, **3** (2), 1–17.

Adelman, M (1990), 'The 1990 oil shock is like the others', *The Energy Journal*, **11** (4), 1–13.

Ailleret, P. (1955), 'Estimation des besoins énergétiques', *Revue Française de l'Énergie*, **6** (September), 418–21.

Akerlof, G. (1970), 'The market for lemons: quality, uncertainty and the market mechanism', *Quarterly Journal of Economics*, **84** (3), 488–500.

Allais, M. (1943), *À la Recherche d'une Discipline Économique*, Paris: Imprimerie Industrial.

Allais, M. (1949), 'Rendement social et productivité sociale', *Econometrica*, **17**, 29–135.

Allais, M. (1952a), 'Étude théorique des conditions générales de l'aménagement économiquement optimum de la production, de la distribution et de l'utilisation des combustibles solides', *Annales des Mines*, **5**, 3–45.

Allais, M. (1952b), 'Étude théorique des conditions générales de l'aménagement économiquement optimum de la production, de la distribution et de l'utilisation des combustibles solides', *Annales des Mines*, **8**, 3–75.

Allais, M. (1961a), 'Les aspects essentiels de la politique de l'énergie', *Annales des Mines*, **VI**, 201–31.

Allais, M. (1961b), 'Les aspects essentiels de la politique de l'énergie (suite)', *Annales des Mines*, **IX**, 249–88.

Allais, M. (1989), *La Théorie générale des surplus*, Grenoble: Presses Universitaires de Grenoble.

Allais, M. (1994), *Traité de l'Économie Pure*, 3rd edn, Paris: Clément Juglar.

Anderson, D. (1981), *Regulatory Politics and Electric Utilities*, Boston, MA: Auburn House.

Arrow, K. (1966), 'Discounting and public investment criteria', in A. Kneese and S. Smith (eds), *Water Research*, Baltimore, MD: Resources for the Future, Johns Hopkins University Press.

Arrow, K.J. and G. Debreu (eds) (1959), *Theory of Value: An Axiomatic Analysis of Economic Equilibrium*, Cowles Foundation Monograph, No. 17, New York: Wiley.

Arrow, K. and M. Kurz (1970), *Public Investment, the Rate of Return and Optimal Fiscal Policy*, Baltimore, MD: Resources for the Future, Johns Hopkins University Press.

Arrow, K. and R. Lind (1970), 'Uncertainty and the evaluation of public investment decisions', *American Economic Review*, **60** (3), 364–78

Averch, H. and L.L. Johnson (1962), 'Behaviour of the firm under regulatory constraint', *American Economic Review*, **52** (December), 1052–69.

Badel, L. (ed.) (1996), *La Nationalisation de l'Électricité en France: nécessité technique ou logique politique?*, Paris: Presses Universitaires de France.

Bailey, E. and L. White (1974), 'Reversals in peak and off-peak prices', *Bell Journal of Economics and Management Science*, **5** (Spring), 75–92.

Barjot, D. and H. Morsel (1996), 'La nationalisation de l'électricité: nécessité technique ou logique politique?', in Badel (ed.), pp. 7–22.

Bates, R.W. and M.G. Webb (1968), 'Government control over investment planning in the nationalised electricity supply industry', *Bulletin of the Oxford University Institute of Economics and Statistics*, **30** (1), 37–53.

Baumol, W. (1968), 'On the social rate of discount', *American Economic Review*, **58** (4), 788–802.

Baumol, W. (1977), 'On the proper tests for a natural monopoly in a multiproduct industry', *American Economic Review*, **67** (5), 809–22.

Baumol, W.J. and D.F. Bradford (1970), 'Optimal departures from marginal cost pricing', *American Economic Review*, **60** (3), 265–83.

Baumol, W., P. Joskow and A. Kahn (1994), 'The challenge for federal and state regulators: transition from regulation to efficient competition in electric power', submitted by the Edison Electric Institute to FERC.

Baumol, W., J. Panzar and R. Willig (1982), *Contestable Markets and the Theory of Industry Structure*, New York: Harcourt, Brace, Jovanovich.

Baumol, W. and G. Sidak (1995a), 'Stranded costs', *Harvard Journal of Law and Public Policy*, **18**, 835–49.

Baumol, W. and G. Sidak (1995b), *Transmission Pricing and Stranded Costs in the Electric Power Industry*, Washington, DC: AEI Press.

Baumstark, L. and A. Bonnafous (2000), 'La relecture théorique de Jules Dupuit par Maurice Allais face à la question du service public', in P. Dockès, L. Frobert, G. Klotz, J.-P. Potoer and A. Tiran (eds) (2000), *Les Traditions Économiques Françaises, 1848–1939*, Paris: CNRS éditions, pp. 397–412.

Beltran, A. and J.-F. Picard (1987), 'EDF, pour la modernisation', in C. Andrieu (ed.), *Les Nationalisations de la Libération*, Paris: Presses de la Fondation Nationale des Sciences Politiques, pp. 330–38.

Bergougnoux, J., F. Careme and J.-J. Mosconi (1986), 'Tarification et financement; quelques approches dans le cas d'électricité en France', *Économies et Sociétés*, Série E.N. (2), 175–201.

Bernard, P. (1986), 'Éléments pour une rétrospective de la tarification: principes, modalités, procédures', in F. Cardot (ed.), *La France des Électriciens, 1880–1980*, Paris: Presses Universitaires de France, pp. 173–84.

Bierman, H. and S. Smidt (1960), *The Capital Budgetting Decision*, London and New York: Macmillan.

Blackford, M. (1970), 'Business men and the regulation of railroads and public utilities in California during the progressive era', *Business History Review*, **44** (3), 307–19.

Blaug, M. (1962), *Economic Theory in Retrospect*, Cambridge: Cambridge University Press.

Bohi, D. and M. Russell (1978), *Limiting Oil Imports: An Economic History and Analysis*, Baltimore, MD and London: Resources for the Future, Johns Hopkins University Press.

Boiteux, M. (1949), 'La tarification des demandes en pointe: application de la théorie de la vente au coût marginal', *Revue Générale d'Électricité*, **58** (August), 321–40. Translated as (1960), 'Peak load pricing', *Journal of Business*, **33** (April), 157–79.

Boiteux, M. (1951), 'Le revenu distribuable et les pertes économiques', *Econometrica* (April), 112–33.

Boiteux, M. (1956a), 'Sur la gestion des monopoles publics astreints à l'équilibre budgétaire', *Econometrica*, **24** (1), 22–40.

Boiteux, M. (1956b), 'La vente au coût marginal', *Revue Française de l'Énergie*, **78** (December), 113–17.

Boiteux, M. (1957), 'Le Tarif Vert d'Électricité de France', *Revue Française de l'Énergie* (January), 137–51.

Boiteux, M. (1960), 'L'énergie électrique; données, problèmes et perspectives', *Annales des Mines* (October), 81–97.

Boiteux, M. (1964), 'Electric energy: facts, problems and prospects', in Nelson (ed.), pp. 3–18.

Boiteux, M. (1969), 'Le service public de l'électricité et la concurrence', *Revue Française de l'Énergie*, **215** (October–November), 105–12.

Boiteux, M. (1971), 'On the management of public monopolies subject to budgetary constraints', *Journal of Economic Theory*, **3** (3), 219–40.

Boiteux, M. (1986), 'Faut-il renoncer au calcul économique?', in B. Munier (1986), *Marchés, Capital et Incertitude. Essais en l'honneur de Maurice Allais*, Paris: Economica, pp. 81–7.

Boiteux, M. (1989), 'Maurice Allais et l'économie appliquée', *Annales des Mines* (June), 38–40.

Boiteux, M. (1996), 'Intervention', in Badel (ed.), p. 237.

Borenstein, S., J. Bushnell and F. Wolak (2002), 'Measuring market inefficiencies in California's restructured wholesale electricity market', *American Economic Review*, **92** (5), 1376–405.

Bouneau, C. (1996), 'Les effets de la Grande Crise et de la guerre sur la reconstruction du réseau électrique français', in Badel (ed.), pp. 141–56.

Bousquet, G. (1947), 'Maurice Allais et l'économie pure', *Revue d'Économie Politique*, **3** (May–June), 477–85.

Brennan, T. and J. Boyd (1996), 'Stranded costs, takings, and the law and economics of implicit contracts', discussion paper 97-02, Resources for the Future, Washington, DC, October.

Breyer, S. (1982), *Regulation and Its Reform*, Cambridge, MA: Harvard University Press.

Breyer, S. and P. MacAvoy (1974), *Energy Regulation by the Federal Power Commission*, Washington, DC: Brookings Institution.

Brown, G. and M. Bruce Johnson (1969), 'Public utility pricing and output under risk', *American Economic Review*, **59** (March), 119–28.

Brown, S. and D. Sibley (1986), *The Theory of Public Utility Pricing*, Cambridge: Cambridge University Press.

Bungener, M. (1986), 'L'électricité et les trois premiers plans: une symbiose réussie', in H. Rousso (ed.), *De Monnet à Massé: Enjeux Politiques et Objectifs Économiques dans le Cadre des Quatre Premiers Plans (1946–1965)*, Paris: CNRS.

Bungener, M. and M. Joël (1989), 'Le genèse de l'économétrie au C.N.R.S.', *Les Cahiers pour l'histoire du C.N.R.S.*, 4 (October), 45–78.

Buzelay, A. (1971), *Vérité des Prix et Services Publiques*, Paris: Librarie Générale de Droit et de Jurisprudence.

Byatt, I. (1963), 'The genesis of the present pricing system in electricity supply, *Oxford Economic Papers*, n.s.**15** (1), 8–18.

Byatt, I. (1979), *The British Electrical Industry 1875–1914*, Oxford: Clarendon.

Campbell, R. (1968), *The Economics of Soviet Oil and Gas*, Baltimore, MD: Resources for the Future, Johns Hopkins University Press.

Caron, F. (1993), 'L'industrie: secteurs et branches', in F. Braudel and E. Labrousse (eds), *Histoire Économique et Sociale de la France IV, 3, 1950–1980*, Paris: Presses Universitaires de France, pp. 1231–320.

Carr, J. (1966), 'Social time preference versus social opportunity cost in investment criteria', *Economic Journal* (December), 933–4.

Chapuis, C. (1998), 'Chernobyl: France', *The Energy Journal*, **9** (1), 31–4.

Chevalier, J., P. Barbet and L. Benzoni (1986), *Économie de l'Énergie*, Paris: Presses de la Fondation Nationale des Sciences Politiques.

Chick, M. (ed.) (1990), *Governments, Industries and Markets*, Aldershot and Brookfield, US: Edward Elgar.

Chick, M. (1991), 'Competition, competitiveness and nationalisation', in G. Jones and M. Kirby (eds), *Competitiveness and the State*, Manchester: Manchester University Press, pp. 60–77.

Chick, M. (1994), 'Nationalisation, privatisation and regulation', in M. Rose and M. Kirby (eds), *Business Enterprise in Modern Britain*, London and New York: Routledge.

Chick, M. (1995), 'The political economy of nationalisation: the electricity industry', in R. Millward and J. Singleton (eds), *The Political Economy of Nationalisation in Britain 1920–1950*, Cambridge: Cambridge University Press, pp. 257–74.

Chick, M. (1998), *Industrial Policy in Britain 1945–1951: Economic Planning, Nationalisation and the Labour Governments*, Cambridge: Cambridge University Press.

Chick, M. (2002), 'Le Tarif Vert retrouvé: the marginal cost concept and the pricing of electricity in Britain and France, 1945–1970', *The Energy Journal*, **23** (1), 97–116.

Chick, M. (2003), 'Productivité, politique tarifaire et investissements dans les entreprises électriques nationalisées françaises et britanniques, 1945–1973', *Annales Historiques de l'Électricité*, **1** (June), 71–102.

Chick, M. (2004), 'The power of networks: defining the boundaries of the natural monopoly network and the implications for the restructuring of electricity supply industries', *Annales Historiques de l'Électricité*, **2** (May), 30–56.

Chick, M. (2006a), 'The marginalist approach and the making of fuel policy in France and Britain, 1945–72', *Economic History Review*, **LIX** (1), 143–67.

Chick, M. (2006b), 'Sécurité nationale, conflit et ravitaillement en carburant et en énergie électrique dans la Grande-Bretagne en guerre', in D. Varaschin (ed.), *Les Entreprises du Secteur de l'Énergie sous l'Occupation*, Arras: Artois Presses Université, pp. 235–47.

Clarke, R. (1978), A. Cairncross (ed.), *Public Expenditure Management and Control: the Development of the Public Expenditure Survey Committee*, London: Macmillan.

Clemens, E. (1941), 'Price discrimination in decreasing cost industries', *American Economic Review*, **31** (4), 794–802.

Coase, R. (1945), 'Price and output policy of state enterprise: a comment', *Economic Journal*, **55** (217), 112–13.

Coase, R. (1946), 'The marginal cost controversy', *Economica*, n.s., **13** (51), 169–82.

Colson, C. (1890), *Transports et Tarifs*, Paris: Rothschild.

Crafts, N. and G. Toniolo (1996), *Economic Growth in Europe since 1945*, Cambridge and New York: Cambridge University Press.

Crew, M., C. Fernando and P. Kleindorfer (1995), 'The theory of peak-load pricing: a survey', *Journal of Regulatory Economics*, **8**, 215–48.

Crew, M. and P. Kleindorfer (1978), 'Reliability and public utility pricing', *American Economic Review*, **68** (1), 31–40.

Crew, M. and P. Kleindorfer (1986), *The Economics of Public Utility Regulation*, Cambridge, MA: MIT Press.

Darmois, G. (2004), *Pourquoi Privatiser? EDF et l'Enjeu de l'Énergie*, Paris: Débats, Belin.

Dasgupta, P. and G. Heal (1979), *Economic Theory and Exhaustible Resources*, Cambridge: Cambridge University Press.

Dean, J. (1951), *Capital Budgeting*, New York: Colombia University Press.

Dean, J. (1954), 'Measuring the productivity of capital', *Harvard Business Review*, **32** (January–February), 120–30.

Debreu, G. (1952), 'A classical tax-subsidy problem', *Econometrica*, **22** (1), 14–22.

Delavesne, Y. (1960), 'L'industrie du pétrole', *Annales des Mines*, **VI** (June), 45–58.

Derthick, M. and P. Quirk (1985), *The Politics of Deregulation*, Washington, DC: Brookings Institution.

Desrousseaux, J. (1965), 'La table ronde des charbonnages 1963–1965', *Revue Française de l'Énergie*, **174** (October), 30–36.

Dessus, G. (1949a), 'Les principes généraux de la tarification dans les services publics', report to the Comité d'Études de la Tarification, Union Interationale des Producteurs et Distributeurs d'Énergie Électrique (UNIPEDE), Brussels, 19–24 September, Paper VI.5. Reprinted in translation as 'The general principles of rate-fixing in public utilities', in Nelson (ed.) (1964), pp. 31–49.

Dessus, G. (1949b), 'Perspectives commerciales sur les fournitures d'énergie électrique à l'industrie', *Revue Française de l'Énergie* (September), 20–26.

Dokic, J. and P. Engel (2001), *Ramsey: Vérité et Succès*, Paris: Presses Universitaires de France.

Drèze, J. (1964), 'Some postwar contributions of French economists to theory and public policy', *American Economic Review*, **54** (4), part 2, 1–64.

Dupuit, J. (1844), 'De la mesure de l'utilité des travaux publics', *Annales des Ponts et Chaussées*, 2nd series, 2nd semester, Mémoires et Documents, **116**, viii, 332–75.

Ebel, R. (1961), *The Petroleum Industry of the Soviet Union*, New York: American Petroleum Institute.

Eckstein, O. (1958), *Water Resource Development*, Cambridge, MA: Harvard University Press.

Ekelund Jr, R. and R. Hébert (1999), *Secret Origins of Modern Microeconomics: Dupuit and the Engineers*, Chicago and London: University of Chicago Press.

Estrin, S. and P. Holmes (1983), *French Planning in Theory and Practice*, London: George Allen & Unwin.

Etner, F. (2000), *Histoire de la Pensée Économique*, Paris: Economica.

Feinstein, C.H. (1972), *Statistical Tables of National Income, Expenditure and Output of the U.K., 1855–1965*, Cambridge: Cambridge University Press.

Feldstein, M. (1964), 'The social time preference discount rate in cost–benefit analysis', *Economic Journal*, **74** (294), 360–79.

Fisher, I. (1907), *The Rate of Interest*, New York: Macmillan.

Fisher, I. (1930), *The Theory of Interest*, London and New York: Macmillan.

Florio, M. (2004), *The Great Divestiture: Evaluating the Welfare Impact of the British Privatizations 1979–1997*, Cambridge, MA and London: MIT Press.

Foreman-Peck, J. and R. Millward (1994), *Public and Private Ownership of British Industry, 1820–1990*, Oxford: Clarendon.

Fourastié, J. (1979), *Les Trente Glorieuses: (ou la Révolution Invisible de 1946 à 1975)*, Paris: Fayard.

Fourquet, F. (1980), *Les Comptes de la Puissance, Histoire de la Comptabilité Nationale et du Plan*, Paris: Recherches.

Frost, R. (1991), *Alternating Currents*, Ithaca, NY and London: Cornell University Press.

Gaspard, R. and P. Massé (1952), 'Le choix des investissements énergétiques et la production d'électricité en France', *Revue Française de l'Énergie*, **35** (October), 5–15.

Gilbert, R. and E. Kahn (eds) (1996a), *International Comparisons of Electricity Regulation*, Cambridge: Cambridge University Press.

Gilbert, R. and E. Kahn (1996b), 'Competition and institutional change in U.S. electric power regulation', in Gilbert and Kahn (eds), pp. 179–230.

Gilbert, R., E. Kahn and D. Newbery (1996), 'Introduction', in Gilbert and Kahn (eds), pp. 1–24.

Giraud, A., P. Guillaumat and O. Guichard (1967), 'Trois documents definissent la politique pétrolière Française', *Revue Pétrolière* (November), 21–7.

Glachant, J.-M. (1989), 'Maurice Allais et la fondation d'une seconde école Française de tarification rationnelle des entreprises publiques', *Économies et Sociétés*, serie Œconomica, PE, no. 11, 109–40.

Glachant, J.-M. and D. Finon (2005), 'A competitive fringe in the shadow of a state-owned incumbent: the case of France', *The Energy Journal*, special edition on European electricity liberalisation (Summer), 181–204.

Glyn, A. (1984), *The Economic Case Against Pit Closures*, Sheffield: National Union of Mineworkers.

Goldman, M. Barry, H.E. Leland and D. Sibley (1984), 'Optimal nonuniform pricing', *Review of Economic Studies*, **51** (2), 305–19.

Gordon, R. (1981), *An Economic Analysis of World Energy Problems*, Cambridge, MA and London: MIT Press.

Gordon, R. (1982), *Reforming the Regulation of Electric Utilities*, Lexington, MA: Lexington Books.

Gordon, R. (1992), 'Energy intervention after *Desert Storm*: some unfinished tasks', *The Energy Journal*, **13** (4), 1–15.

Gouni, L. (1961), 'La politique d'ensemble de l'énergie', *Revue Française de l'Énergie*, **129**, 340–58.

Gray, H. (1940), 'The passing of the public utility concept', *Journal of Land and Public Utility Economics*, **16** (1), 8–20.

Green, R. (2005), 'Restructuring the electricity industry in England and Wales', in Griffin and Puller (eds), pp. 98–144.

Green, R. and D. Newbery (1992), 'Competition in the British electricity spot market', *Journal of Political Economy*, **100** (5), 929–53.

Griffin, J. and S. Puller (eds) (2005), *Electricity Deregulation: Choices and Challenges*, Chicago and London: University of Chicago Press.

Hannah, L. (1979), *Electricity Before Nationalisation: A Study of the Development of the Electricity Supply Industry in Britain to 1948*, London: Macmillan.

Hannah, L. (1982), *Engineers, Managers and Politicians*, London: Macmillan.

Hartshorn, J. (1967), *Oil Companies and Governments*, London: Faber & Faber.

Hausman, W. and J. Neufeld (1984), 'Time-of-day pricing in the U.S. electric power industry at the turn of the century', *Rand Journal of Economics*, **15** (1), 116–26.

Havlik, H. (1938), *Service Charges in Gas and Electric Rates*, New York: Columbia University Press.

Heald, D. (1980), 'The economic and financial control of the UK nationalised industries', *Economic Journal*, **90** (358), 243–65.

Hecht, G. (1998), *The Radiance of France: Nuclear Power and National Identity after World War II*, Cambridge, MA and London: MIT Press.

Helm, D. (2003), *Energy, the State and the Market: British Energy Policy since 1979*, Oxford: Oxford University Press.

Helm, D. (2005a), 'The assessment: the new energy paradigm', *Oxford Review of Economic Policy*, **21** (1), 1–18.

Helm, D. (2005b), *Climate-change Policy*, Oxford: Oxford University Press.

Helm, D. (2005c), 'Climate-change Policy: a survey', in Helm (2005b), pp. 11–29.

Henney, A. (1994), *A Study of the Privatisation of the Electricity Supply Industry in England and Wales*, London: EEE.

Hirsh, R. (1989), *Technology and Transformation in the American Electric Utility Industry*, Cambridge and New York: Cambridge University Press.

Hirsh, R. (1999), *Power Loss: The Origins of Deregulation and Restructuring in the American Electric Utility System*, Cambridge, MA: MIT Press.

Hirshleifer, J. (1958a), 'Peak loads and efficient pricing: comment', *Quarterly Journal of Economics*, **72** (3), 451–62.

Hirshleifer, J. (1958b), 'On the theory of optimal investment decisions', *Journal of Political Economy*, **66** (4) (August), 329–52.

Hirshleifer, J., J. DeHaven and J. Milliman (1960), *Water Supply: Economics, Technology and Policy*, Chicago: University of Chicago Press.

Hirst, E. and L. Baxter (1995), 'How stranded will electric utilities be?', *Public Utilities Fortnightly* (15 February), 30–32.

Hopkinson, J. (1892–93), 'The costs of electricity supply', Presidential Address to the Junior Engineering Society, *Transactions*, **3**, 33–46.

Hotelling, H. (1931), 'The economics of exhaustible resources', *Journal of Political Economy*, **39** (2), 137–75.

Hotelling, H. (1938), 'The general welfare in relation to problems of taxation and of railway and utility rates', *Econometrica*, **6** (3), 242–69.

Hughes, T. (1983), *Networks of Power: Electrification in Western Society, 1880–1930*, Baltimore, MD: Johns Hopkins University Press.

Hunt, S. (2002), *Making Competition Work in Electricity*, New York: John Wiley.

Hunter, M. (1917), 'Early regulation of public service corporations', *American Economic Review*, **7** (September), 569–81.

Hutter, R. (1950a), 'Qu'est-ce que le coût marginal?', *Revue Générale des Chemins de Fer* (February), 53–63.

Hutter, R. (1950b), 'La théorie économique et la gestion commerciale des chemins de fer: le problème tarifaire', *Revue Générale des Chemins de Fer* (July), 318–32.

Jamasb, T. and M. Pollitt (2005), 'Electricity market reform in the European Union: Review of progress towards liberalisation and integration', *The Energy Journal*, European Electricity Liberalisation Special Issue, 11–41.

Jeanneney, J.-M. (1956), *Forces et Faiblesses de l'Économie Française*, Paris: A. Colin.

Jeanneney, J.-M. (1997), *Une Mémoire Républicaine*, Paris: Seuil.

Jeanneney, J.-M. and Claude-Albert Colliard (1950), *Économie et Droit de l'Électricité*, Paris: Domat Monschrétien.

Joly, H. (1996), 'Les dirigeants des entreprises électriques face à la nationalisation: ressources personnelles et trajectoires ultérieures', in Badel (ed.), pp. 243–55.

Joskow, P. (1974), 'Inflation and environmental concern: structural change in the process of public utility price regulation', *Journal of Law and Economics*, **17** (2) (October), 291–327.

Joskow, P. (1976), 'Contributions to the theory of marginal cost pricing', *Bell Journal of Economics*, **7** (1), 197–206.

Joskow, P. (1979a), 'Public Utility Regulatory Policies Act of 1978: electric utility rate reform', *Natural Resources Journal*, **19** (October), 787–809.

Joskow, P. (1979b), 'Electricity utility rate structures in the United States: some recent developments', in W. Sichel (ed.), *Public Utility Rate Making in an Energy Conscious Environment*, Boulder, CO: Westview, pp. 1–22.

Joskow, P. (2000), 'Deregulation and regulatory reform in the U.S. electric power sector', in S. Peltzman and C. Winston (eds), *Deregulation of Network Industries: The Next Steps*, Washington, DC: AEI-Brookings Joint Centre for Regulatory Studies, pp. 113–88.

Joskow, P. (2001), 'California's electricity crisis', *Oxford Review of Economic Policy*, **17** (3), 365–88.

Joskow, P. (2005), 'The difficult transition to competitive electricity markets in the United States', in Griffin and Puller (eds), pp. 31–97.

Joskow, P. (2006), 'Markets for power in the United States: an interim assessment', *The Energy Journal*, **27** (1), 1–36.

Joskow, P., D. Bohi and F. Gallop (1989), 'Regulatory failure, regulatory reform, and structural change in the electrical power industry', *Brookings Papers on Economic Activity: Microeconomics*, Washington, DC: Brookings Institution, pp. 125–208.

Joskow, P. and D. Jones (1983), 'The simple economics of industrial cogeneration', *The Energy Journal*, **4** (1), 1–22.

Joskow, P. and E. Kahn (2002), 'A quantitative analysis of pricing behaviour in California's wholesale electricity market during summer 2000: the final word', *The Energy Journal*, **28** (4), 1–35.

Joskow, P. and R. Schmalensee (1983), *Markets for Power: An Analysis of Electric Deregulation*, Cambridge, MA: MIT Press.

Joskow, P. and R. Schmalensee (1986), 'Incentive regulation for electric utilities', *Yale Journal on Regulation*, **4** (1) (Fall), 1–49.

Joskow, P. and J. Tirole (2000), 'Transmission rights and market power on electric power networks. I: Financial rights', *Rand Journal of Economics*, **31** (3), 450–87.

Kahn, A. (1988), *The Economics of Regulation: Principles and Institutions*, Cambridge, MA: MIT Press. First published in two volumes: *The Economics of Regulation: Principles and Institutions* (I: *Economic Principles*, 1970; II: *Institutional Issues*, 1971), New York: John Wiley & Sons.

Kay, J. and D. Thompson (1986), 'Privatisation: a policy in search of a rationale', *Economic Journal*, **96** (381), 18–32.

Kipping, M. (2002), *La France et les Origines de l'Union Européenne, 1944–1952*, Paris: CHEFF.

Kissinger, H. (1982), *Years of Upheaval*, Boston, MA: Little Brown.

Kissinger, H. (1990), *Years of Renewal*, New York: Simon & Schuster.

Koopmans, T. (1939), *Tanker Freight Rates and Tankship Building*, Amsterdam: Haarlem.

Krapels, E. (1980), 'Oil and security: problems and prospects of importing countries', in G. Treverton (ed.), *Energy and Security*, Farnborough, UK and Montclair, NJ: Gower, pp. 40–73.

Krutilla, J. and O. Eckstein (1958), *Multiple Purpose River Development*, Baltimore, MD: Resources for the Future: Johns Hopkins University Press.

Kuisel, R. (1984), *Le Capitalisme et l'État en France. Modernisation et Dirigisme au XXième siècle*, Paris: Gallimard.

LaCasse, C. and A. Plourde (1995), 'On the renewal of concern for the security of oil supply', *The Energy Journal*, **16** (2), 1–23.

Laffont, J.-J. and J. Tirole (1991), 'The politics of government decision-making: a theory of regulatory capture', *Quarterly Journal of Economics*, **106** (4), 1089–127.

Lanthier, P. (1979), 'Les dirigeants des grandes entreprises électriques en France, 1911–1973', in M. Lévy-Leboyer (ed.), *Le Patronat de la Seconde Industrialisation*, Paris: Éditions Ouvrières, pp. 111–13.

Laqueur, W. (1972), *The Struggle for the Middle East: The Soviet Union and the Middle East, 1958–1968*, Harmondsworth: Penguin.

Lerner, A. (1944), *The Economics of Control: Principles of Welfare Economics*, London and New York: Macmillan.

Lévy-Leboyer, M. and H. Morsel (1994), *Histoire de l'Électricité en France, 1919–1946*, Poitiers: Fayard.

Lind, R. (ed.) (1982), *Discounting for Time and Risk in Energy Policy*, Baltimore, MD: Resources for the Future, Johns Hopkins University Press.

Little, I. (1953), *The Price of Fuel*, Oxford: Clarendon.

Lorie, J. and L. Savage (1955), 'Three problems in rationing capital', *Journal of Business*, **28** (4), 229–39.

Lucas, N. (1985), *Western European Energy Policies*, Oxford: Clarendon.

Lynch, F. (1984), 'Resolving the paradox of the Monnet Plan: national and international planning in French reconstruction', *Economic History Review*, 2nd series, **37** (2), 229–43.

Maass, A. (ed.) (1962), *Design of Water Resource Systems*, Cambridge, MA: Harvard University Press.

MacAvoy, P. and R. Pindyck (1975), *Price Controls and the Natural Gas Shortage*, Washington, DC: American Enterprise Institute for Public Policy Research.

MacGregor, I. (1986), *The Enemies Within: The Story of the Miners' Strike, 1984–85*, London: Collins.

Madelin, H. (1975), *Oil and Politics*, Farnborough, UK: Saxon House.

Malégarie, C. (1947), *L'Électricité à Paris*, Paris: Ch. Béranger.

Maleville, G. (1996), 'Le Rôle de Paul Ramadier', in Badel (ed.), pp. 315–20.

Malterre, M.A. (1956), 'L'influence de la crise de Suez sur l'évolution de l'économie française durant le premier semestre 1957: extracts from a report by M.A. Malterre to Economic Council', *Revue Française de l'Énergie* (December), 118–26.

Margairaz, M. (1996), 'Le précipité d'une double histoire', in Badel (ed.), pp. 83–93.

Marglin, S. (1963a), *Approaches to Dynamic Investment*, Amsterdam: North-Holland.

Marglin, S.A. (1963b), 'The social rate of discount and the optimal rate of investment', *Quarterly Journal of Economics*, **77** (1), 95–111.

Massé, P. (1945), *Les Réserves et la Régulation de l'Avenir*, 2 vols, Paris: Hermann.

Massé, P. (1954), 'Quelques problèmes d'optimum économique', in *Stratégies et Décisions Économiques Études Théoriques et Applications aux Entreprises*, Paris: CNRS.

Massé, P. (1959), *Le Choix des Investissements*, Paris: Dunod. Translated as P. Massé (1962), *Optimal Investment Decisions: Rules for Action and Criteria for Choice*, Englewood Cliffs, NJ: Prentice-Hall.

Massé, P. (1965), 'The French Plan and economic theory', *Econometrica*, **33** (2), 265–76.

Massé, P. (1967), 'L'électricité en France', *Revue Française de l'Énergie*, **190** (May), 343–60.

Massé, P. (1984), *Aléas et Progrès: Entre Candide et Cassandre*, Paris: Economica.

Matláry, J. (1997), *Energy Policy in the European Union*, Basingstoke and London: Macmillan.

Maull, H. (1980a), *Europe and World Energy*, London: Butterworth.

Maull, H. (1980b), 'Oil and influence: the oil weapon examined', in G. Treverton (ed.) (1980), *Energy and Security*, Farnborough, UK: Gower, pp. 3–39.

McCraw, T. (1984), *Prophets of Regulation*, Cambridge, MA: Belknap Press of Harvard University Press.

McKean, R. (1958), *Efficiency in Government through Systems Analysis*, New York: Wiley.

Meade, J. (1936), *An Introduction to Economic Analysis and Policy*, Oxford: Clarendon.

Meade, J. (1948), *Planning and the Price Mechanism*, London: Geo. Allen & Unwin. French translation by G. Lenoan (1952), *Plans et Prix, Entre Socialisme et Libéralisme*, Paris: M. Rivière.

Meade, J. and J. Fleming (1944), 'Price and output policy of state enterprise', *Economic Journal*, **54** (December), 321–39.

Meadows, D., D. Meadows, J. Randers and W. Behrens (1972), *The Limits to Growth: A Report for The Club of Rome's Project on the Predicament of Mankind*, New York: Universe Books.

Meek, R. (1963a), 'An application of marginal cost pricing: the "Green Tariff" in theory and practice. Part 1', *Journal of Industrial Economics*, **11** (3), 217–36.

Meek, R. (1963b), 'An application of marginal cost pricing: the "Green Tariff" in theory and practice. Part II', *Journal of Industrial Economics*, **12** (1), 45–63.

Meek, R. (1968), 'The new bulk supply tariff for electricity', *Economic Journal*, **78** (309), 44–66.

Merrett, A.J. and A. Sykes (1962a), 'Financial control of state industry: I. The present confusions', *The Banker*, **112** (March), 156–64.

Merrett, A. and A. Sykes (1962b), 'Financial control of state industry: II. New approaches', *The Banker*, **112** (April), 227–34.

Merrett, A. and A. Sykes (1963a), 'Incomes policy and company profitability', *District Bank Review*, **147** (September), 18–30.

Merrett, A. and A. Sykes (1963b), 'Return on equities and fixed interest securities, 1919–1963', *District Bank Review*, **148** (December), 17–34.

Merrett, A. and A. Sykes (1966), 'Return on equities and fixed interest securities, 1919–1966', *District Bank Review* (June), 29–44.

Middleton, R. (1996), *Government Versus the Market: The Growth of the Public Sector, Economic Management and British Economic Performance, c. 1890–1979*, Cheltenham, UK and Brookfield, US: Edward Elgar.

Millward, R. (1971), *Public Expenditure Economics*, Maidenhead: McGraw-Hill.

Millward, R. (1976), 'Price restraint, anti-inflation policy and public and private industry in the UK', *Economic Journal*, **86** (342), 226–42.

Millward, R. (2005), *Private and Public Enterprise in Europe: Energy, Telecommunications and Transport, 1830–1990*, Cambridge and New York: Cambridge University Press.

Milward, A. (1984), *The Reconstruction of Western Europe*, London: Methuen.

Milward, A. (1992), *The European Rescue of the Nation State*, London: Routledge.

Milward, A. (2002), *The Rise and Fall of a National Strategy 1945–1963*, London: Whitehall History Publishing, Frank Cass.

Mitchell, B., W. Manning and J. Acton (1978), *Peak-Load Pricing: European Lessons for U.S. Energy Policy*, Cambridge, MA: Ballinger.

Mohring, H. (1970), 'The peak load problem with increasing returns and pricing constraints', *American Economic Review*, **160** (4), 693–705.

Monnier, L. (1983), *La Tarification de l'Électricité en France*, Paris: Economica.

Moore, J. (1986), 'Why privatise?', in J. Kay, C. Mayer and D. Thompson (eds) (1986), *Privatisation and Regulation: The UK Experience*, Oxford: Clarendon, pp. 78–93.

Morlat, G. and F. Bessière (eds) (1971), *Vingt-cinq Ans d'Économie Électrique*, Monographies de Recherche Opérationnelle, 11, Paris: Dunod.

Morsel, H. (ed.) (1996), *Histoire Générale de l'Électricité en France, vol. 3 1946–1987*, Poitiers: Fayard.

Munby, D. (ed.) (1978), *Transport*, London: Penguin.

Nelson, J. (ed.) (1964), *Marginal Cost Pricing in Practice*, Englewood Cliffs, NJ: Prentice-Hall.

Newbery, D. (1999), *Privatization, Restructuring and Regulation of Network Utilities*, Cambridge, MA and London: MIT Press.

Newbery, D. (2005a), 'Introduction', *The Energy Journal*, Special Issue, European Electricity Liberalisation, **26**, 1–10.

Newbery, D. (2005b), 'Electricity liberalisation in Britain: the quest for a satisfactory wholesale market design', *The Energy Journal*, Special Issue, European Electricity Liberalisation, **26**, 43–70.

Newbery, D. and R. Green (1996), 'Regulation, public ownership and privatisation of the English electricity industry', in Gilbert and Kahn (eds), pp. 25–81.

Nissel, H. (1976), *The Electric Rate Question: Europe Revisited*, Washington, DC: Electricity Consumers Resource Council.

O'Mahony, M. and M. Vecchi (2001), 'The electricity supply industry: a study of an industry in transition', *National Institute Economic Review*, **177** (3), 85–99.

Okogu, B. (1992), 'What use the IEA emergency stockpiles? A price-based model of oil stock management', *The Energy Journal*, **13** (1), 79–96.

Paine, C.L. (1937), 'Some aspects of discrimination by public utilities', *Economica*, n.s., **4** (16), 425–39.

Parkinson, C. (1992), *Right at the Centre*, London: Weidenfeld & Nicolson.

Parra, F. (2004), *Oil Politics: A Modern History of Petroleum*, London and New York: I.B. Tauris.

Payne, P.L. (1988), *The Hydro*, Aberdeen: Aberdeen University Press.

Pearce, D. (1971), *Cost–Benefit Analysis*, London: Macmillan.

Perron, R. (1996), *Le Marché du Charbon: Un Enjeu entre l'Europe et les Etats-Unis de 1945 à 1958*, Paris: Publications de la Sorbonne.

Phillips, Jr, C. (1984), *The Regulation of Public Utilities*, Arlington, VA: Public Utilities Reports.

Picard, J. (1951), 'Le charbon Américain et l'approvisionnement Français', *Revue Française de l'Énergie* (December), 66–72.

Picard, J.-F., A. Beltran and M. Bungener (1985), *Histoire(s) de l'EDF: Comment Se Sont Prises les Décisions de 1946 à Nos Jours*, Paris: Dunod.

Posner, M. (1973), *Fuel Policy: A Study in Applied Economics*, London: Macmillan.

Pratten, C. (1990), *Applied Macroeconomics*, Oxford: Oxford University Press.

Quennouëlle-Corre, L. (2000), *La direction du Trésor 1947–1967: L'État-banquier et la Croissance*, Paris: CHEFF.

Ramsey, F. (1927), 'A contribution to the theory of taxation', *Economic Journal*, **37** (145), 47–61.

Randall Curlee, T. and A. Wright (1988), 'Spinning wheels: a review article', *The Energy Journal*, **9** (2), 3–16.

Ray, G. (1982), 'Europe's farewell to full employment?', in D. Yergin and M. Hillenbrand (eds) (1982), *Global Insecurity: A Strategy for Energy and Economic Renewal*, London: Penguin, pp. 200–229.

Ray, G. and L. Uhlmann (1979), *The Innovation Process in the Energy Industries*, Cambridge and New York: Cambridge University Press.

Robinson, C. (1974), *The Energy Crisis and British Coal*, Lancing: Institute of Economic Affairs.

Robinson, C. and E. Marshall (1981), *What Future for British Coal?*, Lancing: Institute of Economic Affairs.

Rostow, E. (1948), *A National Policy for the Oil Industry*, New Haven, CT: Yale University Press.

Rothschild, M. and J. Stiglitz (1976), 'Equilibrium in competitive insurance markets: an essay in the economics of imperfect information', *Quarterly Journal of Economics*, **90** (4), 629–49.

Rueff, J. and L. Armand (1960), *Rapport sur les obstacles à l'éxpansion économique*, Paris: Imprimerie Nationale.

Schumpeter, J. (1954), *History of Economic Analysis*, pbk (1994), London: Routledge.

Scott, R. (1994), *The History of the International Energy Agency: The First Twenty Years*, 2 vols, Paris: OECD.

Sharkey, W. (1982), *The Theory of Natural Monopoly*, Cambridge: Cambridge University Press.

Sherman, R. and M. Visscher (1978), 'Second-best pricing with stochastic demand', *American Economic Review*, **68** (1), 41–53.

Solomon, E. (1956), 'The arithmetic of capital budgeting decision', *Journal of Business*, **39** (April), 124–9.

Solomon, E. (1959), *The Management of Corporate Capital*, Glencoe, IL: Free Press.

Solow, R. (1974), 'The economics of resources or the resources of economics', *American Economic Review*, **64** (2), 1–14.

Soult, F. (2003), *EDF: Chronique d'un Désastre Ineluctable*, Paris: Calmann-Lévy.

Spierenburg, D. and R. Poidevin (1994), *The History of the High Authority of the European Coal and Steel Community*, London: Weidenfeld & Nicolson.

Stasi, P. (1956a), 'Les prix de l'électricité en France et à l'étranger', *Revue Française de l'Énergie*, **17** (76) (June), 331–6.

Stasi, P. (1956b), 'Les prix de l'électricité en France et à l'étranger', *Revue Française de l'Énergie*, **17** (78) (September), 434–40.

Steiner, P. (1957), 'Peak loads and efficient pricing', *Quarterly Journal of Economics*, **71** (4), 585–610.

Stelzer, I. (1970), 'Utility pricing under inflation, competition and environmental concerns', *Public Utilities Fortnightly*, 17–23 (3 December).

Stern, J. (2005), *The Future of Russian Gas and Gazprom*, Oxford: Oxford University Press.

Stevens, P. (2003), 'Economists and the oil industry: facts versus analysis, the case of vertical integration', in L. Hunt (ed.), *Energy in a Competitive Market*, Cheltenham, UK and Northampton, MA, US: Edward Elgar.

Stigler, G. (1971), 'The theory of economic regulation', *Bell Journal of Economics and Management Science*, **2** (1), 3–21.

Stigler, G. and C. Friedland (1962), 'What can regulators regulate? The case of electricity?', *Journal of Law and Economics*, **5** (October), 1–16.

Stiglitz, J. (1976), 'Monopoly and the rate of extraction of exhaustible resources', *American Economic Review*, **66** (4), 655–61.

Stoft, S. (1997), 'What should a power market want?', *Electricity Journal*, **10** (5), 34–45.

Straus, A. (1994), 'Le financement de l'industrie électrique par le marché financier en France des années 1890 aux années 1980', in M. Trédé-Boulmer (ed.), *Le Financement de l'Industrie Électrique, 1880–1980*, Paris: Presses Universitaires de France, pp. 233–58.

Teisberg, T. (1981), 'A dynamic programming model of the US strategic petroleum reserve', *Bell Journal of Economics*, **12** (2), 526–46.

Tietenberg, T. (1996), *Environmental and Natural Resource Economics*, New York: Harper Collins.

Tinbergen, J. (1959), 'Tonnage and freight', *De Nederlandsche Conjunctur*, reprinted in L. Klaasen, L. Koyck and H. Wilteven (eds) (1959), *Jan Tinbergen: Selected Papers*, Amsterdam: North-Holland, pp. 93–111.

Tobin, J. (1963), 'How planned is our economy?', *New York Times Magazine*, 13 October.

Toman, M. and M. Macauley (1986), 'Risk aversion and the insurance value of strategic oil stockpiling', *Resources and Energy*, **8** (2), 151–65.

Turvey, R. (1968), *Optimal Pricing and Investment in Electricity Supply*, London and Cambridge, MA: Allen & Unwin.

Viala, A. (1960), 'L'importation charbonnière', *Revue Française de l'Énergie*, **124** (December), 116–26.

Vietor, R. (1984), *Energy Policy in America since 1945*, Cambridge: Cambridge University Press.

Vietor, R. (1994), *Contrived Competition: Regulation and Deregulation in America*, Cambridge, MA and London: The Belknap Press of Harvard University.

Viscusi, W., Kip, J. Harrington and J. Vernon (2005), *Economics of Regulation and Antitrust*, Cambridge, MA: MIT Press.

Weart, S. (1979), *Scientists in Power*, Cambridge, MA and London: Harvard University Press.

Webb, M. (1966), 'Rate of discount and inflation with particular reference to the electricity supply industry', *Oxford Economic Papers*, **18** (3), 352–8.

Wenders, J. (1976), 'Peak-load pricing in the electric utility industry', *Bell Journal of Economics*, **7** (1), 232–41.

Weyman-Jones, T. (1986), *Energy in Europe*, London and New York: Methuen.

Weyman-Jones, T. (2003), 'Yardstick competition and efficiency benchmarking in electricity distribution', in L. Hunt (ed.) (2003), *Energy in a Competitive Market*, Cheltenham, UK and Northampton, MA, US: Edward Elgar, pp. 35–60.

Willig, R. (1978), 'Pareto-superior nonlinear outlay schedules', *Bell Journal of Economics*, **9** (1), 56–69.

Wilson, T. (1945), 'Price and output policy of state enterprise', *Economic Journal*, **55** (December), 454–61.

Wolak, F. (2005), 'Lessons from the Californian electricity crisis', in Griffin and Puller (eds), pp. 145–81.

Yergin, D. (1991), *The Prize: The Epic Quest for Oil, Money and Power*, New York: Simon & Schuster.

Zannetos, Z. (1966), *The Theory of Oil Tankship Rates: An Economic Analysis of Tankship Operations*, Cambridge, MA: MIT Press.

Zannetos, Z. (1987), 'Oil tanker markets: continuity amidst change', in R. Gordon, H. Jacoby and M. Zimmerman (eds), *Energy: Markets and Regulation: Essays in Honor of M.A. Adelman*, Cambridge, MA and London: MIT Press, pp. 235–57.

Zimmerman, M. (1987), 'The evolution of civilian nuclear power', in R. Gordon, H. Jacoby and M. Zimmerman (eds), *Energy: Markets and Regulation: Essays in Honor of M.A. Adelman*, Cambridge, MA and London: MIT Press, pp. 83–106.

Index